Triumphant Plutocracy

A History of the Gilded Age; the Government and Economics of the United States, 1870-1920 – a Senator's Autobiography

By Richard Franklin Pettigrew

PANTIANOS
CLASSICS

Published by Pantianos Classics

ISBN-13: 978-1-78987-321-4

First published in 1922

Contents

Foreword - American Public Life

The American people should know the truth about American public life. They have been lied to so much and hoodwinked so often that it would seem only fair for them to have at least one straight-from-the-shoulder statement concerning this government "of the people, by the people and for the people," about whose inner workings the people know almost nothing.

The common people of the United States, like the same class of people in every other country, mean well, but they are ill-informed. Floundering about in their ignorance, they are tricked and robbed by those who have the inside information and who therefore know how to take advantage of every turn in the wheel of fortune. The people voted for Roosevelt because he talked of "trust-busting" at the same time that he was sanctioning the purchase of the Tennessee Coal and Iron Company by the Steel Trust. They supported Wilson "because he kept us out of war" at the same time that Wilson was making preparations to enter the war. The rulers can negotiate "secret treaties" at home and abroad. The people, knowing nothing of either the theory or the practice of secret diplomacy, commit all sorts of follies for which they themselves must later foot the bill.

At the present moment the American people are being taught "Americanism" — taught by the same gentry who are making away with billions of dollars, sometimes "legally" and sometimes without any sanction in the law.

The most prominent among the leaders of the Americanization campaign were the most prominent among the war profiteers. They are the owners of resources and industries — the owners of America. It is from them that the preparedness agitation came in 1915 and 1916, and it is from them that the new preparedness agitation is coming now.

Here is a newspaper story in the New York Herald (November 7, 1920) which illustrates the point. The story, evidently inspired by the War Department, is devoted to a description of certain big guns and certain new forms of tanks that the government is at the present time busy manufacturing. The country was caught napping once, says the writer, but the War Department is going to be sure that the same thing does not happen again. Therefore, it is building up its machinery now, while the country is still at peace. In this work the War Department is assisted "by some of the leading industrial spirits of the country, who are keeping up the same enthusiastic devotion to the service of their country they displayed in the war. A little army of dollar-a-year men, headed by Benedict Crowell, former Assistant Secretary of War, has mobilized itself under the name of Army Ordnance Association and is giving its valuable time to the country without costing the government a single cent."

Who are the members of this "little army" of patriots? The Herald gives the answer in full. Besides Mr. Crowell, there are, in the Army Ordnance Association, William Wheeler Coleman, president of the Bucyrus Company of Milwaukee, Wis.; Charles Eliot Warren, past president of the American Bankers' Association; Ralph Crews, of the law firm of Sherman & Sterling, New York City; Guy Eastman Tripp, chairman of the board of directors of the Westinghouse Company; Samuel McRoberts, of the National City Bank of New York; Waldo Calvin Bryant, president of the Bryant Electric Company; Frank Augustus Scott, former chairman of the War Industries Board; Robert P. Lament, president of the American Steel Foundries of Chicago, and C. L. Harrison, of the First National Bank of Cincinnati.

What do these patriotic business men hope to gain by their devotion to the preparedness program of the War Department? The answer appears later in the same articles: "It is this desire to keep abreast of the world's performances in ordnance that has prompted the War Department to ask for an increased appropriation next year. The department's appropriation last year was $377,246,944. The estimates for this year call for an appropriation of approximately $814,000,000." The difference, or $435,000,000, represents the value of contracts that will go to the business interests of the United States.

Again, bankers, lawyers, manufacturers and business men are going to save the country — not by keeping us out of war, but by getting ready for the next war. It is these men who dominate the life and thought as well as the industries of these United States, and it is just such men that have been in control of the United States ever since I entered the Senate thirty years ago.

It is fifty years since I began to take an interest in public affairs. During those years I have been participating, more or less actively, in public life — first as a government surveyor, then as a member of the Legislature of Dakota; as a member of the House of Representatives and, finally, as a member of the United States Senate. Since 1880 I have known the important men in both the Republican and Democratic parties; I have known the members of the diplomatic corps; I have known personally the last ten presidents of the United States, and I have known personally the leading business men who backed the political parties and who made and unmade the presidents. For half a century I have known public men and have been on the inside of business and politics. Through all of that time I have lived and worked with the rulers of America.

When I entered the arena of public affairs in 1870, the United States, with a population of thirty-eight millions, was just recovering from the effects of the Civil War. The economic life of the old slave-holding South lay in ruins. Even in the North, the Panic of 1873 swept over the business world, taking its toll in commercial failures and unemployment and an increase in the number of tenant farmers. The policy of sending carpet-bagging rascals into the embittered South hindered reconciliation, and sectional differences prevented any effective co-operation between the two portions of the country. The result was a heavy loss in productive power and in political position. Through this period, the United States was an inconsequential factor in international affairs.

The transformation from that day to this is complete. With three times the population; with sectionalism practically eliminated; with the South recovered economically and the economic power of the North vastly increased; with more wealth than any other five nations of the world combined; with the credit of the world in her hands; with large undeveloped, or only slightly developed resources; with a unified population and a new idea of world importance, the United States stands as probably the richest and most influential among the great nations.

I witnessed the momentous changes and participated in them. While they were occurring I saw something else that filled me with dread. I saw the government of the United States enter into a struggle with the trusts, the railroads and the banks, and I watched while the business forces won the contest. I saw the forms of republican government decay through disuse, and I saw them betrayed by the very men who were sworn to preserve and uphold them. I saw the empire of business, with its innumerable ramifications, grow up around and above the structure of government. I watched the power over public affairs shift from the weakened structure of republican political machinery to the vigorous new business empire. Strong men who saw what was occurring no longer went into politics. Instead, they entered the field of industry, and with them the seat of the government of the United States was shifted from Washington to Wall Street. With this shift, there disappeared from active public life those principles of republican government that I had learned to believe were the means of safeguarding liberty. After the authority over public affairs had been transferred to the men of business, I saw the machinery of business pass from the hands of individuals into the hands of corporations — artificial persons — created in the imagination of lawyers, and given efficacy by the sanction of the courts and of the law. When I turned to the reading of American history, I discovered that these things had been going on from the beginnings of our government, that they had grown up with it, and were an essential part of its structure. From surprise and disgust I turned to analysis and reason and, for the past twenty years, I have been watching the public life of the United States with an understanding mind. For a long time I have known what was going on in the United States. Today I think that I know why it is going on.

When I look back over the half century that has passed since I first entered public life, I can hardly realize that the America, which I knew and believed in as a young man in the twenties, could have changed so completely in so short a time. Even when I know the reason for the change, it is hard to accept it as a reality.

Many of the public men who have lived and worked in the United States during the past century have written their impressions of public affairs. Benton, Blaine, Grant and Sherman discussed the public life of the middle of the last century. Since then, there have been many autobiographies and memoirs. I have read these books carefully, and it seems to me that not one of the writers is at the same time a student and a realist.

First of all, they have written about politics, with very little or no attention to the economic forces that were shaping politics. In the second place, too many of them have written the agreeable things and left the disagreeable ones unsaid. In the third place, they have written what they believed should have happened rather than what actually did happen. Fourth, and by far the most important, each of these men has written as a member of a ruling class, pleased with himself, and satisfied that rule by his class was the best thing for the community. The pictures that these men give are like the decisions of our courts — built of precedents rather than of realities.

It is my ambition to tell my fellow-countrymen what has happened during the half century that I have known public life. I know what went on, because I saw it. I want others to have the same knowledge. During my public career I have received very definite impressions, and I am anxious to pass those impressions on to others. I want to do this because I believe that my country is in danger; I believe that the liberties of the American people are already well-nigh destroyed; I believe that we are moving forward to a crisis of immense significance to the future of the American people, and the ideas and ideals for which the United States has stood before the world. We are far along on the road to empire, and we are traveling faster towards that goal than any nation in history ever traveled.

It is with that purpose and in that spirit that I have written this book, and it is in that spirit that I ask them to consider and ponder what I have said there.

1. Land Grabbing

My first struggle with the business interests, after I entered the Senate in 1889, came over the question of land-grabbing. At that time the Federal Government still owned millions of acres of valuable timber, mineral and agricultural land that might easily have been utilized for public advantage instead of for private gain. The attorneys and other representatives that the vested interests maintained in Washington were busy grabbing this land. I set myself to save it for the people.

I was thoroughly familiar with the public Land Laws of the United States as I had been a practicing lawyer before the Land Department, a surveyor on the public domain, and beside that I had planted a timber claim with white ash trees which stand today. I, therefore, sought appointment upon the Senate Committee on Public Lands, of which Preston B. Plumb, of Kansas, was Chairman. In that position I had an excellent opportunity to see land grabbing from the inside.

The House passed a bill to repeal the timber culture law "and for other purposes" in February, 1890. When the bill reached the Senate it was referred to the Committee on Public Lands, and Chairman Plumb appointed Senator Walthall of Mississippi and me as a sub-committee to consider the bill. I gave the matter very careful attention and, after some weeks of study and work, I reported the bill to the Senate in such a form that it involved a complete revision of the Federal land laws. The bill, containing nineteen sections, finally passed the Senate on the 16th of September, 1890.

Immediately, upon its passage, a conference was requested and Senators Plumb, Walthall and Pettigrew were appointed as Conference Committee on the part of the Senate. In the House the bill was referred to the Committee on Public Lands, which reported it back, early in the next session of Congress, agreeing to the Conference asked for by the Senate and appointing three conferees, Payson of Illinois, Holman of Indiana and Pickler of South Dakota. Plumb did not act with the Conference Committee. Walthall of Mississippi and myself took full charge of the work and, after many conferences, we finally agreed upon and did report to each house a bill just as the Senate had passed it, with five additional sections, making twenty-four in all. The 24th section was as follows:

"SEC. 24, p. 1103, 51st CONGRESS, MARCH 3, 1891.
"That the President of the United States may from time to time set apart and reserve, in any State or Territory having public land bearing forests in any part of the public lands wholly or in part covered with timber or undergrowth, whether of commercial value or not as public reservations and the President shall by public proclamation declare the establishment of such reservations and the limits thereof."

I give this section in full, first, because it resulted in departure in public policy that was highly advantageous to the people of the United States, and second, because it led to one of the most bitterly fought parliamentary struggles in which I have ever participated.

Section 24 was placed in the bill at my suggestion to take the place of the timber culture law, which never had produced any timber. I had offered this section in the Senate Committee on Public Lands, but the Western Senators were opposed to "locking up" the country in forest reservations. In conference, while I had some difficulty, I secured an agreement which included this section in the bill.

Nothing was done under Section 24 until after Cleveland commenced his second term and then he, as President, appointed a commission of eastern people to go out into the Western country — Dakota, Wyoming, Colorado— and establish the forest reservations. These men rode about the country in a Pullman car, and prescribed the boundaries of forest reservations without any discriminating judgment. For example, they established the reservation, of Black Hills in South Dakota, and embraced within its boundaries the city of Deadwood, and the towns of Leed, Custer and Hill City, which contained thousands of people who were mining, home-building and getting the timber necessary for these activities from the surrounding forests. Once these reservations were established it became impossible to cut any timber upon them; consequently the people who had made their homes in the reserved area were practically compelled to move.

Since no law had been passed for the administration of these newly created reserves, the country was completely locked up. No new people could go in and settle, and those already there found themselves restricted on every hand. The result was a general dissatisfaction with the whole policy of forest reservations.

I realized that, unless some change was made, the whole policy would be discredited, and therefore I secured legislation suspending reservations already located until proper legislation could be secured for their administration.

Finally, at my request, Wolcott, who was then at the head of the Geological Survey, prepared an amendment to the Sundry Civil Appropriation Bill, which I offered in the Senate, providing for the administration of these forests. After this law for administration was enacted, the Secretary of the Interior informed me that he would make the boundaries of the Black Hills Forest Reservation whatever I might recommend. I went out to the Black Hills, held meetings of the people, and explained to them the purpose of the Forest Reservation. In every instance they passed resolutions in favor of being embraced with the Forest Reservation as administered under the new laws. By this direct appeal to the people most intimately concerned I was able to enlarge the reservation by over 200,000 acres.

When I returned to Washington, the Secretary of the Interior asked me to suggest such rules and regulations as would best enable his Department to administer the forest reservations laws. In accordance with this request I wrote out the rules and regulations which were afterwards adopted by him.

I remember in one of the regulations that I provided for sowing the Black Hills spruce seed upon the snow in all the open parks and denuded places, so that when the snow melted these seeds would sink down into the moist ground and immediately sprout and grow; and. today, there are many thousands more acres of forest in the Black Hills reservations than there were when the law was enacted.

Thus far matters had gone very nicely. I had had a hard fight to get the policy of forest reservation adopted and the reservations themselves established. Now came the real fight — to hold them for the people.

In the amendment which was added to the Sundry Civil Appropriation Bill I inserted a provision that permitted any settler, who was embraced within a Forest Reservation, to exchange his land, acre by acre, for other government land, outside of the reservation. Such a provision enabled settlers who had taken land before the establishment of reservations to take up a new quarter section in case they did not care to live under the reservation regulations.

The Conference Committee of the two houses that considered the Sundry Civil Bill changed the wording of this section in such a way that the land grant railroads, which had received in all nearly two hundred million acres of land, could exchange their land, if embraced within a forest reservation, for the very best land the Government had remaining on the public domain outside of the reservation. Allison of Iowa was Chairman on the part of the Senate and Joe Cannon of Illinois, Chairman on the part of the House. The Conference report came to the Senate the day before the end of the session. Therefore it was not printed, but was rushed through after having been read hurriedly by the clerk. I listened to the reading, but I did not notice this change of wording in my amendment, and so this monstrous proposition became a law.

Of course, the conferees knew what they were doing when they slipped through this provision. Under it, the Interior Department ruled that the land grant railroads could exchange their odd sections, embraced within a forest reservation, for the best remaining acres of the public domain. The right to make this exchange was worth at least fifty millions of dollars to the land grant railroads.

I did not discover this change, made by the Conference Committee, until I learned that the Department of the Interior was permitting the railroads to make these exchanges. As soon as I discovered this, I looked up the law and found what an enormous fraud had been practiced through the cunning of Senator Allison of Iowa, Chairman of the Committee on Appropriations, and Joe Cannon, Representative from Illinois, a banker and lawyer, and Chairman of the Committee on Appropriations in the House. Nearly ten years had dragged along, from the time I began the fight in favor of forest reservations,

11

until this fraud was perpetuated on the American people by these two representatives of business.

In order to meet the situation I presented an amendment to the Sundry Civil Bill on May 31, 1900 (56th Congress, 1st Session, pages 6289 to 6298 of the Congressional Record), which reads as follows:

"And said superintendents, assistant inspectors, supervisors and rangers shall, under the direction of the Secretary of the Interior, examine all lands within the boundaries of any forest reservation that belong to any land-grant railroad company, and have not heretofore been sold in good faith for a valuable consideration, and report to the Secretary the character and value of said land, and pending such examination and report none of said lands shall be exchanged for other lands outside of said reservation."

It may be well to state at this point that the Central and Union Pacific Railroad had received grants by an Act of Congress, 20 miles wide, from the Missouri River on the west boundary of the State of Iowa, straight across the continent to the Pacific Ocean, through the length of the States of Nebraska, Wyoming, Utah, Nevada, and California. The road has the odd sections on a strip 10 miles wide on each side of the tracks. The Northern Pacific Road received a grant of land 40 miles in width from some point in the State of Minnesota, clear through to the Pacific Ocean. This grant extended through the States of Minnesota, North Dakota, Montana, Idaho and Washington, and the area granted included the odd sections throughout this entire region. These grants embraced the good and the bad land alike. Of necessity they included large areas on the tops of the Rocky Mountains and the Cascade Range and a great deal of desert land. Whether by design or not, when the forest reservations were created, they embraced, indiscriminately, forested and non-forested districts. By some chance they also embraced large areas of desert land. These deserts were probably embraced intentionally so that the railroads could exchange their odd sections of worthless desert land for lands of great value outside the reservation.

After I had presented the amendment just referred to, I made a statement of these facts, after which the following significant debate took place. I quote it in order to show where certain Senators lined up when it came to an issue between private interest and the public welfare. (Cong. Record, May 31, 1900, 1st session, 56th Congress, p. 6288.)

Mr. PETTIGREW: "Mr. President, the amendment I propose is a provision for the protection and administration of forest reservation. Three years ago in an appropriation bill we provided for the protection and administration of these reservations, and provided that any actual and bona-fide settler who had taken a claim within a forest reservation afterwards created could exchange his land if he desired to do so, for a like area of the public domain. It was the intention of the law to allow a settler whose land was embraced in any forest reservation to exchange his land, if he desired to do so, for lands outside of the reservations, acre for acre.

12

"But certain words were inserted under which the Department has decided that a land-grant railroad can exchange the worthless lands — lands from which the timber has all been cut, tops of mountains, the inaccessible and snow-capped peaks of the Rockies and Sierra Nevadas — for the best land the Government has, acre for acre. So they have swapped lands on the Cascade Range, which are covered forever with ice and snow, not worth a tenth of a cent an acre, for lands worth from six to ten dollars in the valleys of Washington and Oregon and Idaho and Montana, thus depriving the settlers of a chance to secure these lands, besides enlarging the grants of the railroads to that extent.

"Now, my amendment simply provides that these lands shall be inspected and examined by the officers who have charge of the reservations, and they shall report to the Secretary the character of the lands that belong to these companies, so that in the future we can make a proper adjustment — not an adjustment by which they shall receive a thousand times more than which they surrender — and that while the appraisement is going on no more exchanges shall be made. That is all that the amendment aims to accomplish, and it is one in the interest of the public beyond all questions, suspending the operation of a law which Congress would never have passed if it had been discussed."

Mr. ALLISON: "I wish to say that this amendment, as it appears to me, is general legislation. Certainly on the statement made by the Senator from South Dakota, it changes the existing law. I hope he will not press it on this bill, because if he does we shall be obliged to make the point of order that it is proposed general legislation."

Mr. PETTIGREW: "I wish to say that I do not believe it is subject to the point of order, because it prescribes the duties of these officers who are provided for and the method of the expenditure of the appropriation now in the bill. Therefore, I do not believe it is subject to the point of order. It seems to me if it is passible to insert the amendment we ought to do it and protect the Government and the people of this country against the execution of a law which we never would have passed if we had known what it contained."

Mr. PETTIGREW: "I should like to ask the chairman of the Committee on Appropriations if the Secretary of the Interior did not think the law should be entirely repealed?"

Mr. ALLISON: "The Secretary did."

Mr. PETTIGREW: "Did he not think there were great frauds being practiced under it?"

Mr. ALLISON: "I have no doubt that is all true, but that is a subject we cannot deal with now."

(The amendment is read again.)

Mr. PENROSE: "I make the point of order that this is general legislation and contrary to the rule."

THE PRESIDENT (pro tempore): "The Chair has overruled that point of order. It has already been made. The question is on agreeing to the amendment."

"The amendment was agreed to."

Allison of Iowa, Tom Carter of Montana, Chandler of New Hampshire, Piatt of Connecticut, Aldrich of Rhode Island, Penrose of Pennsylvania, Walcott of Colorado, Hawley of Connecticut, all joined in the fight against me to see that the land-grant railroads were given this vast graft at the expense of the people of the United States and against the public welfare. This is but a typical case. The lawyers in the Senate always lined up against the people of the United States and in favor of the railroads and the other predatory interests who are the real government of the United States. This Senate debate is significant because it shows that rascality, graft, and public plunder are not political questions, especially in so far as the Senate of the United States is concerned.

Observe that Allison of Iowa, who had inserted the amendment making possible the exchange of these railroad lands, was among the first to attack my amendment and to insist that it should not go into the bill. Observe further that Tom Carter, Chairman of the Republican National Committee, took the same side. It was he who figured in the scandalous affair during Harriman's second campaign for election, at which time he collected from Cramp, the shipbuilder, $400,000 and told Cramp where the money was to be expended. When Tom Carter died he left a large fortune. This same debate was participated in by Bill Chandler of New Hampshire, Stewart of Nevada and finally by Penrose of Pennsylvania, who arose and for the second time raised the point of order against my amendment. Penrose is still in public life and he is still a faithful servant and representative of the great predatory interests. He has never been a representative of the people of Pennsylvania or of the United States.

Despite all of this opposition my amendment was adopted without a roll-call. The reason is plain. Neither these men nor their backers desired to have the amendment become a law, but the scandal connected with the exchange of the railroad lands had gained such publicity, and the amendment was so clearly in the public interest that they did not dare to kill it openly. Besides, this was an amendment to the Sundry Civil Bill and could be changed in conference, and the conference report forced through the Senate on the last day of the session. Allison of Iowa was called "Pussyfoot Allison" by his fellow Senators because of his cunning, his unscrupulous rascality, and his suavity, and he could be relied upon to throw out of the bill as reported from the conference committee anything that threatened property interests.

So the bill passed the Senate and went to conference.

Allison was chairman of the conference on the part of the Senate and Joe Cannon on the part of the House. The conference struck out my amendment, adopted by the Senate, and inserted in its place the following:

14

"That all selections of Land made in lieu of a tract covered by an unperfected bona-fide claim or by a patent included within a public forest reservation as provided in the Act of June 4, 1897, shall be confined to vacant surveyed non-mineral public lands which are subject to Homestead entry not exceeding in area the tract covered by such claim or patent."

The conference simply struck out the Senate amendment and inserted the original clause that they had placed in the Sundry Civil Bill of 1897 and under which the fraudulent exchange had taken place. The change would have permitted the railroads to continue the exchange of their worthless lands for the best of the government land and thus to plunder the public domain.

The Conference report came up in the Senate on the day before adjournment. I was watching to see what had been done with my amendment, for I knew Allison and Cannon were but paid attorneys of the railroads. When the amendment was read (56th Congress, 1st Session, Congressional Rec, p. 6690):

Mr. PETTIGREW: "I should like to understand the paragraph in relation to non-mineral lands. As I understand it, as read from the Secretary's desk, it permits a continued exchange by the land-grant railroad companies of the worthless lands in the forest reservations for the best land the Government has. Is that correct?"

Mr. ALLISON: "I do not so understand it. The amendment provides for the exchange of surveyed lands only, and not of unsurveyed lands."

Mr. PETTIGREW: "But it allows the exchange?"

Mr. ALLISON: It allows the exchange of surveyed lands."

Mr. PETTIGREW: "Mr. President, this conference report provides that lands where a railroad company has cut off all the timber or the land on the snow-capped peaks of the mountains, if they are within a forest reservation, can be exchanged for the best lands the Government owns, acre for acre, for timber lands. Hundreds of thousands of acres have already been exchanged, and yet, although the Senate placed upon this bill an amendment which would stop that practice, the conference committee brings in a report to continue it."

I wish to call particular attention to the statements made by Allison and Wolcott, that only surveyed land could be exchanged. This statement is specifically contradicted by the wording of their own amendment. The falsity of the statement was well known to them, yet they made it for the purpose of deceiving the Senate.

A number of the faithful friends of the plutocrats distinguished themselves signally in this debate. Among them were Senators Wolcott of Colorado and Hawley of Connecticut.

Senator Wolcott, who came into the Senate without a dollar, retired from that body with a large fortune. He was always eager to get into the Record as having produced laughter on the part of the Senators. He considered his effort in the interest of the robbery of the public domain particularly worthy of credit.

Old Hawley of Connecticut was always a champion of the interests. As long as I know him he was mentally incapacitated from comprehending anything except the interests of the big business groups with which he always acted. He had an intellect like the soil of Connecticut, so poor by nature that it could not be exhausted by cultivation.

The amendment, as modified by the Committee on Conference was finally agreed to, because if we did not agree to the Senate Civil Sundry Bill with this amendment in it, an extra session would have been necessary. Thus the fraud was perpetuated, and the continued grabbing of public lands made possible.

The frauds thus deliberately ratified by Congress after all the facts were known caused me to wonder what forces were in control of the Government, and convinced me that the lawyers who composed two-thirds of both Houses of Congress were but the paid attorneys of the exploiters of the American people, and that both political parties were but the tools in the hands of big business that were used to plunder the American people. The frauds begun under Cleveland, a Democratic President, were enlarged and completed under McKinley, a Republican President. Millions of acres of forest reservation were established in Montana, all within the grant of the Northern Pacific Railroad, where there was no timber or forests, only a little scrub pine that never was and never will be of any value for lumber or any kind of forest products, and that was done so that the Northern Pacific Railroad could exchange its odd sections of worthless desert for scrip, acre for acre, and this scrip sells for from $8 to $10 per acre, and can be located on any land the Government owns anywhere within our broad domain, and the desert for which this scrip was exchanged was not and is not worth ten cents per acre.

This is the story of one small event in the great drama of American public life that had been unfolding all around me. I have told it in detail because it shows, as well as anything that I ever learned, the fate that lay in wait for any measure aimed to promote the public welfare. When I began this fight for the enactment of forest legislation, I believed that we were enjoying a system of popular government in the United States. By the time the fight was ended, I understood that the country was being run by plunderers in the interest of capital.

2. The Land for the People

Powerful interests were out to plunder the public domain. I had felt their grip. They were shrewdly advised. I had faced their spokesman in the Senate and the House. They were sinister. Many a man, under my eyes, had tried to thwart them, and not one such had remained an enemy of the vested interests and at the same time continued in public life. Nevertheless, I went, straight ahead, trying to save the land for the people. I knew how enormously rich was the public domain; I had an idea of its possibilities. I wanted to have it used in the future, not for the enrichment of the few, but for the well being of the many.

In order to protect the public in their sovereign rights over the remainder of the public domain, I worked out what I believed was a feasible plan for keeping the public domain in the hands of the public. After I had secured the forest legislation and the passage of the law administering forests, I introduced the following bill in the Senate on March 22, 1898 (55th Congress, 2nd Session):

A Bill

To preserve the public lands for the people. Be it enacted by the Senate and House of Representatives of the United States of America, in Congress assembled.

That the public lands of the United States, except reservations, be and they are hereby donated to the States and Territories in which they may be located on the sole condition that all such public lands shall be held in perpetual ownership by such States and Territories to be used by the people residing therein free of rent under such regulations as may be prescribed by the legislatures of such States and Territories each for itself.

This bill had three purposes:

1. To make use and not ownership the criterion in the distribution of nature's gifts to individual citizens.

2. To keep the title to the public domain, including agricultural land, mineral land, timber land, waterpower, and all other natural gifts, perpetually in the whole people, and thus to prevent any greater quantities from getting into the grip of the few.

3. To localize control over the administration of the lands, so as to bring the problem closer to the people.

Could this first step be taken, I believed that we should be in a position to go forward with a general program for the conservation of all resources.

The bill was referred to the Committee on Public Lands, of which I was a member, and to the members of that committee, individually and collectively, and on the floor of the Senate, I presented my arguments. In support of my proposition that the public domain should be leased but never sold, I stated that the public domain in my own state amounted to 20,000,000 acres of grazing land. Then I showed that if these lands were conveyed to the State of South Dakota, with the privilege of leasing, they could be leased to cattlemen for ten cents an acre, which would produce a revenue of $2,000,000 a year. Then I showed that this money derived from farm leases could be used to build great reservoirs on the heads of all streams and store the flood-water, and thus irrigate and make productive large areas of this semi-arid land.

In my own state, the opportunities for irrigation by means of artesian wells were unusual. I pointed out to the Senate that almost anywhere in the middle half of the state the artesian basin could be tapped at depths varying from

300 to 2,000 feet, each well releasing a flow almost marvelous in quantity. Many of these wells exhibit a pressure strong enough to drive heavy machinery, and from most of them water could be elevated 30 or 40 feet into reservoirs by the force of the head behind the artesian supply. Nature had thus made provision for irrigation on an extended scale in South Dakota, and all that was needed was the money with which to provide for the distribution of the water.

I called the attention of the Senate to the fact that Dakota land was only one part of the public domain, and that the Dakota problem was only one aspect of the whole problem of conservation. I showed them that the United States had 500,000,000 acres of arid and semi-arid land, large areas of which could be irrigated to advantage, either through stream conservation or through the sinking of artesian wells.

Furthermore, I showed that the Government, through its control of the lakes and streams of the country, had an' opportunity to adopt constructive relief measures designed to meet the recurring floods and droughts in the lower reaches of the rivers. Many of the streams are navigable. Successful navigation depends on the maintenance of a steady flow of water. Many were used for the generation of power. Again, there is a need to conserve the spring surplus to cover the needs of the late summer. Each spring this water, so sorely needed later, is allowed to run off from the land, not only wasting the supply but, through floods, overflowing the banks and destroying temporarily or permanently large areas of fertile and cultivated land.

For the purpose of preventing this destruction, particularly along the Mississippi, Congress had for many years appropriated money for the construction of dykes and levees, under the theory that such work was for the benefit of commerce. Here was a twofold problem: Millions of acres of arid land, on the one hand, required only water to make them produce splendid crops. On the other hand, the interests of commerce, of power development and of the dwellers along some of the larger rivers, demanded an intelligent regulation of stream flow.

It was estimated at that time by the Government authorities that 72,000,000 acres of land could be thus reclaimed and made to produce crops sufficient to support 15,000,000 people. The benefit that commerce, industry and agriculture would derive from such a plan would be incalculable. Therefore, I moved an appropriation of from one to two hundred million dollars to begin the building of such reservoirs as were most urgently needed and the establishment of irrigation projects in the districts that would yield the most immediate results.

I further showed that if the storm water was all stored in these reservoirs, it would reduce the floods on the great rivers — the Missouri and the Mississippi— and obviate the necessity of building embankments to reclaim the lands heretofore flooded by these great rivers. Thus, the leasing of the land held the title for all the people, while it made the land available for such as were able to utilize it.

For my part, I stated that I would prefer to have Congress turn over its arid and semi-arid land, lying within its boundaries, to the State of South Dakota, because I believed the problem would be practically and honestly worked out to the great advantage of the people of that state. The same thing I insisted was true of Idaho, of Montana, of Wyoming, of Colorado, of Nevada, of Utah, New Mexico, Arizona, Western Kansas, Western Nebraska and North Dakota. I insisted that the nation could not afford longer to neglect this great opportunity for material advancement, which I considered of fully as much importance, if not of more importance, to the future greatness and prosperity of this country than the clearing out of harbors along the small streams of the coast, or even the development of the great harbors themselves.

The arguments fell on deaf ears. These questions arose during the days following the Spanish War and preceding the conquest of the Philippines. We had started upon a career of conquest rather than one of internal improvement. The Administration, backed by many of the people, believed that it was of great benefit to this country that we should annex 10,000,000 people in the Philippines. Instead of spending hundreds of millions in conquering the Philippines, it would have been far better economy and better business judgment to spend it in reclaiming the arid lands of the west.

At the time that I presented these arguments to the Senate, I considered them weighty. I consider them weighty today. I believe that they represented the only statesmanlike approach to the problem of resource conservation and that they suggested a line of action that might have been followed lo the advantage of the people of the United States. Yet I was unable to persuade the committee to report the bill back to the Senate in any form.

There was no question of choosing between two policies. The committee had no policy on this subject. On the subject of the public domain they had only one conclusion — that the only way to make a state or territory prosperous was to get the title of the public domain out of the Government and into the hands of some private interest, by selling it, or giving it away, or doing anything to get rid of it.

There was not a single member of the committee on public lands that was in favor of the sovereign ownership of the natural resources. They wanted to deed not only the land, but the minerals underneath the land, and also to convey the water power so that these utilities, of no value except that which the community gave them, could be used to enrich individuals and exploit the whole population. Everyone was opposed to public utilities being used for any other purposes than that of enriching individuals, and corporations were being rapidly formed for the purpose of more thoroughly performing this work of exploitation.

Two-thirds of both houses were lawyers, and they believed that the rights of property, no matter how acquired, were the only sacred thing in connection with humanity, and the only legitimate subjects for the consideration of a well-ordered legislative chamber in an intelligently directed state. The same point of view has prevailed ever since, and therefore no policy of reclaiming and utilizing the public domain for the benefit of the people of the United States has ever been adopted. Instead, the 65th Congress, at its second session, passed the infamous Shield's Water Power Bill.

The natural resources of the United States, a hundred years ago, were the richest possessed by any modern nation. Like the air and the sunlight, they existed in almost limitless abundance. But the "land-hog," in his multitude of corporate forms, came upon the scene and today the timber (except 170,000,000 of acres embraced within the forest reservations), coal, copper, iron and oil that once belonged to the American people are in the hands of a few very rich men who, with their agents and attorneys and hangers-on, administer these free natural gifts for their own profit. At the present moment, the one great resource remaining in the hands of the whole people — the "white coal" of our streams and rivers — is being gobbled up by the public utility corporations, which plan to charge four prices for a commodity that should go to the people at its cost of production.

I made my fight in the land because it was so basic and so important from the point of view of economic strategy; because it was so rich; because, by holding and using it for their common advantage, the American people might have remained free; because this same land, in the hands of a small and unscrupulous ruling caste, will not only enable the members of that caste to live parasitically upon the labor of the remainder of the community, but will give them the right to decide who among the citizens of the United States shall be able to earn a living and who shall be condemned to slow starvation.

I lost my fight on the land because every branch of the government machinery was manned by the agents and attorneys of the interests which were busy grabbing the public domain; because, through their control of the press, they kept the public in ignorance of the things that were really transpiring, and because the people, lulled by soft words such as "liberty" and "constitutional rights," were busily pursuing their daily occupations, secure in the belief that the Government would protect them. So I lost the fight because those who wanted the land were keen and powerful, though few in number; while the many, from whom the few stole it, were basking in the belief that they were citizens of a "free country."

3. Banks and Bankers

My life in the West taught me the power of the land-grabbers. My experience in the East gave me an insight into the power of the banker. The land-grabber cornered land. The banker corners money and credit. Both are able through their monopolies to plunder the producers of the product of their toil.

We learned, through our experiences with the Eastern bankers, that the institution which can issue money and extend credit holds the key to the whole business world. The banks, under the present laws, can do both, and this fact makes them the dictators of business life.

Perhaps a little story, "The Evolution of a Banker," will help to show what the banker does to his fellowmen.

In 1868 placer gold was discovered high up on the sides of Mount Shasta, in Northern California. The report of this discovery was quickly known in other placer mining camps farther south, and a great stampede occurred. Five or six hundred miners, at one time, went to Shasta, staked out their claims, and commenced mining.

Of course there was every variety of the genus homo, from the saloon-keepers, gamblers and highwaymen to miners, speculators and prospectors — a motley crowd. Among the others there was Robert Waite, an educated fellow — a sort of graduate — who could talk on every subject from the Bible to Hoyle. Then there was Silver Jack who, when he was not mining, was shooting up the mining camps or robbing stage-coaches.

When they arrived at Shasta, all of the members of the crowd, with one exception, staked out claims and went to work. The diggings were good. The returns were high.

In the camp lived the usual hangers-on, and among them there was one man who among all of his fellows had staked out no claim. Everybody else worked at something. He never worked. The others were equal and demo-cratic. He held himself aloof. He was better dressed than the others; he was never about in the daytime, but in the early evening he might be seen loiter-ing about the gambling houses. He neither swore nor drank; he talked but little, and he was known by everybody.

As the weeks went by he opened a little office and began to lend money to miners who had a good claim and who were dissipating their earnings, at four per cent a month. Time passed, and he opened a bank. Because of his personal habits and rather agreeable appearance, the miners deposited their savings with him. He paid the depositors ten per cent a year, and loaned the money to other miners, who were willing to give their claims as security, for four per cent a month. Under these conditions the bank flourished and the banker made money.

But one day he sold the bank and moved to San Francisco, and there opened a bank on a large scale, and became known as one of the great finan-ciers of the Pacific Coast. A few years afterward, when he had become fa-mous, he removed to New York and entered the circle of the great financiers of the world, and became widely known as a manipulator of moneys and credits.

At a banquet which he gave to celebrate the thirtieth year of his entry into the banking business, he grew enthused with wine, and in his speech gave a sketch of his life and told how he was the first banker in Shasta in '68. There-upon the miners at Shasta — those of the old-timers who still remained — held a meeting to discuss the question. And they said:

"Why this man is not the man who started the first bank in Shasta; or, if he is, then his name was -so-and-so, and we remember him well."

And they thereupon appointed a committee of three to make an investigation and ascertain how the great banker got his start, and the committee reported that he had gone with the stampede to Shasta, had taken no claim and done no work whatever; but that he slept days and crawled around at night and stole from each of the miners so little of the day's production that he did not miss it. The committee therefore resolved that he had changed his name but had not changed the methods of doing business which he inaugurated at Shasta in the early days. He was still stealing so little from each of his fellow men that they did not miss it, and had thus accumulated an enormous fortune and become one of the greatest financiers of the world.

The committee further concluded that no person or corporation should be permitted to do a banking business under any circumstances; that the medium of exchange was the life-blood of business and the most important of all public utilities and that, therefore, it should be controlled by the government alone; that every post-office should be a savings bank, and that the government should establish commercial banks everywhere and loan money to the people at just what it cost to do the business above what was paid the depositors who placed their surplus in the Postal Savings Banks, so that if the Postal Banks paid three per cent to depositors, the Government commercial banks would loan this money to the people of the locality where it was deposited for not to exceed three and a half per cent. And thus this great engine of exploitation, now operated to plunder the producers of wealth in the United States, would be turned into a great public benefaction and compel the bankers — parasites on society — to join the ranks of the producing classes.

The banking business is a parasite business; the banker is a member of a parasite class; yet so completely does he dominate the present order of society that, instead of being punished by society and compelled to take a position and earn his living like the masses of the people, through the pursuit of some useful occupation, the banker is generously rewarded; laws are passed in his favor and he is encouraged and assisted in his efforts to pluck his fellow men.

For years, under our National Bank Act, the banker could subscribe for Government bonds, deposit them in the Treasury, and have the Treasury issue to him the full face value of the bonds in currency. Thus he retained the bonds and at the same time was able to secure an equal amount of money which he could use for his private profit in the banking business. The issue of money was thus made a function of private banking institutions. They could not only lend money; they could actually create it.

During my visit to Japan, I received some interesting sidelights on our banking business as the Japs saw it.

Before going to Japan I talked with the Japanese Minister in Washington, and secured from him all of the books published in English giving the history and the economic development of Japan. I also secured two large volumes on the Japanese banking system written by Soyeda, a Jap educated in England, who was then the Treasurer of Japan. When I arrived Soyeda met me; and he not only entertained me very graciously, but talked with me on many occasions.

I had noticed in reading his book on Japanese banking that Japan had at first adopted the American National Banking system, but had abandoned it after four years of trial. I asked Soyeda why this was.

He explained that four years had convinced them that the system was entirely unworkable because under it the bankers could cause an expansion of the currency whenever it was profitable for the bankers to expand, and a contraction of the currency whenever it was profitable for them to contract. The resulting panics benefited the creditor class and ruined the producing class: that in fact our banking system worked in Japan just as it worked here — expanding the currency to gratify the greed of the bankers when expansion was to their profit, and contracting it in the interest of the bankers whenever it was to their advantage to contract the volume of money.

Japan has concluded that all money should be issued by the Government and its volume regulated by index numbers so as to maintain a steady range of prices; that is, when the volume of money was unduly expanded, it would cause a rise in all prices and lead to the expansion of business and a new credit; that whenever the money was unduly contracted in volume, it would lead to a decline of all prices, cause panics, and allow the creditors to take possession of the property of the producers.

And so the Japanese established a central bank and branches, and the nation issued its own currency. In other words, the Japs discovered a great economic law, well known to some people of the United States, but the officials of Japan had the honesty and character to act upon this law instead of following our example of leaving the issue of money and the control of its volume in the hands of a few manipulators to be used as an engine for exploiting the producing population.

This Japanese situation was interesting to me. I had left the Republican party in 1896 on this very issue.

The Japs with their keen sense of values and their willingness to experiment learned in four years what the American people had not learned in forty — that the banking power in private hands makes the bankers the autocrats of the business world.

This lesson came to me with double force. When I returned to America I found Congress debating the extension of National Bank charters. Aldrich of course was for the extended charters. In the Senate (March 2, 1901), two days before my term as Senator expired, he said:

"The present charters of the National Banks expire from time to time, commencing July 14, 1920. The law is that new plates shall be issued to all banks in extending their charters. The preparation of these plates will take nearly a year, and it is desirable that this bill should be passed at this session.

There can be no objection to it. It is simply a matter of form, as certainly the time of the charters will be extended in the next Congress."

Mr. PETTIGREW: "Mr. President, I do not believe that the charters ever ought to have been issued, and I am certainly opposed to their being renewed. I believe the system is a pernicious one and has a tendency to breed panics, to expand the currency when it ought to be contracted, and to contract it when it ought to be expanded. Japan adopted this system, and after thorough investigation repealed the law, and for this very reason.

"Under this system, which is a branch of our financial system, the banks can produce a panic whenever they please, and wreck the property of this country or any other country where the system exists. The subject ought to be studied and thoroughly investigated. These charters never should be renewed, and a remedy should be offered by which we could have an elastic currency rather than one which produces too much when there is already too much and too little when there is already too little, and puts the control of the volume of the money of the country in the hands of a combination of national bankers. I therefore object to the bill."

The bill therefore went over to the next session. Then, after my term of service in the Senate expired, the bill was passed.

The experiences of the American banking system during the great war confirmed my view in every particular. The Federal Reserve Act, passed in 1913, had made possible the centralization of banking power. The war did the work. As Roger Babson recently stated the matter:

"In 1914 we had 30,000 banks, functioning in a great degree in independence of one another. Then came the Federal Reserve Act, and gave us the machinery for consolidation, and the emergency of five-years' war furnished the hammer-blows to weld the structure into one."

Mr. Alexander is right about the strength of the American banking system. Under the Federal Reserve Act the vast power of the thirty thousand American banks is concentrated in the hands of a little club with headquarters in Wall Street. This club holds in its hands the power to make or to destroy any businessman in the United States; the power to make or wreck financial institutions and inaugurate panics; the power to issue credit, even money. The bankers at the center of the financial web are endowed with the power of government.

The right to issue money is, as I have said, fundamental. This right is exercised by the New York Bankers' Club, thinly disguised as the Federal Reserve Board. On November 3, 1920, the amount of Federal Reserve notes outstanding was $3,588,713,000.

What was the basis of this huge issue of paper money? Commercial paper!

The member banks were permitted to lend money (or credit) to their patrons; to take commercial paper in exchange for their loans; to deposit this paper under the authority of the Board, and to issue currency against it. This currency was again loaned out, the paper redeposited, etc., so that the Federal Reserve Bank of New York was able to earn, by this pyramiding of credits, over 200 per cent in the frugal year of 1920, in a market where the rate of interest never ran over 8 per cent on standard securities.

Through their authority over money and credit, the bankers thus became the arbiters of the business destiny of the United States. No one elected them. No one can recall them. There is no way in which they can be made the object of public approval or disapproval. They are as far above public responsibility as was William Hohenzollern in Germany before 1914. Self-elected dictators of American life, they make and unmake; they wreck and rule. They are the heart of business America — the center of the exploiting -system that sits astride the necks of the people.

The United States emerged from the Great War with the best credit of any of the larger nations. Its wealth was the greatest; its income the largest, and its bank assets and resources exceeded those of any other country; but this very economic position, centered as it is in the hands of bankers, will be used by them to exploit the peoples of Latin America and Asia as they have during recent years exploited the people of the United States. Exploitation is the profession of the banker, and those in charge of the American banking institutions have the greatest exploiting opportunity that has ever come to the bankers in any of the modern nations.

4. Money

My experiences with the world of affairs have convinced me that the power in our public life was exercised through the bankers. My study of banking showed me that the grip which the bankers were able to maintain on the economic system depended largely upon their ability to control money. There were two ways in which they exercised this control. One was by determining who should issue money. The other was by specifying its character. The bankers of the United States have been in a position to decide both of these questions in their own interest.

The Constitution of the United States says that the Congress shall have power to coin money, to regulate the value thereof and of foreign coins, and to fix the standard of weight and measures. The Constitution does not empower Congress to delegate the right to issue money to any person or combination of persons.

Yet the Congress has always delegated the right to issue money to the banks. The power thus conferred by Congress upon the banks to issue money has been used by the bankers to exploit and plunder the people of the United States.

While I was a member of the House of Representatives (1880) I had become acquainted with Peter Cooper of New York. The renewal of the National Bank charters was under discussion in the House at the time and of course the whole question of currency and of our economic system was covered in the debate. One day Peter Cooper of New York placed upon our desks a pamphlet dealing with the money question, I read this pamphlet with great interest, because Peter Cooper was called a "greenbacker" and was supposed to be in favor of what they called "fiat" money. Again and again throughout the debate his name had been mentioned and he had been abused by the speakers.

The foundation theory of Peter Cooper's pamphlet was that the law of supply and demand applied to money just as it applies to other commodities, so that an abundance of money would be registered in the rise in the price of all those things whose value is measured in terms of money. In other words, that the law of supply and demand (the theory that quantity affects price) applies to money as well as to corn, oats, and potatoes. Therefore, the proof of a too great abundance of money lay in the universal rise of prices; and, conversely, the proof of money scarcity was the universal decline in prices. Following this theory, it became evident that while the price of any one commodity would rise or fall, according to the variations in the supply of and the demand for that commodity, a general rise or fall of all prices indicated that money was too abundant or too scarce. Peter Cooper held that money was redeemed whenever it was exchanged by the possessor for the things which he desired more than he desired the money, and that there should be no other form of redemption. In other words, money should be issued by the government and its volume so regulated as to maintain a steady range of prices.

I was so interested in this pamphlet that I went to New York, made the personal acquaintance of Peter Cooper, and talked with him many times and quite fully upon social and economic questions. These talks, and the ideas which I had secured from my reading, convinced me that so long as the banks controlled the issue of money, they would be able to determine the economic life of the United States.

Shortly after my entrance into the Senate, the whole question was dramatized in the struggle over the free coinage of silver

The big business interests had become convinced that if the United States was to take her position as one of the great exploiting nations of the world she must follow the example of England — the world's premier empire — and establish a gold basis for the currency. It was in opposition to this policy of imperialism that we advocated the free and unlimited coinage of silver.

We were demanding that, in this respect, the United States should take a position worthy of her great traditions and refuse to strike hands with the international plunderers who were busy with their work of economic aggression in all parts of the world Those of us, who were opposing British or any other brand of imperialism, were, with equal insistence, demanding that the United States adopt a money system calculated to protect the borrower as against the lender, and so designed as to take out of the hands of private individuals the huge power that money-lending conferred.

Many of the leaders of American public life were urging that the United States must wait for England to move, but the absurdity of such a proposition was apparent on its face. Indeed, her leading statesmen declared that fact in so many words. Thus Gladstone is credited with the following statement in a speech to the House of Commons. (London Times, March 1, 1893):

"I suppose there is not a year which passes over our heads which does not largely add to the mass of British investments abroad. I am almost afraid to estimate the total amount of property which the United Kingdom holds beyond the limits of the United Kingdom, but of this I am well convinced, that it is not to be counted by tens or hundreds of millions. One thousand millions ($5,000,000,000) probably would be an extremely low and inadequate estimate. Two thousand millions ($10,000,000) or fifteen hundred millions than that, is very likely to be nearer the mark. ('Hear! Hear!') I think under these circumstances it is rather a serious matter to ask this country to consider whether we are going to perform this supreme act of self-sacrifice. I have a profound admiration of cosmopolitan principles. I can go a great length, in moderation (laughter), in recommending their recognition and establishment, but if there are these two thousand millions ($10,000,000,000) or fifteen hundred millions ($7,500,000,000 of money which we have got abroad, it is a very serious matter as between this country and other countries.

"We have nothing to pay them; we are not debtors at all; we should get no comfort, no consolation, out of the substitution of an inferior material, of a cheaper money, which we could obtain for less and part with for more. We should get no consolation, but the consolation throughout the world would be great. (Loud laughter.) This splendid spirit of philanthropy, which we cannot too highly praise — because I have no doubt all this is foreseen — would result in our making a present of fifty or a hundred millions ($500,000,000) to the world. It would be thankfully accepted, but I think the gratitude for your benevolence would be mixed with very grave misgivings as to your wisdom. I have shown why we should pause and consider for ourselves once, twice, and thrice before departing from the solid ground on which you have, within the last half century, erected a commercial fabric unknown in the whole history of the world — before departing from the solid ground you should well consult and well consider and take no step except such as you can well justify to your own understanding, to your fellow countryman, and to those who come after us." (Cheers.)

How could England be expected to abandon an economic system that was yielding hundreds of millions in yearly profits to her bankers and investors?

Again and again this issue has been raised at international conferences.

The first conference was held in 1867 at the invitation of France, and met at Paris on June 17, 1867. Eighteen of the principal European countries and the United States participated They voted unanimously against the single silver standard, and every nation participating in that conference voted in favor of the single gold standard but the Netherlands, and they also voted to establish the 25-franc gold pieces as an international coin.

The next conference met, at the invitation of the United States, at Paris, August 16, 1878. Twelve countries were represented. Germany refused to send delegates. It was proposed by the United States, first, that it is not to be desired that silver shall be excluded from free coinage in Europe and the United States; second, that the use of both gold and silver as unlimited legal tender may be safely adopted by equalizing them at a ratio fixed by international agreement.

Then the convention resolved — what? Simply this, and nothing more: That the difference of opinion that had appeared excluded the adoption of a common ratio between the two metals, and then adjourned.

The next, or third, conference was called by France and the United States, and was held in 1881, nineteen countries being represented. The delegates from Sweden said that they had better reaffirm the declaration of 1878, and the conference reaffirmed that declaration and adjourned never to meet again. The declaration of 1878 was that the differences of opinion which had appeared excluded the adoption of a common ratio between the two metals.

The next conference was held at Brussels in 1892. At that conference the United States proposed, not the free and unlimited coinage of silver at any ratio, but simply this: The United States had at first sent an invitation to Great Britain, asking that government to join us in a convention to adopt both metals at a ratio to be agreed upon. Great Britain refused to accept the invitation to the conference to discuss the question of agreeing upon a ratio for the coinage of the two metals, but, when we changed the invitation so as to provide for simply meeting and discussing the question of the enlarged use of silver, Great Britain joined in the conference, and this was the program of the United States in the conference of 1892:

That in the opinion of this conference it is desirable that some measure should be found for increasing the use of silver in the currency system of the nations.

That was all. No greater or broader resolution would be accepted by Great Britain. Neither would she join us in a conference to discuss the question of the ratio. But what more? Mr. Wilson, a delegate from Great Britain, immediately said:

"Her Majesty's Government did not find it possible to accept an invitation conveyed in terms which might give rise to a misunderstanding by implying that the Government had some doubt as to the maintenance of the monetary system which had been in force in Great Britain since 1816."

Speaking of Sir Charles Freemantle and himself, he said:

"Our faith is that of the school of monometallism pure and simple. We do not admit that any other than the simple gold standard would be applicable to our country."

Early in the session the leading delegate from Germany declared:

"Germany, being satisfied with its monetary system, has no intention of modifying its basis...In view of the satisfactory monetary situation of the Empire, the Imperial Government has prescribed the most strict reserve for its delegates, who, in consequence, cannot take part either in the discussion or in the vote upon the resolution presented by the delegates of the United States."

Germany, in that conference, then refused to discuss or vote one way or another upon a proposition simply for the enlarged use of silver.

Austria-Hungary, although represented in the conference, instructed their delegate to take no part in the conference, in its discussion or votes.

The delegate from the Netherlands declared:

"That Holland would not enter into a bimetallic union without the full and complete participation of England, is a part of the formal instructions furnished us by our government."

France made the same declaration practically; in fact, absolutely the same declaration, that she would not participate in any agreement unless England joined.

The convention adjourned to meet again at some future time, to be called again, some time within the then coming year, but it never reassembled. Afterwards, the Congress of the United States passed a bill providing for nine delegates to a monetary conference whenever we could find anybody who would confer with us; and we were unable to find anyone who would join in a conference and who would talk with us about this question, and the law lapsed by limitation of time.

The United States had become a capitalist nation — producing surplus wealth; exporting it in the form of goods and investment funds, living on the interest that these investments produced, and thus saddling upon the backs of the undeveloped countries of the world the burden of taking care of those nations which were rich enough to bind the poorer peoples to them by the lending of money.

The gold standard was a part of the harness that the eastern bankers had used to drive the western farmers. The fight was lo.st by the free silverites. The gold standard won the day and with that victory went the triumph of protection, the establishment of a trust-controlled government, the degradation of labor, and the assurance of plutocracy's power.

The Government of the United States has allowed interested parties — creditors and bankers — to manipulate its credit and volume of money in such a way as to produce panics and, by this means, to plunder those who toil. These panics have come at stated intervals. M. Juglar (a French authority) has fully analyzed the three phases of American business life into prosperity, panic and liquidation, which three constitute themselves into a 'business cycle" which ordinarily occupies about ten years. These ten years may be apportioned roughly as follows: Prosperity, five to seven years; panics, a few months to a few years; liquidation, three or four years.

On the next page is a list, with dates, of all the panics in the United States during the last century, with the corresponding dates for France and England.

What evidence could be more conclusive of the utter failure of a system of economic life than these successive breakdowns in the machinery of production and exchange? Yet here is the record upon which the present economic system must stand condemned in the eyes of every thinking human being — the record of disaster following disaster, with neither the inclination nor the ability, on the part of the masters of business life, to put a stop to these successive stoppages of economic activity.

The figures just cited show that, during the past century, panics have occurred in England and France at the same time that they occurred in the United States. These three countries are linked together by the "gold standard," and their governments are capitalistic governments — administered by the banks and creditor classes for the benefit, not of the people, but for the benefit of the rich. Furthermore, all three countries

France	England	United States
1804	1803	....
1810	1810	....
1813-14	1815	1814
1818	1818	1818
1825	1825	1826
1830	1830	1829-31
1837-39	1836-39	1837-39
1847	1847	1848
1857	1857	1857
1864	1864-66	1864
....	1873	1873
1882	1882	1884
1889-90	1890-91	1890-91
1894	1894	1893-94
1897	1897	1897
1903	1903	1903
1907	1907	1907
1913	1913	1913

have the same, or about the same, distribution of wealth. In each of these countries the workers are robbed of what they produce by the same process. The creditor classes, through their privileges, are able to manipulate the money and credit through panics, so as to produce, first, a rise in prices — by expansion of money and credit, then a withdrawal of both, followed by a sudden drop in prices, and then liquidation. Or, in other words, a gathering in of all property produced by toil. With the liquidation, the cycle is completed and there follows a new cycle of ten years more, of prosperity, panic and liquidation.

I have had an excellent opportunity to observe the effect of these successive economic disasters upon the producing class. I went to the Territory of Dakota in 1869 and located at Sioux Falls, near the northwest corner of the State of Iowa. At that time, all of the land in Dakota was owned by the Government and was subject to entry under the Homestead and Pre-emption laws, and could only be secured by actual settlers. The result of the panic of 1873 caused very many of these homesteaders to commute their homesteads, because the price of farm products had declined below the cost of production. As a result, the movement for farm tenancy was begun. The United States publishes no figures on farm tenure previous to 1880, but by that year the percentage of tenant farmers in the rich Middle West was for Illinois, 23.7 per cent; Michigan, 31.4 per cent; Iowa, 23.8 per cent; Missouri, 27.3 per cent; Nebraska, 18 per cent, and Kansas, 16.3 per cent.

The next great disaster to the producing classes culminated in the manufactured panic of 1893. Grover Cleveland had been elected President of the United States upon the tariff issue in 1892, and when he took office in 1893 he called a meeting of Congress for the purpose of repealing the purchasing clauses of the Sherman law of 1890, which provided that the Treasurer of the United States should purchase and coin not less than two million dollars' worth of silver and not more than four and a half million dollars' worth during each month, thus adding to the volume of circulating medium. The cutting-off of four and a half millions of silver by the repeal of the Sherman law purchasing clauses, with its consequent decline in the volume of money, proved disastrous. The prices of all farm products fell sharply, causing the ruin of the agricultural classes and a prolonged panic nearly as disastrous as that of 1873.

The members of the House of Representatives, who believed in bimetallism, called a meeting a day or two before Congress was to assemble, and 201 members of the House declared that they were in favor of both gold and silver as money, because there was not gold enough in the world to furnish a circulating medium. Two weeks afterwards, when the vote was taken in the House of Representatives on the bill to completely democratize silver by repealing the purchasing clause of the Sherman Act, one hundred of these members had been bought over, through patronage and money and party pressure, to the interests of the bankers, and thus the bill was passed.

The panic of 1893, resulting from this act, which involved a contraction of the volume of money and a reduction in prices, again drove large numbers of people from the land and reduced agricultural production below a remunerative point. As a result of this panic and the panic of 1873, the lands in Dakota, which had all been owned by the cultivators, passed into the hands of the mortgage companies, the banks, the creditors, so that in the county where I reside — Minnehaha County, South Dakota — 52 per cent of the farms now are cultivated by tenants. Within my memory, every acre of land in that county belonged to the Government. Both in the panic of 1873 and in that of 1893 the results were the same. The owners and monopolists of money used their monopoly power to squeeze the small producer and to enrich themselves.

The panic of 1893 was followed by the discovery in South Africa of the richest gold deposit in the world and within the next few years these mines produced vast sums of gold to be used as money, and caused a rise in the price of everything that is the product of human toil.

These were the two outstanding economic disasters that occurred during my connection with public affairs. Both arose from similar causes and both produced like results — the concentration of wealth in the hands of the few; the bankruptcy of the small business man and of the farmer; unemployment, distress and lowered wages for the worker; crime, suicide and murder.

The great deposits of gold which had been poured into the currency of the world by the discoveries in California in the early fifties endangered the mortgage-holding classes of all the capitalist nations.

Chevalier, one of the mo.st prominent financiers of Europe, published a book in which he contended that gold must be demonetized; that the continuous use of gold as money would work universal repudiation; that it was dishonest and wicked to pay debts in gold under such a flood as was coming from California and Australia. His voice was potent. Germany and Holland —

31

creditor nations — closed their mints to gold and adopted the silver standard. Maclaren of England, representing the bondholders of the British Empire, made the same argument in the early fifties against the use of gold, which has since been used by gold standard contractionists for more than sixty years against the use of silver. In his argument in favor of the bondholders, Chevalier said:

"Our neighbors on the Continent received the announcement of these remarkable discoveries in a different spirit. From the first they have considered them of the greatest importance and have expressed great solicitude for the maintenance of the standard value."

Immediately that the fact of a great increase in the production of gold was established, the Government of Holland — "a nation justly renowned," says M. Chevalier, "for its foresight and probity," discarded gold from its currency. "They may," says the same author, "have been rather hasty in passing this law, but in a matter of this nature it is better to be in advance of events than to let them pass us."

France appointed a monetary commission which considered the question of demonetizing gold for several years and, finally, reported that it was necessary to demonetize one or the other of the precious metals — that the supply was violating contracts by depreciating money with which debts were paid. Up to this time the creditor classes in England, France and the United States had accepted bimetallism. The rush of California gold endangered their monopoly. The discovery of the Comstock lode threatened to deluge the world with silver, and Mr. Lindeman, Director of the United States Mint, reported in London that there were fifteen hundred millions of silver in sight in one mine on the Comstock.

When gold became very abundant in the middle of the century, the creditor classes wanted to demonetize that metal in order to make money scarce. Then came the flood of silver, and they feared that more than gold,

John Sherman undertook the duty of carrying into effect in the United States the demonetizing of silver. John J. Knox, Comptroller of the Currency, a crafty, scheming, money-making individual, got up a codification of the mint laws. John Sherman introduced the bill, and continually talked about the silver dollar, the inscriptions on it, etc. But when the bill became a law it was found that there was no provision for a silver dollar in the bill, the trade dollar containing 120 grains taking the place of the silver dollar, and thus silver was demonetized, and it was made easy for the creditor classes of the world to corner gold and thus to control money.

How conscientiously this control over money has been exercised is indicated by the actions and utterances of the bankers themselves.

The American Colonies had been in the habit, for a number of years before the Revolution, of issuing what were then known as Colonial Treasury notes; the notes were made receivable by the several provinces for taxes. These Colonial notes being adopted by all the Colonies led to an unexpected degree of prosperity, so great that when Franklin was brought before the Parliament of Great Britain and questioned as to the cause of the wonderful prosperity growing up in the Colonies, he plainly stated that the cause was the convenience they found in exchanging their various forms of labor one with another by the paper money, which had been adopted: that this paper money was not only used in the payment of taxes, but in addition it had been declared legal tender. After Franklin explained this to the British Government as the real cause of prosperity, they immediately passed laws forbidding the payment of taxes in that money.

In 1862, the creditors of the United States, the Bank of England, sent the following circular to every bank in New York and New England:

"Slavery is likely to be abolished by the war power, and chattel slavery destroyed. This, I and my European friends are in favor of, for slavery is but the owning of labor and carries with it the care for the laborer, while the European plan, led on by England, is for capital to control labor by controlling the wages. THIS CAN BE DONE BY CONTROLLING THE MONEY. The great debt that capitalists will see to it is made out of the war must be used as a means to control the volume of money. To accomplish this, the bonds must be used as a banking basis. We are now waiting for the Secretary of the Treasury to make the recommendation to Congress. It will not do to allow the greenback, as it is called, to circulate as money any length of time, as we cannot control that."

In 1872, the ring of bankers in New York sent the following circular to every bank in the United States:

"Dear Sir: It is advisable to do all in your power to sustain such prominent daily and weekly newspapers, especially the agricultural and religious press, as will oppose the issuing of greenback paper money, and that you also withhold patronage or favors from all applicants who are not willing to oppose the Government issue of money. Let the Government issue the coin and the banks issue the paper money of the country, for then we can better protect each other. To repeal the law creating National Bank notes, or to restore to circulation the Government issue of money, will be to provide the people with money, and will therefore seriously affect your individual profit as bankers and lenders. See your Congressman at once, and engage him to support our interests that we may control legislation."

The panic of 1893 was a bankers' panic and in their interest and the ring of gambling bankers in New York sent out the following circular to every bank in the United States:

"Dear Sir: The interests of national bankers require immediately financial legislation by Congress. Silver, silver certificates and Treasury notes must be retired and National Bank notes upon a gold basis made the only money. This will require the authorization of from $500,000,000 to $1,000,000,000 of new bonds as a basis of circulation. You will at once retire one-third of your circulation and call in one-half of your loans. Be careful to make a money stringency felt among your patrons, especially among influential business men. Advocate an extra session of Congress for the repeal of the purchasing clause of the Sherman law, and act with the other banks of your city in securing a large petition to Congress for its unconditional repeal, per accompanying form. Use personal influence with Congressmen and particularly let your wishes be known to your Senators. The future life of National Banks as fixed and safe investments depends upon immediate action, as there is an increasing sentiment in favor of Government legal tender notes and silver coinage."

Mr. Alexander is right about the strength of the American banking system. Under the Federal Reserve Act the vast power of the thirty thousand American banks is concentrated in the hands of a little club with headquarters in Wall Street. This club holds in its hands the power to make or to destroy any business man in the United States; the power to make or wreck financial institutions and inaugurate panics; the power to issue credit, and even money. The bankers at the center of the financial web are endowed with the power of government.

The right to issue money is, as I have said, fundamental. This right is exercised by the New York Bankers' Club, thinly disguised as the Federal Reserve Board. On November 3, 1920, the amount of Federal Reserve notes outstanding was $3,568,713,000.

What was the basis of this huge issue of paper money? Commercial paper!

The member banks were permitted to lend money (or credit) to their patrons; to take commercial paper in exchange for their loans; to deposit this paper under the authority of the Board and to issue currency against it. This currency was again loaned out, the paper redeposited, etc., so that the Federal Reserve Bank of New York was able to earn, by this pyramiding of credits, over 200 per cent in the frugal year of 1920, in a market where the rate of interest never ran over 8 per cent on standard securities.

Through their authority over money and credit, the bankers thus became the arbiters of the business destiny of the United States. No one elected them. No one can recall them. There is no way in which they can be made the object of public approval or disapproval. They are as far above public responsibility as was William Hohenzollern in Germany before 1914. Self-elected dictators of American life, they make and unmake; they wreck and rule. They are the heart of business America; the center of the exploiting system that sits astride the necks of the people.

The United States emerged from the Great War with the best credit of any of the larger nations. Its wealth was the greatest; its income the largest, and its bank assets and resources exceeded those of any other country; but this very economic position, centered as it is in the hands of bankers, will be used by them to exploit the peoples of Latin America and Asia as they have, during recent years, exploited the people of the United States. Exploitation is the profession of the banker, and those in charge of the American banking institutions have the greatest exploiting opportunity that has ever come to the bankers in any of the modern nations.

The banks are again issuing circulars and in April or May, 1920, the order went out from New York, from this club which is our government, to all the Reserve Banks throughout the United States, to call their loans and to refuse credit on all the products of human toil not controlled by the combinations.

The result has been, of course, the reduction in the price of everything that is produced in the way of food and raw material, and to a very low point, causing the ultimate ruin of all those who cultivate the soil. And it was not because there was not plenty of money, for there is more money -several times over in circulation in the United States than ever before in our history. We have secured most of the gold of Europe, and I know of my own knowledge positively that these bankers are financing the bankrupt nations of Europe. For instance, they loaned France a hundred millions a few months ago, and within the last six months they have loaned Norway twenty millions. And so another panic is in progress.

The banking system of this country is so organized and constituted as to take from the producer the result of his effort; purposely so organized; organized with the intention of controlling the volume of money; contracting and expanding credit so as to produce a panic, or apparent prosperity, as suits the purpose of its organizers and managers.

This system of banking was the invention of Lord Overstone, with the assistance of the acute minds of the Rothschild bankers of Europe, and was so constructed as to enhance the importance of capital and overshadow the importance of toil. The system is one based upon a small volume of legal tender money, and the limit of this volume they would make as small as possible, in order that they may control it absolutely. Expansion by the issue of credit, not legal tender; contraction by the withdrawal of credit. Expansion that they may sell the property of the producers, which they have taken in with the last contraction, and then contract again in order to wreck the enterprising and once more reap the harvest of their efforts. This is the banking system of Great Britain, and the banking system of every gold standard country in the world today. It is the banking system of the United States. This is the system the Republican party is pledged to strengthen and perpetuate. There is no hope of relief for the people of this agricultural country in any possible thing the Republican party can or will do. In 1873, fearing that the volume of metallic money would become too large, these manipulators of panics, these gatherers of the products of other people's toil, set about to secure the demonetization of silver and make all their contracts payable in gold. The result has been, as the thinking ones of every nation agree, that in every gold standard country on the globe, agricultural prices have fallen steadily until we have reached a point where the cost of production is denied the producer. The present Federal Reserve law adopted by the United States is but a culmination of all the infamous banking systems ever invented by any age or people, and it has already produced the practical enslavement of the people of the United States.

Banking and the issue of money and credit are the duties of the sovereign and should be performed by the Government for service and not for profit, and for the equal good of the whole population. Section 8, Paragraph 5 of the Constitution of the United States says:

35

"Congress shall have power to coin money, regulate the value thereof and of foreign coins. Congress is not by the Constitution authorized to delegate the power to any person or corporation."

The functions of money are created by law and are legal tender, a measure of value and, as a result, a medium of exchange, and the value of the unit of money depends upon the law of supply and demand, and the volume of money should be regulated so as to maintain a steady range of prices, and this can be done by the use of index number. No substance should be used as money that has any value besides its money value.

And, above all, no metal should be used that has a commodity value, as the volume of money is liable to be affected by hoarding and by being shipped away to other countries, and by being consumed in the arts. In fact, money should never be international. It is the most important tool that a nation can possess for the transaction of its business, and it is more idiotic to ship it out of the country to pay balances than it would be for a farmer to ship his implements, plows and reaper away and sell them for seed; or a manufacturer to strip his factory of its machines and sell them for raw material.

5. The Tariff

Next, perhaps, to the money system, the tariff is the handiest weapon that the American business interests have at their disposal. I believe in a tariff, provided it is accompanied by a free and untrammeled competitive system of production. The purpose of such a tariff would be to give temporary assistance to such industries as are necessary to the sound economic life of a country. Once the competitive system is destroyed, however, the tariff falls to the ground, becomes merely an instrument in the hands of the Government for the plundering of the people through the agency of their monopolistic combinations. Under such circumstances a tariff cannot be justified unless a man is in favor of stealing.

The tariff bills that I saw enacted, two by Republican Congresses and one by a Democratic Congress, aimed to distribute favors and special privileges to those industries that were strong enough to demand them and to enforce their demands. The Wilson Bill, passed by a Democratic Congress, provided almost as much protection as the McKinley and Dingley bills, passed by the Republicans. The commodities on the free list were changed, but the principle of protection was accepted by both great parties. Both were serving business and business demanded protection.

It was to meet this situation that I urged (May 29, 1894) a tariff commission with power to examine the books of every protected industry in order to ascertain the cost of producing these goods in the United States; to compare this cost with the cost of producing them abroad, and thus to determine a fair rate of protection for the home industries. I urged at that time that the tariff commission be established as a permanent bureau in order to make protection a science. The business interests, who were clamoring for protection, did not wish it to be a science. On the contrary, they looked upon it as a sinecure.

I had a further reason for believing in a protective tariff as a means of preventing nations which produced similar lines of goods from trading with one another.

Commerce is a tax on industry. The act of producing wealth has already been finished when commerce begins. A nation should therefore trade only with nations so situated as to soil and climate that their products are different, and are naturally necessary to comfort and happiness. The United States should, therefore, trade chiefly, not with Europe, but with the countries of the tropics, and our industries should be so adjusted that our surplus would pay for those things which we cannot produce; and this would be our condition today if we produced everything to which our soil and climate are adapted.

We should insist that the man who produces the things we can produce shall live here, if he wants us to buy them; shall help support our Government; shall be a taxpayer and a defender of our institutions; we should have the art and the artisan as well as the article, and thus be able to reproduce it. In this way, by varied industry alone, can we bring out all that is in our people, every trait of character, every variety of talent, and can produce an unmatched race of men and an unparalleled civilization.

The United States is endowed by nature with the greatest natural resources of any equal area of the earth's surface. We have the most intelligent, free, vigorous and active people. Our wealth and prosperity depend upon the amount we draw from nature's inexhaustible storehouse and that, in turn, depends upon the industry, frugality and sobriety of the living generation.

Little is left over from one age to another; the nearer we can bring consumer and producer together, the smaller the friction and the less the wear and tear and the expense of energy in making the exchange, and the greater the amount of production. It makes no difference what price we pay each other for our products; if our laws are just there will be an equal and fair distribution of wealth, and, as a result, universal happiness. The theory of free trade is beautiful, and if all the people on earth had an equal chance, were all equally intelligent, moral and industrious, and lived together under the same just laws, free trade might be universally enacted with profit to all.

But these conditions do not exist. Therefore, if we enact free trade our great natural resources and our accumulated wealth would be dissipated throughout the earth, resulting in a slight rise in the scale of living and civilization of all mankind and a great fall in the scale of living and civilization of our own people. An old illustration is apt. If you connect two ponds of water, one large and at a low level, the other small and at a high level, they will both reach the same level — the large one rising a little and the small one falling very much. So it would be with us were we to adopt free trade; for from it results the corollary that our people must do whatever they can do and grow whatever they can produce in competition with all the rest of the world.

What can we economically produce in competition with the starving millions of Asia or the paupers of Europe? England Is trying the experiment; with what result? Great aggregations of wealth; numerous millionaires living in incredible extravagance; but a million of her people on an average are paupers always — twenty-eight out of each one thousand of her population. One person out of every twelve needs relief to keep from starvation; one-half of the people of England who reach the age of sixty are or have been paupers. Is this a pleasant picture — an example fit to follow? India, with the oldest civilization on the globe, has reached a little worse state than England.

India suffers from a widespread famine every four or five years; eighty out of every one hundred of her people never have enough to eat; sixteen out of every one hundred have barely enough to eat; four out of every one hundred live in idleness and luxury, and these are the castes which separate the people so that there is no chance to rise and no future but death.

Free trade is not a panacea, and not even a probable remedy; and while a tariff will enrich us as a nation it will not cause a just distribution of wealth among our own people unless we have just laws which confer equal opportunities.

Pursuant to this theory, I presented in the Senate on June 4, 1897, during the famous debate on the Dingley Tariff, an argument in favor of a duty on nickel (Volume 30, page 1500) to illustrate the point I was making.

"The great issues that are before the people of the United States today reach further than a controversy over the amount of tariff on any item in the pending bill. They are the great questions which determine whether we will march on in the course of freedom and liberty and maintain our republic, or whether we will become a plutocracy — not a plutocracy of natural persons, but a plutocracy of artificial persons; whether we will continue to be what in fact we are today — a government of the corporations, for the corporations and by the corporations, or whether we will go back to what we were in the past — a government of, for, and by the people.

"The provision of the Senate Committee in regard to nickel is equivalent to no duty at all. The Senate Committee has provided as to nickel a duty of six cents per pound, and then has inserted in brackets "except nickel matte." Of course, under that provision, all of the nickel would come in, for nickel matte is simply the nickel extracted from the ore, with such other metals as accompany it in the ore. Then they can be separated in this country. It would all come in free, nickel matte being free. There it is absolute free trade. That provision is a good deal like a good many other provisions in the bill - obscure; not intended to deceive, but having that effect. We can produce all the nickel used in this country, and yet what is the history of this industry? There are nickel mines in Missouri, Pennsylvania, Arkansas, Washington, North Carolina, Colorado, New Mexico, California, Oregon, Nevada and South Dakota."

Mr. QUAY: "The mines in Pennsylvania have been abandoned."

Mr. PETTIGREW: "The Senator from Pennsylvania says that the mines in Pennsylvania have been abandoned. So they have been in every one of the states I have named. Pennsylvania is no exception. So would the Pennsylvania mills be abandoned if you had free trade. Open your doors to the low-paid labor of Asia, compensated in silver, and your mills will be abandoned; the doors will be closed. There is no question about it.

"Let us see what is the history of nickel. We produced in the United States in 1885, 275,000 pounds of nickel; in 1886, 214,000 pounds; in 1887, 205,000 pounds; in 1889, 252,000 pounds; in 1890, 223,000 pounds; in 1891, 118,000 pounds; in 1892, 92,000 pounds; in 1893, 49,000 pounds; in 1894, 9,000 pounds. I have not the figures for 1896, but I understand the production went on declining, one mine after another closing throughout the country.

"When they are all closed, you will pay twice what you now have to pay for nickel. What is the occasion of the decline in the industry? A deposit of nickel was discovered in Canada which is so rich in nickel and copper that the copper pays the cost of production. Therefore, the nickel costs nothing. They can put the price at any figure they choose. The moment they have destroyed the industry in this country you will pay two prices for your nickel again, and no one will dare to open the mines of the United States in view of this known competition, because they know the moment they open the mines and invest their money in the industry the Canadians can come in and put down the price so as to wreck their enterprise and make them. lose their capital.

"What we want, then, is a duty upon nickel sufficiently large, so that it can be produced in this country constantly and so that we shall not be in the hands of a foreign producer, and so that with our high-priced labor we can continue the production. It will not shut out the Canadian nickel, because it can come to this market anyway, no matter what the duty is. Their nickel costs nothing. We have mines in Oregon, for instance, the ore from which has taken the premium, but it is not accompanied with copper in sufficient quantity so that the copper will pay for mining both. Yet men are ready today to go ahead, but not under the provisions of this bill, and put up works costing $150,000 to mine nickel in Oregon and Washington, provided a sufficient duty is placed upon the article so that they can mine it and be safe from absolute ruin by Canadian competition. I hold that there is justice in their claim..

"We can mine nickel profitably in Dakota, but we cannot do it — we cannot get capital to do it — if we know that at our door is a deposit which can put the price where it will absolutely destroy all profit and not even permit us to make enough to pay the cost of production. I hold it is good policy to place a duty upon nickel sufficient so that we can keep our mines open. Then we will always keep the price at a reasonable figure. Then, if the duty is enough so that it will assure the working of the American mines, we will not be at the mercy of the foreigners to double the price when our mines are closed. I hold that it is good, patriotic policy again to open the mines which produced almost enough nickel to supply our wants in the past, and do it by a duty of fifteen cents a pound upon nickel, and not admit nickel matte free."

My argument carried no weight. The tariff was not based on any theory, nor did it appeal to science. Instead, it was an agglomeration of concessions to special interests. When this became clear to me, I adopted another method of approach to the problem. These were the years when the feeling against "trusts" was running high. I, therefore, decided to relate the two problems by introducing an amendment to the tariff bill (55th Cong., 1st Session, p. 1893), providing that trust-controlled products should be admitted free of duty.

In the end, the amendment was rejected, but it occasioned a lively debate, of which I reproduce a part:

Mr. PETTIGREW: "Up to the last national convention the amendment which I have offered was in strict accord with the platform, the principles, and the policies of the Republican party. But the last convention of the Republican party at St. Louis left that plank out of their platform. Previous to that time the Republican party had declared for bi-metallism. Bi-metallism is dangerous to trusts, because trusts do not thrive on rising prices, but flourish when prices decline. Therefore, if the trusts were to be left out, and bi-metallism left out, everything would be in absolute harmony. The platform, accorded apparently with the policies of the convention. If this was accidental, if this provision was left out of the platform by an oversight, if it was not left out because the trusts had gained possession of the convention, and did not desire to abuse each other, then, of course, that will be illustrated by the vote today.

In the platform of 1888 the Republican party declared:

"We declare our opposition to all combinations of capital, organized in trusts or otherwise, to control arbitrarily the condition of trade among our citizens; and we recommend to Congress and the State legislatures, in their respective jurisdictions, such legislation as will prevent the execution of all schemes to oppress the people by undue charges on their supplies, or by unjust rates for the transportation of their products to market. We approve the legislation by Congress to prevent alike burdens and unfair discriminations between the states.

"And that is good Republican doctrine. It was at that time, at the next convention, in 1892, the Republican party declared:

"We reaffirm our opposition, declared in the Republican platform of 1888, to all combinations of capital organized in trusts or otherwise to control arbitrarily the condition of trade among our citizens. We heartily endorse the action already taken upon this subject and ask for such further legislation as may be required to remedy any defects in existing laws and to render their enforcement more complete and effective.

"Today we have a chance to carry out the plank in that platform and enact those necessary laws, to enact one of those protective provisions to carry out this platform by declaring that every article controlled by a trust or by a combination to limit production or increase the price shall be subject to the competition of the world, unless the trust will dissolve. The punishment is, therefore, automatic. The trust can decide whether it will go out of existence or contest the rich American market with the manufacturers of other countries.

"It is absolutely and strictly in accordance with the fundamental principles of protection as laid down by the Republican party since it came into existence, for the Republican doctrine was that by protection we reduce the price of the article to the consumer; that by protection we build up competition at home; that competition lowers the price and does justice to the consumer. But, Mr. President, when you allow the existence of a trust to control that price and then fix a tariff by which they can raise the price to the limit of the tariff, you have overturned every principle of protection. You cannot justify this bill without the amendment..."

Mr. ALLISON: "I asked the Senator from South Dakota, when he introduced the amendment, to allow it to be passed over, in order that it might come in at its proper place and be more maturely considered. I am strengthened in this view by the criticisms that have already been made upon the amendment. It deals with a very important subject, and deals with it in a way that may be effective; or, instead of working justice, it may work injustice. It goes upon the assumption that the way to cure this evil is by punishing the people who are engaged in trusts by placing all the articles manufactured in the country of a like character upon the free list. It assumes also that the tariff itself is the author of the trust.

"I remember very well, as a good many Senators on this floor remember, that we had a long debate on the question of dealing with trusts and the remedies some six or seven years ago. The venerable Senator from Ohio, now Secretary of State, introduced a bill upon that subject. It was referred, I think, to the Committee on Agriculture at first, and reported from that committee. That may not have been the committee. My recollection is not very distinct upon that subject. It was reported back and debated here for a week or two. Then it was referred to the Judiciary Committee and was considered for some weeks by that committee, and then reported back here and debated, and finally passed.

"I submit to the Senate that a matter which may do injustice, which may be an ineffectual remedy, which may only do partially what is sought to be done, should have more mature consideration than can be given to it in debate here from day to day upon the subject. So I appeal again to the Senator from South Dakota to allow the amendment to be passed over for the time being until we have finished these schedules, and then reintroduce it when Senators on both sides of the chamber shall have an opportunity to present modifications or amendments to it. If the Senator will do that I think it will facilitate our work on the tariff bill."

Mr. PETTIGREW: "I wish to make my reply at some length. Mr. President, I will say in answer to the question of the Senator from Iowa that I have no pride with regard to the form of this amendment. All I desire is to accomplish the purpose which is clearly indicated by the amendment. Neither have I any pride in its being my amendment. Let us discuss and point out what defects, if any, there are in the amendment. I think the subject is of sufficient importance for the Senate to consider it until we perfect the amendment.

Where it is attacked in good faith, I believe the Senator attacking it should offer an amendment to the amendment which will cure the defect. Of course, I understand that when a Senator wishes to find an excuse for going against the amendment he can find it, and he can find it in technical quibbles. Capable and able lawyers can readily raise plenty of those,...We have asserted in all our arguments to the American people that the tariff produces competition, and competition reduces prices. On every stump we have told the people how an imported article, Fuller's Earth, for instance, was worth from nineteen to thirty-two dollars a ton, but we discovered it in this country and began its production under a very small duty, when the price fell to twelve dollars a ton in a year and a half. It was the same with nails. It seems to me that if we wish to perpetuate the principles of protection and defend this bill, we must carry out that policy which we have so often advocated and give to the American consumer a competitive market. That is all I desire. Cannot we perfect an amendment, then, that will accomplish that object?

"But, Mr. President, I have my doubts about some Senators wanting to do this. I think it has been developed in this debate, and in the votes that have been taken, that some Senators do not want to do this. They do not want to give to the people of this country a competitive market...

"Mr. President, in regard to this amendment, I have this to say: I am perfectly willing it shall go over until tomorrow, so that we may discuss and perfect it. The American people are against the trust. They are not willing to allow any Senator in this body to vote against this amendment simply because its phraseology does not suit him. Neither are Senators going to crawl out by a quibble that amendment will not accomplish the object it has in view. It is the duty of any Senator who objects to the amendment to perfect my amendment, and I shall be glad to accept such an amendment."

Later in the same debate Senator Piatt of Connecticut had a discussion over the duty on Fuller's Earth. During the discussion, Senator Piatt accused me of not being a protectionist "except in spots." To this charge I replied (Cong. Record, 55th Cong., 1st Sess., p. 2041, June 26, 1897):

"Further, Mr. President, I do not know that I care to disclaim or admit the charge as to whether I am a protectionist or not. I believe that the nation should do its own work. I believe that a varied industry is necessary to the development of the best traits of character and the highest civilization among any people. I believe that it is the nation's duty to encourage that varied industry which will enable every talent among its people to be developed to its fullest extent.

"Because I refused to vote for 185 per cent duty on woolen goods, the Senator from Connecticut stands up here to say that I am a protectionist only in spots. Because I refused to vote for 700 per cent duty on the lower grades of silk, used by the poor people of this country, the Senator from Connecticut says I am a protectionist only in spots.

"Well, if to be a protectionist all over a man must vote for 700 per cent duty on the cheaper articles and for 10 per cent on the higher-priced articles that are used by the rich, I am only a protectionist in spots. If to be a protectionist I must vote for an extra duty on sugar purely and absolutely in the interest of the most corrupt and demoralizing trust ever organized in this country, at the behest and dictation of a political caucus, then I am a protectionist only in spots. If I must vote for every trust, if I must vote for every combination, vote special privileges to the few, high rates of duty, differential duty, in order that they pay be encouraged in their raids upon the people of this country, then, Mr. President, I am not a protectionist all over.

"Is the Republican party a protection party? Why, Mr. President, the issue of protection has departed from our politics. When New England made her trade with the cotton Democrats of the South for the purpose of putting a duty on cotton, thinking to break Up the Solid South, she abandoned the only principle, the only issue, that gave the party character, and it has left you nothing with which to fight the next campaign. All the Republican party stands for today, inasmuch as protection is no longer an issue and the South is broken up, is as the champion of the trusts and the gold standard, as the special representative of the classes against the masses."

Thus I had tried three lines of attack. First, I had tried to have a tariff commission to determine tariff schedules on a scientific basis. Second, I had tried to show to what extent particular schedules were working hardship. Third, I had attempted to rationalize the tariff by denying protection to trusts. I failed along all three lines, and I failed because the tariff was not a scientific means of regulating industry, in the interest of public welfare, but a cleverly disguised method used by certain industrial freebooters to increase their profits.

During the twelve years that I was a member of the Senate of the United States no effort was ever made to pass a tariff bill in the interests of the people of the United States; they were entirely left out of consideration. Two-thirds of the Senate were always lawyers and they were simply interested in passing a tariff bill that would enrich their clients and at the same time humbug the American people into the belief that it was being done in their interest.

Allison of Iowa was from an agricultural state, and you would have supposed that he would have looked after the interests of the people of Iowa; but he never did. He was in the Senate as the representative of the transportation, the financial and industrial combinations. Piatt of Connecticut, another lawyer, was in the same category. The committees were all packed in the interests of business, and a majority of each committee that had charge of the tariff or any other branch of legislation were men (attorneys, as a rule) who were there to look after the exploiters of the people of the United States. I also state without hesitation or qualification that no trust legislation was ever considered by any committee in the Senate except with a view to allowing the trusts to prosper and flourish and, at the same time, so word the law as to humbug and deceive the American people. That the leaders were in the employ of the great industrial combinations and that they exercised considerable cunning in their practices to bring about this result. The tariff and the trusts always received the fostering care of the lawyers of the Senate and House and were never framed or intended to be framed to protect the interests of the people of the United States.

6. The Trusts

I was in the Senate when the Sherman Anti-Trust Law was passed in 1890. I was there representing a state that was rabidly opposed to trusts in theory and trusts in practice. For twelve years I worked and voted to drive the trusts out of American politics, and yet, as if in ironical comment on the futility of my efforts, the Steel Trust — greatest of them all — was organized during my last year in the Senate (1901).

The people of South Dakota lived on the land and still believed in the necessity for competition. They had grown up under the conviction that our civilization is founded upon the theory of evolution, upon the doctrine of the survival of the fittest, upon the law of competition. The result of this theory in the past was feudalism, or the supremacy of brute strength and physical courage, and its resulting paternalism. But feudalism, by the operation of the law of competition and evolution, destroyed itself by the subjugation of the weaker by the stronger and the creation of monarchical forms of government in its place.

My history had taught me these facts. Coming from a state that was still under the control of farmers, small shop-keepers and professional men, I believed that this theory of competitive life held out the soundest answer to the many public questions then confronting the country. Despite all my efforts, I witnessed the abandonment of the old theory and the adoption of a new practice — the practice of trust organization. Competition, under this theory, ceased to be the life of trade, and became an irksome form of activity that should be dispensed with at the earliest convenient moment.

We, the American people, have abandoned the doctrine we often repeated and so much believed, that competition is the life of trade, and have adopted the doctrine that competition destroys trade. The practice of this new economic theory calls for the organization of trusts and combinations to restrict production, to maintain and increase prices, until practically all of the important articles manufactured in the country are produced by combinations and trusts. Thus the fundamental principle of the early American civilization is overturned, and those who do not combine — the farmer, the individual proprietor, the professional man and the toilers on the land — are at the mercy of those who do combine.

The rapid growth of trusts in the United States began with demonetization of silver, and the formation of trusts was the means adopted by some of the most far-seeing and shrewdest men, having control and direction of capital invested in manufacturing and transportation, to avert losses to themselves by reason of falling prices, which lead to overproduction and under-consumption. They realized that the first effect of a decline in prices is to stimulate production, because the producers hope to make up the difference in price by larger sales at less expense. They also foresaw what the average producer fails to see, that when the decline of prices is general the purchasing power is less in the whole community, and therefore an increased production can find no market at any price, so that there exists at the same time an overproduction of things which are most needed and an under-consumption of these very things, because of the inability to purchase them.

The organizers of the trusts did not go into the causes of falling prices. In most cases they knew nothing about the natural effects of throwing the entire burden upon one metal constituting the basis of the money of the world, which had formerly rested upon both gold and silver. So they made the common error of mistaking effect for cause, and attributed the decline in prices to overproduction. Therefore they combined and formed trusts to restrict production and keep up prices. The effect of the successful operations of trusts is to compel higher prices to be paid for the finished product, or for transportation, while they do not check the decline in the value of raw material nor in the rates of wages, nor do their managers wish to do so.

I do not desire to be understood as charging that the trusts are able to withstand the general fall of prices. The ability of the consumer to pay fixes the limit beyond which prices cannot be forced, and that is the only limit upon the powers of a trust to regulate prices when the combination of domestic producers is so perfect as to defy competition at home and the tariff duty upon the imported article excludes the competition in our markets of foreign producers.

Many people, during the nineties, insisted that there were no trusts. Today there are persons who believe that the trusts have been "busted" by our bluff and scholarly chief executives. The trusts were growing into positions of power in the late nineties; they received an immense impetus through the economic and political events surrounding the Spanish-American War. The first fifteen years of the new century has witnessed a rounding out of the trusts and an expansion into wider fields of activity.

My particular attention was attracted to the Sugar Trust because I had come into such intimate contact with its workings in connection with my fight over the annexation of Hawaii.

Prior to August, 1887, there was life and free competition in all branches of the sugar trade. The producers of raw sugars all over the world sought in the ports of the United States a market in which numerous strong buyers were always ready to take their offerings at a price varying with the supply and demand. There was the same healthy competition among the sugar refiners as among the producers and importers of raw sugar. This was manifested by constant efforts to improve the product and to lessen the cost of refining by the introduction of better processes.

The distribution of the raw and refined sugar to the consumer through the usual trade channels from the importers and the refiner by way of the jobber, the wholesale grocer, and the retail grocer to the family was also untrammeled. Each bought where he could purchase to the best advantage and sold upon terms agreed upon between him and the buyer, and not dictated by any third party.

But in 1887 the enormous profits amassed by the Standard Oil Trust suggested to a few of the leading refiners the possibility of controlling the sugar trade in the same way. It was then claimed for the first time that the individual refineries through competition were unable to make sufficient money to continue in business.

This seems a little strange in view of the fact that most of the refiners who had the misfortune to die or had retired from business before that time are known to have left or still possess large fortunes. Those millions, however, no doubt seemed insignificant in comparison to the potentialities of wealth offered by the adoption of trust methods.

So the sugar trust was formed in the fall of 1887 by a combination between twenty-one corporations, some of which were formed out of existing unincorporated firms for the express purpose of entering the trust, which was called the Sugar Refineries Company.

One of the first acts of the new trust was to close up the North River Sugar Refinery. This led to an action by the attorney-general of New York in behalf of the people for the forfeiture of the charter of the company, at the end of which the Court of Appeals declared the trust illegal, and the charter of the North River Company was forfeited. The trust was thereby compelled to abandon its organization and reorganize under the laws of New Jersey as the American Sugar Refining Company, a single corporation, in which were combined all the parties to the original trust.

While my amendment to the tariff act, providing that trust-made products should be admitted free of duty, was under consideration in the Senate, Senator Sewell of New Jersey entered the debate with a remarkable question. Said he (55th Cong., 1st Session, p. 1740):

Mr. SEWELL: "How does the Senator know that there is a sugar trust? The American Sugar Refining Company is a corporation of my state, with a very large capital and doing a large business. It is not in a trust with anybody, as I understand it. They surrendered everything of that kind three or four years ago."

Mr. PETTIGREW: "Mr. President, that is a strange question and a remarkable proposition. The American Sugar Refining Company was formerly a combination of twenty-one refineries. They closed the North River Refinery. The courts of New York declared that combination to be a trust. Then these same people formed a corporation under the laws of New Jersey.

"I notice that almost every rotten corporation in this country is organized under the laws of New Jersey. I do not knew whether the laws need fixing or not; but something is the matter. At any rate, all such corporations go there whenever they want to get up a combination to get away with somebody and to be sure that they will not be troubled. They formed a combination there of all these refineries, and then they proceeded to close refineries, raised the price to the limit of the tariff, and took from the people of this country untold millions. Under this amendment any combination or corporation for this purpose, to control production and increase the price, is a trust, and therefore the American Sugar Refining Company is a trust, and the courts can so decide.

"What is more, Mr. President, the president of the American Sugar Refining Company testified that they controlled the price of sugar — I read his testimony yesterday — that they fixed the price for their customers, and that they fixed it for everybody else. I also showed yesterday that the American Sugar Refining Company controlled every refinery in this country but four, and then I showed by the testimony of a St. Louis grocer that they controlled those four; for when this St. Louis grocer refused to sign a contract by which he was to bind himself to buy no other than sugar made by the trust at a price fixed by them — when he refused to sign that contract to take their refined sugar on commission — they refused to sell any sugar at all; and when he applied to the four independent refineries, he could not buy a pound of sugar from them. So that, after all, the combination embraces not only all the refineries in the trust, but all the others."

After we passed the McKinley law, which was particularly favorable to the trust, Mr. Havemeyer was called before the Senatorial investigating committee, and he gave this testimony:

Mr. HAVEMEYER: "We undertake to control the price of refined sugar in the United States. That must be distinctly understood."

Senator ALLEN: "And the price of refined sugar in the United States is higher to the American people in I consequence of the existence of the American Sugar i Refining Company than it would be if the different companies in your organization were distinct and independent companies?"

Mr. HAVEMEYER: "For a short time it is.

Senator ALLEN: "And what difference does it make for the consumers in this country in a year in your judgment?"

Mr. HAVEMEYER: "It has been in three years past three-eighths of a cent more on every pound they ate, as against doing business at a loss."

In other words, the fact that they were in a trust and that they controlled the price, according to his own statement, added three-eighths of a cent to every pound of sugar consumed in this country.

Senator ALLEN: "And that would be about how much in round numbers?"

Mr. HAVEMEYER: "It is a large sum in the aggregate."

Senator ALLEN: "How many millions?"

Mr. HAVEMEYER: "I should say it was close to $25,000,000 in three years."

How did I know there is a trust in sugar? It has been told to everybody, until there is not a boy six years old who can read and write who does not know there is a sugar trust.

Senator ALLEN: "And you intend to keep your hold upon the American people as long as you can?"

Mr. HAVEMEYER: "As long as the McKinley bill is there we will exact that profit."

"We will exact that profit. Is there competition? Is there any show for competition? They say they fix the price and that they are going to continue to do it so long as you keep the duty on; and yet the Senator wants to know how I know there is a sugar trust. It would be astonishing if I did not know it."

That discussion took place at a time (1897) when it was still possible to feign surprise at the mention of "trusts" in the United States. After 1901, when the Steel Trust was organized, the matter was decided for good. After that everybody recognized the fact that there were trusts; that these trusts were managed by corporations; that the object of their management and manipulation was to increase the profits and the power in the hands of the business interests.

During the twelve years that I was a member of the United States Senate Congress did nothing effective for the control of the trusts. The Anti-Trust Act was passed in 1890, but no effective means were ever provided for its enforcement. The act of 1890 was passed by outraged farmers as a protest against the exploitation under which they were suffering. By the time I introduced my amendment to the Tariff Act in 1897, it was taken for granted that combinations of capital should exist, and that these combinations should get what they could.

A careful review of all legislation from the pas-sage of the Sherman Anti-Trust Law in 1890 to the present time convinces me that it was the consistent policy of Congress to protect rather than to destroy the trusts and to build up and foster the trusts and thus create these great combinations to exploit the American people. Before I left the Senate they were talking about them as "benevolent institutions" and today they regard them as one of the bulwarks of our civilization.

Whatever possibilities there may have been in the act of 1890 disappeared with the "rule of reason" introduced by the Supreme Court. Not "restraint of trade" but "unreasonable restraint of trade" was the meaning of those who framed this law. Finally, in 1920, came the decision in favor of the continuance of the Steel Trust on the ground that public policy demanded it. I know of no better comment on the situation than the interview given out by Judge Gary after the Court's decision was announced:

"The decision as made will immeasurably add to the general feeling of confidence in the value of property and in the opportunities of business enterprise." (Boston "Globe," March 2, 1920.)

Judge Gary summarizes the entire policy of the Federal Government with regard to combinations and trusts. They were organized to protect property, and Congress has done everything in its power, during the last thirty years, to make trust organizers feel secure and happy.

7. Railroads

Predatory power in the United States centers in three institutions — the bank, the trust and the railroad. In previous chapters I have described my relations with the money power and with the masters of organized industry. During my two terms in the Senate I had many a struggle with the representatives and bankers and trust magnates. I also had numerous encounters with the spokesman of the railroads, which were, perhaps, the most powerful and aggressive of the vested interests during the last two decades of the nineteenth century.

Before I went to the United States Senate in 1889, I had built and operated a railroad from Sioux Falls to Yankton, S. D. I also began to organize and build the Midland Pacific Railroad, from Sioux Falls, S. D., to Puget Sound. For several years I had engineers on the road locating the line through to Seattle, crossing the Rocky Mountains near the mouth of Yellowstone Lake. Consequently I was thoroughly familiar with the costs of railroad building and operation.

When I entered the Senate I was of the opinion that the highways of the United States should be owned and operated by the Government, for the benefit of the people of the United States — operated for service and not for profit. At the beginning of my term I knew very little of the general operation of the railroads by the great combinations which then controlled them, but a short time in the Senate clinched this conviction by showing me that the railroads were robbing the Government as well as the people of the United States.

For instance, I found that J. L. Bell, who was Second Assistant Postmaster-General, had been a railroad employee at a salary several times as great as that which he received as Second Assistant Postmaster-General, and that he had resigned his position with the railroads to become Assistant Postmaster-General, and in that capacity to direct the railroad mail service. Thus the railroads had taken charge of the Post Office Department just as they have taken charge of the courts and the Interstate Commerce Commission — by the simple expedient of putting their man in control. This railroad man commissioned in the public service to look after railroad interests invariably proceeded to exploit the public in the interests of the special interests for which he was working.

Nowhere did I see this principle more amply illustrated than in the case of railway mail pay. For carrying the mail, during the time I served in the Senate of the United States, the railroads received ten times as much per pound as the express companies paid for carrying express matter on the same train, and generally in the same car. In addition, when the railway mail-cars were established, the companies rented to the Government for $6,000 per year cars that cost less than $3,000, so that the annual rental was double the value of the car. To complete the work, the railroads and their attorneys in both houses of Congress franked great quantities of Government publications and shipped them through the mails, back and forth, all over the United States, during the thirty days of each year when the mail was being weighed for the purpose of determining the amount of compensation that the railroads were to receive. From an investigation of the matter in the early years of my service I know that this practice was continued during the twelve years that I was a member of the Senate, and that millions of pounds of Government documents were shipped back and forth every year under a frank of some member of Congress or member of the Senate, during the thirty days the mail was being weighed to determine the compensation of the railroads, and that J. Laurie Bell, Second Assistant Postmaster-General and his successors, employee of the railroads rather than of the Government, superintended the job.

This abuse was so open and so flagrant that I offered an amendment to the Post Office Appropriation Bill, reducing the compensation for carrying the mails twenty per cent, and an investigation verified the facts that I have stated; yet the committee would not report in favor of reducing the pay of the railroads one cent. Two-thirds of the Senate and House were lawyers — very many of them in the direct pay of the railroads on a salary, or a fee, and nothing whatever could be accomplished.

When the Senate investigated this question and brought the employees of the Second Assistant Postmaster-General before the Committee, they deceived the Committee in the interest of the railroads whom they were serving. I quote some of the evidence from the Congressional Record:

Mr. PETTIGREW: "I will read first from the report of the Postmaster-General under the head of 'Weighing the Mails,' from the report of 1896:

"'The Department takes every precaution at its command to insure honest weighing of the railroad mails. But this has not prevented one or two attempts on the part of the railroad officials to pad the mails during the weighing season.'

'What are the facts? The Seaboard Air Line procured 16 tons of public documents franked by some member of the House of Representatives or of the Senate. They can secure them without the connivance at all of the persons who frank them. They ship them back and forth to their station agents. They ship this franked matter during the weighing season to a station, and have their agents take out the packages from the bags, redirect them, and mail them again. So they kept these 16 tons of frankable matter going for thirty days. The Department determined to have a reweighing. They had a reweighing for thirty days more, and then the railroad company secured an extra edition of a newspaper that weighed 5 tons; they shipped that back and forth along the line, and distributed it over the line during the thirty days, and when the Postmaster-General complained, they asked him what he was going to do about it. And Mr. McBee, the manager of the road, asked the Postmaster-General why the Seaboard Air Line had been singled out as a subject for criticism for stuffing the mails during the reweighing period, when it was well known that all railroads practiced the same fraud upon the Government. So it is the general practice. There is no doubt about it. Everybody knows it. We do not need to investigate the matter much to learn that fact..."

There is a great profit in carrying the mail which pays 2 cents postage, and so the railroads have organized on their own hook a postal system which defrauds the Government out of hundreds of thousands, and I believe millions, of dollars a year because that branch of the service, the carrying of letters, is profitable.

The railroads did not stop with the exploitation of the Government — they were criminal in their treatment of the public. The railroads gave very low rates to their favorites, and very high rates to the rest of the people. They determined whichmen should prosper and do business and which men should be made bankrupt by their discriminations. They also determined, through their rates, which town should grow and which should languish. A prosperous town could be destroyed and its industries closed by giving to its rival town a railroad rate of one-half or less, and this was done constantly. The Interstate Commerce Commission was created for the purpose of correcting this and similar abuses. Eleven years after the law was passed creating the Commission, I find this statement in the annual report (1898):

"We are satisfied from investigations conducted during the past year and referred to in another portion of this report, as well as from information which his perfectly convincing to a moral intent,...that a large part of the business at the present time is transacted upon illegal rates. Indeed, so general has this rule become that in certain quarters the exaction of the published rate is the exception. From this, two things naturally and frequently result: First, gross discriminations between individuals and gross preference between localities; and these discriminations and preferences are almost always in favor of the strong, and against the weak. There is probably no one thing today which does so much to force out the small operator, and to build up those trusts and monopolies against which law and public alike beat in vain, as discrimination in freight rates. Second, the business of railroad transportation is carried on to a very large extent in conceded violations of law. Men who in every other respect are reputable citizens are guilty of acts which, if the statute law of the land were enforced, would subject them to fine or imprisonment."

Further on, the report of the Interstate Commerce Commission says: "Discriminations are always in favor of the strong and against the weak. This condition the law seems powerless to control." Thus the railroads were above the law. The United States judges, generally selected from the ranks of the corporation and railroad attorneys, go upon the bench to construe the law, which they do in the interest of their former employers.

A prominent oil refiner of Pennsylvania, writing under date of October 4, 1899, after setting forth his complaint against the railway discrimination in favor of the Standard Oil Company, gives his experience as follows:

"I manufacture 35,000 barrels of oil per month. Seventy per cent of that is marketed in Europe where the railroads are controlled by the governments. We have no difficulty in competing with the Standard Oil Company in those countries, because our tonnage is carried as cheap by the Government as that of the Standard Oil Company, although the Standard Oil Company ships one thousand times more to the interior of the several countries than I do. The reason that I am obliged to send 70 per cent of my oil across the Atlantic Ocean to be marketed is because I cannot transport it over the railroads of the United States at the same rates as the Standard Oil Company."

How much influence the railroads exerted in building up the trusts may be readily inferred from the following instance:

The Tin Plate Trust was endeavoring to make terms with an independent producer; he replied that he felt no desire to change his methods; his company was making money, doing well in fact, and were quite satisfied with their plant and its ownership. The promoter of the trust advised the president of the company that it would be better to sell out; but finding his offers of no avail to secure the property he proceeded to threats. "You are enjoying certain concessions in your freight rates," he said. "All your profits would cease if these freight rates were withdrawn; if you will not sell to us, we will see what we can do." In a few days the manager of the railway wrote the independent mill owner that the rates conceded the company would have to be withdrawn, because," etc. The mill-owner called a meeting of the stockholders and bondholders, explained the situation, and in two weeks the mill was turned over to the trust.

So much for the attitude of the railroads toward the Government and towards the people of the United States. Now, a word as to another phase of their activity — the financing.

The railroads of the United States when they were constructed were bonded for more than they actually cost, and then those who were manipulating them issued common and preferred stock for considerable more than the amount of the bonds. Thus both bonds and stocks are simply gambling chips which can be used to swindle the American public.

Railroad securities should be the most stable of all securities because the railroads are the highways of the nation, and their service is absolutely essential and reasonably uniform. Yet for many years these railroad securities have been the football of gamblers.

While I was in the Senate the price of the leading railroad stocks fluctuated from 30 to 300 per cent in a single year, and the price of the bonds from 5 to 100 per cent. At the same time, the bulk of the stocks paid no dividends, and large numbers of the bonds paid no interest. To show how largely fictitious these stocks and bonds were considered, see the following table from the report of the Interstate Commerce Commission.

We see from this statement that three and one-half billion of the five and a half billion of railway stock paid no dividends, while nearly a billion of the bonds received no interest, and six hundred millions more of stock and bonds paid only a return between 1 and 3 per cent. These facts are only noted in order that the notion of the total value of railways may not be erroneously inferred from a merely nominal capitalization.

The situation is well summed up in the case of the Union & Central Pacific Railroads which were conceived in the womb of the Republican Party; were born into the world as the full-fledged children of corruption and iniquity, and which never for one day drew an honest breath. Ames and his associates (who were, like Ames, the most prominent bankers and business men of their day) organized the Credit Mobilier, came to Washington, and acted as midwives for the Congress of the United States while it gave birth to these twins.

Per cent paid	Stocks	Per cent of total stock	Funded debt (exclusive of equipment trust obligations)	Per cent of total funded
Nothing paid ..	$3,570,155,239	66.26	$ 852,402,622	15.82
From 1 to 2...	142,496,300	2.65	176,996,988	3.28
From 2 to 3...	118,096,361	2.19	162,789,940	3.02
From 3 to 4...	96,348,397	1.79	673,945,852	12.51
From 4 to 5...	385,381,689	7.15	1,766,290,104	32.77
From 5 to 6...	409,778,699	7.60	928,046,512	17.22
From 6 to 7...	198,603,262	3.69	562,732,833	10.44
From 7 to 8...	244,736,724	4.54	229,716,648	4.26
From 8 to 9...	127,852,050	2.37	27,762,600	51.
From 9 to 10...	6,698,055	.13	5,014,300	.09
10 and above...	88,121,545	1.63	4,236,300	.08
Total.....	$5,388,268,321	100.	$5,389,934,599	100.

Ames and his associates distributed the stock of the Credit Mobilier among the Senators and members of the House of Representatives, every Republican member with a particle of influence receiving a share, while almost all of the prominent Democratic leaders were taken care of in the same manner. Thereupon laws were passed by which the Government of the United States gave these two roads a land grant of half of all the land ten miles wide on each side of the track from Omaha to San Francisco, and in addition furnished a sum of money more than sufficient to build and equip the roads. In exchange for this grant of money, the Government received a second mortgage. The roads never paid any interest to the Government, and in 1896 when the second mortgage fell due the managers of the roads selected a reorganizing committee of professional exploiters to devise ways and means to swindle the Government out of its money, — principal and interest. This reorganization committee consisted of Marvin Hughitt, President of the Chicago and North Western Railroad, Chauncey Depew, President of the New York Central, and Louis Fitzgerald, T. J. Coolidge and Oliver Ames, who represented the Goulds of New York and the Ames crowd of Boston.

I met this proposal of the reorganization committee by introducing a resolution directing the Secretary of the Treasury to proceed at once to foreclose the mortgage held by the Government on the Union Pacific and the Kansas Pacific companies; to pay off the prior liens and the floating indebtedness; to assume control of all the property of the two roads, including the Federal land grants; to take possession of the roads, and to pay the necessary costs by the sale of three per cent bonds.

I will let the Congressional Record tell the rest of this story:

Mr. PETTIGREW: "Mr. President, I wish to call the especial attention of the Committee on Pacific Railroads to this resolution, for I think it outlines a method by which to solve this much-discussed question in a businesslike manner, and in the only way it can be solved with credit to the Government. We have only the interests of the whole people to consider. There are no equities in this case in favor of the present stockholders of these roads, and I will show that the reorganization committee of the stockholders of the roads are entitled to no consideration whatever, as they represent the heartless and unscrupulous scamps that have been robbing the Government and the public for a generation, casting reproach upon our Government and our people that must make every honest citizen blush with shame.

'The stockholders and owners of the first mortgage bonds on the Union and Kansas Pacific Railroads have appointed a committee to reorganize the road and to settle with the Government for its second mortgage upon the property. This reorganization committee proposes to issue one hundred million of fifty-year 4 per cent bonds on about 1,900 miles of road — that is, the road from Omaha to Ogden, which is the main line of the Union Pacific, and about 400 miles of road from Kansas City west, which is the Kansas Pacific Railroad...

"This 1,900 miles of railroad can be reproduced for $23,600 per mile, and yet the Government of the United States is asked to go into partnership with a party of dishonest men, and bond and stock the road for $123,600 per mile, and the public whom this road serves is to be called upon to pay interest on this vast sum...

"But they go further than this, and tell us how they will distribute this vast amount of stocks and bonds. They propose that the Government shall take $34,000,000 of the bonds, which is just equal to the principal of the Government's claim against the roads, and shall take $20,000,000 of the preferred stock in full payment for all the defaulting interest; that the first-mortgage bonds, which amount to $34,000,000, shall be taken up and a like number of these new bonds issued in their place; and for every $1,000 of bonds issued to the present holders of the first-mortgage bonds of these roads, $500 of preferred stock shall be issued as a bonus, the remainder of the stock and the remainder of the bonds to be the property undoubtedly of the conspirators in this stupendous transaction.

"Let us see who are the men who compose this reorganization committee of the Union and the Kansas Pacific railroads. This reorganization committee is composed of five members, Louis Fitzgerald, T. J. Coolidge and Oliver Ames being three out of the five members of the reorganization committee (who represent the old management of the road, the Goulds of New York and the Ameses of Boston), the other two being Marvin Hughitt and Chauncey Depew. While every one of the receivers who are now managing and operating the road is in the interest of this gang of highwaymen who have plundered the public with this instrumentality in the past, three of the receivers, namely S. H. H. Clark, who was formerly manager and for years president of the road, has been and is the representative of the Gould interest; Mr. Mink, of Boston, was comptroller of the company and has been for years its vice-president, and is also an executor of the will of the late Fred L. Ames, and is of course the direct and immediate representative of the Boston crowd of highwaymen who, through the use of this highway — the Union and the Kansas Pacific Railroads — have robbed the public and the Government for the past thirty years. The third receiver, who has always acted with this interest, is E. Ellery Anderson, who has also been for' several years a Government director, and was placed there for the purpose of protecting the Government's interests, but has never undertaken to protect the Government's interests, and has always acted in the interest of the old and dishonest management. The other two receivers of the road, Coudert and Doane, seem to have a leaning in the same direction, for they have been Government directors, and have never remonstrated against the frauds which have disgraced the management of these roads, and of which they must have had knowledge.

'If this reorganization plan is carried through with the assistance of the Government the road will have to earn 4 per cent of $100,000,000 of bonds and 5 per cent at least on $75,000,000 of preferred stock, and the people along the line of the road will be charged a rate sufficient to accomplish this result, even if no dividend whatever is paid upon the $60,000,000 of common stock. This interest charged, then, will amount to $7,750,000 a year, which would be an unjustifiable burden upon the people who are served by the road. The only reasonable and proper thing for the Government of the United States to do is to take possession of the road, issue its own bonds bearing 3 per cent interest as provided by the resolution which I have offered, pay the first-mortgage bonds of $34,000,000, refund to the Government of the United States the $53,000,000 now due to the Government from these companies, take up and pay the floating debt of these roads of $12,000,000, and thus get possession of the bonds and stocks which are held as collateral security for this floating debt, and thus acquire title to $98,000,000 par value of the branch lines' bonds and stock, the market value of which is at least $42,000,000 at the present time, thus taking possession of all the branch lines of these roads, amounting to 4,000 miles of track, and operate the whole as one great system.

"In this way the Government would realize every dollar these roads owe it. The interest charged would be only 3 per cent on $100,000,000 of bonds, or $3,000,000 per annum, instead of $7,750,000 under the plan proposed by the reorganization committee. The rates for carrying freight and passengers would therefore be much less. There would be no incentive for discrimination in favor of persons or places; every man and every town would have an equal opportunity, and the scandal of our Government connected with the Union Pacific management would disappear from the pages of our history."

I have devoted more space to the Union & Central Pacific than I would were it not for the fact that their history, management and method are a true picture of the railroad situation in the United States.

55

Before I leave the subject I should like to quote an interesting passage from the autobiography of Charles Francis Adams, who was made President of the Union Pacific Railroad in 1884. Mr. Adams, in referring to the dealings between the Union Pacific and the Government with regard to the second mortgage which the Government held on the road, on page 192 writes:

"I was sent over to Washington to avert the threatened action of the Government, and then and there I had my first experience in the most hopeless and repulsive work in which I ever was engaged — transacting business with the United States Government and trying to accomplish something through Congressional action. My initial episode was with a prominent member of the United States Senate. This senator is still (1912) alive though long retired. He has a great reputation for ability and a certain reputation, somewhat fly-blown it is true, for rugged honesty. I can only say that I found him an ill-mannered bully and by all odds the most covertly and dangerously corrupt man I ever had opportunity and occasion carefully to observe in public life. His grudge against the Union Pacific was that it had not retained him. While he took excellent care of those competing concerns which had been wiser in this respect, he never lost an opportunity of posing as the fearless antagonist of corporations when the Union Pacific came to the front. For that man, on good and sufficient grounds, I entertained a deep dislike. He was distinctly dishonest — a senatorial bribe taker."

Early in my term of service in the Senate, the railroads began to combine and to pool the freight and to agree upon rates. The combination of the railroads was in violation of the Anti-Trust Law, but the law had been framed to make it as easy as possible for the corporations to evade its provisions, and the railroads cared nothing about the Anti-Trust Law because their lawyers were in the executive offices and on the bench. When the Joint Traffic Association was organized in violation of the Sherman Anti-Trust Law, and suit was brought by the Government to dissolve it on that account, it was found that the Association was a combination of thirty-two of the leading roads in the United States to pool the business, agree upon the division of traffic, and have uniform rates, so far as the public was concerned; that Hobart, Vice-President of the United States, was one of the arbitrators and drew a salary as such arbitrator for this Joint Traffic Association, and when the suit was brought before the United States Court in New York, Judge Lacombe announced from the bench that he was disqualified from sitting on the case because he owned the stocks and bonds of the defendant railroads, and he said: "I am of the opinion that there is no judge in this Circuit but that is suffering a like disqualification."

In 1874, the Senate of the United States, in response to a general demand, appointed a Special Committee on Transportation, composed of William Windom, of Minnesota, John Sherman, of Ohio, Roscoe Conkling, of New York, H. G. Davis, of West Virginia, T. M. Norwood of Georgia, J. W. Johnson, of Virginia, John H. Mitchell, of Oregon, and S. B. Canover, of Florida. The committee occupied the entire summer of 1874 in making an exhaustive examination of the subject, and in their report we find the following:

"In the matter of taxation, there are today four men representing the four great trunk lines between Chicago and New York, who possess, and who not unfrequently exercise, powers which the Congress of the United States would not dare to exert. They may at any time, and for any reason satisfactory to themselves, by a single stroke of the pen, reduce the value of property in this country by hundreds of millions of dollars. An additional charge of five cents per bushel on the transportation of cereals would have been equivalent to a tax of forty-five millions of dollars. No congress would dare to exercise so vast a power upon a necessity of the most imperative nature, and yet these gentlemen exercise it whenever it suits their supreme will and pleasure, without explanation or apology. With the rapid and inevitable progress of combination and consolidation, these colossal organizations are daily becoming stronger and more imperious. The day is not distant, if it has not already arrived, when it will be the duty of the statesman to inquire whether there is less danger in leaving the property and industrial interests of the people thus wholly at the mercy of a few men who recognize no responsibility and no principle of action but personal aggrandizement."

All of these facts convinced me that the only possible remedy was the Government ownership of the railroads. I therefore prepared and introduced a bill for this purpose (Senate Bill No. 1770) on the 18th day of December, 1899. This bill provided that the railroads should be operated under the Post Office Department, and operated for service and not for profit, and that the owners should receive United States bonds for the actual value of the property. At that time the roads would have cost the Government between four and five billions, although they were capitalized at from eight to nine billions, including the stocks and the bonds. I also included in this bill a provision that all rates should be absolutely uniform, alike for everybody in proportion to the service rendered; that passenger fares should not exceed one cent per mile, and I showed conclusively that passengers should be carried in this country at a profit at one cent per mile, provided no passes were granted. I knew the extent of the pass abuse. I knew that every politician and every lawyer of any prominence, and every judge, and every congressman, and everybody else that had any pull, rode upon a pass, and that the public was charged two prices for riding, in order to pay the railroads for carrying free those people who could best afford to pay their fare.

I also provided for a Commission of Transportation in this law, under the Post Office Department, to operate the roads and to remove the control, as far as possible, from political influence. The bill also provided that the express business should be done by the Government, and I showed that the express business could be done at a cost to the public of less than one-half the price charged by the express companies if done by the Government through the Post office on Government railroads.

When I introduced the bill and had it printed, some of my friends came to me and said: "Well, what will your friend James J. Hill think of your introducing a bill for the government ownership of the railroads?" I said: "James J. Hill is a big man; he is one, out of the whole railroad system, that is not a stock gambler, and I sent him the first copy of the bill that was printed." Some months afterward, when I met Mr. Hill, the first thing he said was: "I received your Railroad Bill, and you are entirely right about it If the railroads are going to combine — and" said he, "they are going to combine — the only way the public can be protected from robbery is to have the Government own the railroads."

Needless to say, my bill received scant consideration and little support from the champions of privilege who dominated the House and Senate, nor need I add that its introduction marked me as a man who should be eliminated from public life at the earliest possible moment. I am now of the opinion that the Government of the United States should take the railroads and cancel all the outstanding stocks and bonds without making any payment to the holders of the same. There are no innocent owners. The railroads are the highways of the nation and have been built and paid for more than once by the American people, but are now in the hands of a gang of gambling scoundrels who are using these highways to enrich themselves and their favorites and to rob and exploit the whole population. To take the roads without paying anything to these thieves is not confiscation or robbery, but simply returning the stolen property to its rightful owners.

The Interstate Commerce Commission has just issued a report showing that, out of 627,930 stockholders in the various railroads of the United States, the majority of stock is owned by only 8,031 persons OF 1.3 per cent of all the stockholders.

The Commission, through its Bureau of Statistics, has discovered that of a total of 97,475,776 shares of all the railroads, 50,873,322 shares are held by the small minority, an average of 6,130 shares each. The balance of 46,602,454 shares is owned by 649,629 stockholders, an average of 75 shares each. The 8,031 stockholders who own the majority stock include holding companies of railroads, as well as other corporations. It also includes the stock held by voting trustees and estates. The Interstate Commerce Commission's Report distributes these holdings as follows:

	Shares
Held by other railway companies	24,638,407
By other corporations or partnerships	11,565,838
By voting trustees	5,307,043
By estates	1,333,961
By individuals (males)	6,945,205
By individuals (females)	1,082,868

The report shows that of 100,000 stockholders in the Pennsylvania Railroad, the largest twenty own 8.9 per cent of the total stock outstanding; that of the 27,000 stockholders in the New York Central, 25.1 per cent is held by the largest twenty stockholders. The largest twenty shareholders in the Illinois Central own 41.6 per cent; in the Southern Pacific 23 per cent; in the Southern Railway, 37.7 per cent; in the Chicago & Northwestern, 20.9 per cent; in the Great Northern 18.5 per cent; in the Northern Pacific, 19.8 per cent; in the Chicago, Milwaukee & St. Paul, 18.5 per cent; in the Lehigh Valley, 18.1 per cent; in the Baltimore & Ohio, 17.4 per cent; in the New York, New Haven & Hartford, 15.3 per cent; in the Erie, 19.7 per cent; in the Atchison, Topeka & Santa Fe, 14.3 per cent.

One hundred per cent of the stock of the Pennsylvania Company, which owns all the Pennsylvania Lines west of Pittsburgh and Erie, is owned by 17 shareholders, including the Pennsylvania Railroad Company, which is the holding concern. The entire stock of the Philadelphia & Reading, one of the principal coal roads, is owned by thirteen stockholders, including the Reading Company; and 99.5 per cent of the stock of the C. B. & Q. is owned by the twenty largest shareholders out of a total of 326 shareholders.

The largest blocks of stock of the Erie; Philadelphia & Reading; Wabash; Southern; Chicago, Milwaukee & St. Paul; Great Northern; Northern Pacific; Chicago, Rock Island & Pacific and Union Pacific are held by corporations or partnerships other than railways.

Of the Wabash stock, 46,000 shares are held in Amsterdam, Holland, and 36,000 shares by fourteen New York and one Boston concern. Of the Chicago, Milwaukee & St. Paul, 216,000 shares are held by eleven New York concerns; the bulk of the stock of the Virginia Railway is held by the Tidewater Company; the stock of the Bessemer & Lake Erie is owned by the United States Steel Corporation.

Virtually all the corporations that are among the largest shareholders of the various railroads do business with these railroads and obtain special advantages.

The earlier reports of the Interstate Commerce Commission show that the largest industrial monopolies of the country were favored by the railroads to the extent of hundreds of millions of dollars in rebates, drawbacks and differentials; and that the railroads were managed largely in the interest of these monopolies as against the interest of rival concerns and the public generally. This is particularly true with reference to Standard Oil, as disclosed by reports of the Interstate Commerce Commission and by the testimony of witnesses before Congressional Investigation Committees.

The par value of railroad stocks is generally $100 a share, which means that the 97,475,776 shares of the railroads are estimated to be worth $9,747,577,600. The total value of the bonds issued by the various railroads up to December 31, 1916, is estimated at $11,202,607,096.

It is obvious from this record that the control and ownership of the stocks of the railroads of the United States is concentrated in the hands of those who enjoy excessive private fortunes and there is no doubt that a similar or more acute state of concentration exists in all other monopolistic corporations.

It is quite evident, from the facts above adduced, that the Morgan and Rockefeller groups own the controlling interest in the railroads of the United States. The common people who own stocks and bonds in the roads are so few in number that they have neither voice nor power in the management.

THE "WIDOW AND ORPHAN" CRY IS AN OLD "WOLF" CRY OF THE BANKERS AND SPECULATORS WHO HAVE STOLEN THEIR CONTROL OF THE TRANSPORTATION SYSTEMS OF THE COUNTRY. IF THERE ARE ANY CONSIDERABLE NUMBER OF WORTHY WIDOWS OR ORPHANS OR "COMMON PEOPLE" HOLDING STOCKS IT WERE BETTER TO PENSION THESE PEOPLE FOR LIFE AND PROCEED TO TAKE OVER THE RAILROADS.

After many years of investigation devoted to this subject, I am convinced that the highways of the nation should be taken over by the Government and operated for the good of the people.

The Government of the United States took over and operated the roads for a little over two years during the war, at the request of the railroads, under terms and conditions that were absolutely infamous, by which the government was plundered out of billions of dollars. But before the roads were turned over to the Government to operate, these scamps (who ought to occupy cells in our penitentiaries), and I mean by that the bankers of New York, the Federal Reserve Board, the managers and owners of the railroads, and the great industrial trust combinations, organized companies to take over the shops of all of the great railroads controlled by them. These companies were incorporated under the infamous laws of New York and New Jersey and all of the shops of the great railroads were conveyed to those companies, not only the repair shops, but the great factories where they manufacture equipment for the railroads of every kind and sort, so that after the Government began the operation of the roads they had to hire all of their repairs, and buy all of their equipment of these great combinations, and they paid from four to ten times as much as the service and material was worth that they bought of these inside corporations controlled by the biggest stockholders of the railroads.

They also organized terminal companies wherever the terminals were of great value, in all the great cities of the United States, and separated the terminals from the railroads, and then they charged as rent for the use of the terminals, a rental in many instances, as high as one hundred per cent per year on actual cost of the terminal. For these terminals were conveyed to these companies for the purpose of swindling the Government during its operation and to make it appear that the operation by the Government of the roads did not pay, and owing to the enormous prices which these men compelled the Government to pay, not only for terminals and switching facilities, but for repairs and new equipment, accounts for the failure of the roads to be properly operated by the Government. But the roads were not really operated by the Government at all. Ostensibly they were. That was the talk, but the fact is that the management remained in the hands of the old crowd.

I know very intimately the president of one of the great railroads. He was president during the entire time that the Government pretended to operate the roads, and he is still president of the road at a salary of fifty thousand dollars a year. The president of that road is the operating man, and he continued to operate the road just the same as he always had, while the Government had control, and he assured me that that was the case with practically all of the roads. They were simply using the camouflage of government ownership and operation to plunder the Government and the public generally, and he said to me, "We have no interest in making government control popular." But while it was an infamous transaction to turn the roads over to the Government, the crowning infamy was the Cummings bill, by which the railroads were taken back from the Government, to whom they had never been conveyed, and the Government guaranteed dividends on their stock and interest on their bonds.

THE REMEDY IS FOR THE GOVERNMENT OF THE UNITED STATES TO TAKE OVER ALL THE RAILROADS WITHOUT PAYING ONE CENT FOR THEIR STOCKS OR BONDS. The railroads have been paid for by the American people over and over again, and they are the property of the American people. They are the highways of the nation. They are in the hands of a small number of gambling bankers who use the stock and bonds as chips in the gambling game to swindle the public. There are no innocent purchasers of their stocks, and if any of the stocks are owned by widows or orphans, they are widows and orphans of a gambler, and if they are impoverished by the cancellation of these stocks and bonds and the taking over the railroads by the people of the United States, and are unable to work, I am perfectly willing that an asylum should be built to take care of them as long as they live.

The owners of the railroads are entitled to no consideration whatever from the American people. They have forfeited all right to any consideration whatever.

It is now nearly twenty-five years since I introduced a bill in the Senate of the United States to take over and operate the railroad companies for service, and not for profit; operate them by the Post office Department. I showed in an argument in the Senate that the railroads could reduce their freight rates one-half and still be operated at a profit, if all favors granted to big trusts and combinations were eliminated and the service granted to all the people on equal terms. I showed that the practice was for the big stockholders to become interested in some manufacturing enterprise and then cut rates to less than half what they gave to the public, to the favored enterprises. I showed that these people who could afford to pay their fare rode on a pass, and that the common people paid three to four cents a mile, and I provided in this bill that passenger fares should hereafter, under government ownership, be one cent per mile for everybody, and no passes granted to anyone. I showed that express could be carried on government owned railroads for one-third what the public was now paying for this service. I then proposed to buy the roads and pay for them by: using Government bonds, a sum equal to their actual physical value. But since then the conduct of the railroad managers has been such that there is no justification whatever in buying the roads. They should be taken over as the highways of the United States and operated for the general welfare and their stocks and bonds cancelled and destroyed. This is not confiscation or robbery, it is restoring stolen property to its rightful owners and it would be well to put the thieves in jail so that they cannot steal something else.

8. Labor

I have tried in the preceding chapters to describe some of the more important economic changes that have occurred in the United States during the past fifty years. All of them relate to business, to the rich, the powerful. The control of the banks; the right to issue money; the tariff-privileges enjoyed by the favored few; the organization of the trusts, and the manipulation of the railroads— these were the outstanding features of a system that gave property-holders first choice in all of the important economic relations of life.

A visitor to the United States, during these years, would have supposed that the workers did not count for much, one way or the other, but that the very heart and soul of existence consisted in putting more money into the hands of the rich. Indeed, this was the attitude taken by a majority of my colleagues in both houses of Congress.

The whole trend of legislation was toward the granting of privilege. The lawyers, who composed both houses of Congress, were representatives of the business interests. They never asked the question: "What does the public welfare demand?" Instead, their one thought was: "What do my clients want?" Therefore, their actions were always directed toward the protection of property and never toward the protection of the workers.

Perhaps I can best illustrate this point by reference to an experience which I had with a bill requiring the railroads to report accidents.

During the whole twelve years of my service in the Senate, only one bill, even remotely in the interests of labor, became a law. All of the others, and there were hundreds of them, were either reported from the committees adversely, or not reported at all. If reported and passed through the house where they originated, they were always killed in the other body. If a bill originated in the Senate and passed the Senate, the committee in the House would never report it. If a bill passed the House and came to the Senate, the Senate committee would not report it; or, if the committee did make a report, it was done in such a manner that the bill was sure to receive no serious consideration. Although the American Federation of Labor always had its lobbyists at work, and there were other labor organizations that had their representatives urging the passage of legislation, the clever manipulation of bills by bodies of both houses offered a guarantee that nothing definite or effective would ever be accomplished.

Finally, during the last year of my service in the Senate, a bill passed the House requiring railroads to file with the Interstate Commerce Commission monthly reports of accidents — their causes and the names of the persons injured. The bill was referred to the Committee on Interstate Commerce.

Late in the session, the representative of the railroad men, who had been working for a year to have this bill passed, came to me and said he could not get the Senate Committee to report the bill. He asked me to take charge of it and see if I could not secure its passage. This was some time in January, 1901, and my term as a Senator expired on the 4th of March.

I asked him to describe in detail the steps that he had taken to secure its passage. He gave me the information, and concluded with the observation that, in his judgment, the Senate did not intend to pass the bill. I gathered that he came to me as a sort of forlorn last hope.

I finally told him that I would take charge of the bill, provided it was understood that I had full charge, and I promised him that I would make it exceedingly interesting for the Interstate Commerce Committee if it did not allow the bill to pass. I told him, furthermore, that it would be a hot fight in which some bitter enemies would be made for all who supported the bill. I further told him that my method would discourage him, but that, in my judgment, it was the only method that had even a remote chance of success. If I would have his full support under these circumstances, and without any interference, I was willing to take the bill. To this proposition he heartily agreed.

I then went before the Committee on Interstate Commerce at its next session and gave vigorous reasons why the bill should be reported. [1] The railroad attorneys on the committee — Wolcott of Colorado and others — protested that the reports of the railroads would be examined by shyster lawyers and used to begin suits for damage. I said: "That is not the reason why you oppose this bill. Your clients have ordered you to kill this bill because they, the railroads, are not obeying the law as to safety appliances. It costs money to stop killing, so they refuse to obey the law while they continue to kill. You know as well as I do that more people, both employees and passengers, are killed on American railroads than by all the other railroads in the world. An amendment to the bill will prevent the report being used against the roads in damage suits." The next day the Committee reported the bill with four or five amendments, any one of which would have made the law, if passed, practically inoperative. I called up the bill for passage, and showed to the Senate the meaning of the amendments offered, with the result that I had the first amendment rejected by the Senate after a long discussion and bitter struggle on the floor. Thereupon the chairman of the Committee arose in his seat and moved that the bill be recommitted to the Committee, which is a motion that is always agreed to and, therefore, the bill was recommitted to what the railroad lawyers supposed would be its graveyard.

At the next meeting the Committee on Interstate Commerce did not act upon the bill nor report it back to the Senate. I, therefore, introduced a resolution in the Senate to discharge the Committee from further consideration of the bill and place it immediately upon the calendar. This led to a filibuster debate which was intended to wear out the session. Whereupon the chairman of the Committee arose in his seat and said that if I would withdraw my motion he would call a meeting the next day and would report the bill. So the bill was reported from the Committee the next day with amendments which wholly destroyed its original purpose. I moved the immediate consideration of the bill and I stated in the Senate that I had been a member of that body for twelve years and that during that time no labor bill had passed both Houses and become a law; that this sort of a record could not be justified or defended by the Congress of the United States, especially should Congress defeat the present measure. I also stated that the railroads wanted to defeat this bill because, while the Congress of the United States had enacted laws compelling the railroads to use certain safety appliances upon their trains, appliances which cost money — the railroads were not using these appliances, with the result that many accidents occurred which could be traced directly to the absence of these appliances. The bill was particularly obnoxious because its passage would make a public record of these facts. I succeeded, therefore, in defeating all of the amendments but the one which provided that the reports should not be used in court. Thereupon the chairman of the Committee moved to recommit the bill to the Committee.

The next day I offered a resolution to discharge the Committee from further consideration of the measure and place it upon the calendar. The chairman of the Committee immediately arose in the Senate and said he would call an extra session for the next morning and would report the bill if I would withdraw my motion, which, of course, I did. The next day the bill was reported with the same amendment with regard to not using the reports against the railroads and with another amendment destroying the real intent of the bill. I defeated the pernicious amendment in the Senate and the railroad attorneys allowed the bill to pass with the amendment prohibiting the use of the reports against the railroads in any lawsuit.

The session was nearing a close and the opponents of the bill thought they could prevent it from going through the House of Representatives without amendments. The Speaker of the House was Henderson of Iowa, a one-legged soldier, veteran of the Civil War, an honest man — a rare quality in a Speaker of the House — whose sympathy was with the men who toil. The moment the bill passed the Senate, I went over to the House, for I had advised with Henderson several times about the matter, and told him that I had got the railroad bill through with an amendment which would not affect the working of the law, but that if the amended bill was sent to the House Committee, there would be delay and the session would be over before action could be taken. I therefore asked Henderson to have the House concur in the amendment as soon as it came over, and have the bill immediately enrolled and returned to the Senate.

Henderson asked me who had charge of the bill on the floor of the House. I told him the name of the member and when that member arose and stated to the House that the Senate had passed House Bill 10,302, with an amendment, the Speaker immediately said: 'The motion is upon agreeing to the amendment of the Senate to House Bill 10,302. All those in favor say 'Aye,' and all those opposed say 'No.' The ayes have it."

A day passed, and I heard nothing from the bill. I then went to the Clerk of the House, and he told me that he had had the bill enrolled and had sent it over to the Senate. I, therefore, returned to the Senate, and, after waiting a day and finding that the bill did not come, I stated in the Senate that the bill had been lost.

(Congressional Record, Vol. 344, p, 3533, 56th Congress, 2d session, March 2, 1901.)

Mr. PETTIGREW: "I am informed that the Senate amendments were accepted by the House, and that the bill was enrolled and placed in the hands of the messenger to bring to the Senate, and on the way, or somewhere, it has been lost. In other words, there seems to be an effort to steal the bill."

Mr. LODGE: "In connection with what the Senator from North Dakota is saying, I desire to say that I have been engaged in trying to find that bill. My attention was called to the fact that it was lost. It was announced to the Senate that the House had concurred in the amendments of the Senate."

Mr. PETTIGREW: "The bill was enrolled."

Mr. LODGE: "The bill was enrolled in the House, is was signed by the Speaker, according to the records of the House, Mr. Browning, and that is the last of it. Mr. Browning says he delivered it here. There is no record of it here at all. It cannot be found. I have been personally to the room of the Committee on Enrolled Bills and looked over the bunch of bills that was sent, and the bill is not there. I do not know what can be done, but the bill has disappeared between the two houses."

Mr. SPOONER: "Can it not be re-enrolled?"

Mr. LODGE: "The Speaker, I am told, on one occasion, when a bill had disappeared in that way, declined to sign the bill again. It has disappeared between the two houses."

Mr. SPOONER: "It cannot be, if a bill has been lost before it has been signed by the officer of the other house and that, that Congress is powerless about it. Both houses have passed it."

Mr. LODGE: "Certainly they have."

Mr. SPOONER: "I do not see any reason why it cannot be re-enrolled."

Mr. PETTIGREW: "If the bill is lost, it is lost on purpose. There is no question about that. That might do for some half-civilized community, but for the Senate of the United States it is a pretty tough proposition."

After some discussion, the Senate passed a resolution which requested the House to have the bill re-enrolled, signed by the Speaker and sent over to the Senate.

There was nothing further for the Senate to do, so I resolved to take the matter into my own hands. I went over to the House of Representatives, taking with me Louis Kimball, a Civil War veteran, who had been appointed, at my suggestion, messenger to one of the Senate Committees. On the way over to the House I told Kimball what had happened, and then explained my plan to him. I proposed to go to the Clerk of the House and ask him which of his assistants had enrolled the railroad bill. When he told me, I was to attract the attention of this assistant while Kimball went through his desk.

The plan worked like a charm. McConnell was Clerk of the House — a Republican from Pennsylvania, who could be relied upon by the agents of big business to render faithful service. I knew him well. When I reached his desk I asked which of the clerks had enrolled the railroad bill. He indicated the man, and started toward him.

"No," I interposed, "call him over here." I stood stock still till the clerk came.

While I engaged him in conversation about the bill, Kimball went through his desk and, in the back end of the top drawer of the desk, he found the bill, enrolled and ready to be transmitted to the Senate.

"McConnell," said I to the Chief Clerk, "you know what this means. If that bill is not over in the Senate by the time I arrive there, I will ask for the floor and recite to the Senate the circumstances under which we discovered that bill."

Needless to say, the bill was in the Senate chamber before I got back. It was signed at once and sent to the President, who signed it on March 3, 1901, the day before my term as United States Senator expired.

On the day previous. Senator Lodge made the following explanation (March 2, 1901, p. 3537):

"Mr. President, I desire to say a word in regard to the lost bill with respect to which we passed a resolution not long ago. I am informed while the debate was in progress on the North Carolina Claim Bill that the bill had been found in a desk in the enrolling room of the House of Representatives. It seems to have slipped into the drawer of the desk. I wish to say this in justice to the clerks and officers of the Senate. It never came here."

That is the story of the one labor measure that, to my knowledge, passed both houses of Congress and became a law during the twelve years that I was in the Senate. Every means, fair and foul, was employed to kill it, and it was rather by good luck than anything else that we found the bill and got it through in the closing hours of the Session.

During the last year I was in the Senate, that is, from 1899 to March 4, 1901, the Congress of the United States enacted laws upon every conceivable subject, which fill a volume of more than 2,000 pages and these laws were enacted by the attorneys of the property interests of this country who had complete control of both houses, and most of these laws were privileges to the owners of stolen property to exploit the people of the United States.

So much for the standing of labor before Congress — it had no standing at all. And why? Partly because of the lack of organization; partly because of the ignorance and weakness of the leaders; partly because labor can hope to gain little or nothing at the hands of a Congress composed of corporation lawyers and other representatives of the business interests. Perhaps a word with regard to my relations with the American Federation of Labor will help to make my meaning clear.

I became acquainted with Samuel Gompers, President of the American Federation of Labor, many years ago. At that time, I supposed that he represented the labor unions of the United States in the interests of the toiling masses, and that that interest extended to the public in general. But I very soon found that Samuel Gompers and the American Federation of Labor were a combination something in the nature of a trust, organized, even before the great industrial combinations were formed, for the purpose of exploiting everybody except the members of their own combination. I found that Gompers was standing in with the employers of labor and undertaking to get all he could for his crowd, without reference to the general welfare.

On August 8, 1911, Mr. Almont, one of the organizers of the American Federation of Labor, came to me at Sioux Falls, S. D., and said that he had received a letter from Samuel Gompers, or from the office of the American Federation of Labor, requesting Almont to secure a letter from me giving my opinion regarding the trade union movement. I thereupon wrote Gompers the following letter:

"Sioux Falls, August 8, 1911.
"Samuel Gompers, President American Federation of Labor.
"Dear Sir:

"F. C. Almont, one of your organizers, has asked me to write you and give an opinion with regard to the Trade Union Movement.

"The Trade Union should be universal and include every man who toils, not only in the factory, but on the farm. The strike and boycott are but crude and savage and warlike remedies, and I am sure labor will never receive what it earns until the land and implements of production are co-operatively or publicly owned.

"Capital cannot exist without labor and is entirely dependent upon labor, while labor is independent of capital, can and does exist without it. Yet under the present system of production capital exploits labor, and takes more than two-thirds of the earnings of labor, and, until the system is changed, labor will struggle in vain to secure what it produces.
Yours truly,

"R. F. PETTIGREW."

During the fall of 1911, I visited Washington and called upon Gompers. He brought up the subject of my letter, said that he had received and read it and that it was an impertinence to write him such a letter. He began, in a rather excited way, to announce that it was socialism and then to attack the socialists and the socialist doctrine. That interested me very much, so I stayed and

67

talked with him for a long time and got a very fair insight into his theory of the labor movement. Later, I continued the investigation and had at least one meeting with four or five of the principal union officers at the headquarters of the American Federation of Labor at Washington.

After I had thoroughly examined the American Federation of Labor and its processes and purposes, and had ascertained beyond question the relation Mr. Gompers held with the capitalistic and exploiting classes, on December 8, 1916, I wrote the following letter to Gompers:

"December 8, 1916.

"Hon Samuel Gompers,
    "President American Federation of Labor,
        "Washington, D. C.
"Dear Sir:
"The position of the American Federation of Labor as represented by you is that of standing in with the corporations who employ labor to secure a part of what labor is entitled to and make the corporations divide with organized labor what they take from the public.

"You seem to be ignorant of the purpose and objects of the Civic Federation and are getting acquainted with Professor Commons. The only way to make a federation of labor effective is to combine all those who are producers of wealth in a political organization and take charge of the government and then administer the government in the interest of the rights of man. It is now administered in the interests of the rights of property and administered by the men who did not produce any of the property, but who have stolen it from those who did produce it.

"I am enclosing you copy of my article on the distribution of wealth in the United States, also copy of my letter to you of August 8, 1911.

"I very much hope that Congress will pass the Compulsory Arbitration laws, if that is necessary to open your eyes and the eyes of the American Federation of Labor as to what is going on. Commons is right — the Supreme Court will hold that it is constitutional.

"They sent Dred Scott back to slavery and if they will now hold that organized labor can be forced to work, whether they want to or not, and thus send it back to slavery, you will wake up and take possession of the Government and Congress and also of the courts.

"Right after the Dred Scott decision, Lincoln made a speech at Cincinnati, using the following language with reference to the Supreme Court:

"'The people of these United States are the rightful masters of both Congress and the courts, not to overthrow the Constitution, but to overthrow the men who pervert the Constitution.'

"I have wondered if organized labor would still refuse to affiliate with the other laborers — would finally abandon their position as the aristocracy of labor — that of looking with contempt upon their fellow-workers. I wondered if the time will come when you get sufficiently jolted so that you will organize a labor party composed of farmers and other producers of wealth and take charge of the Government of the United States and administer it in the interests of humanity instead of continuing to administer it in the interest of property — stolen property — with organized labor constantly trying to compromise.

"Your position and the position of organized labor has been a matter of great astonishment to me for years and I very much hope that they will pass the compulsory arbitration law, for the extreme measure is necessary to jolt organized labor off from the pedestal upon which it has been roosting on to the ground among its fellow-men.

"Yours very truly,

"R. F. PETTIGREW."

Gompers had always insisted that labor should not go into politics, but that they should select from the two old parties the good men and vote for them without reference as to whether they are Democrats or Republicans, knowing full well that that policy would only result in perpetuating the system of universal exploitation, of which he was one of the representatives.

The people who produce the wealth and do the work in the United States are at least two-thirds of the population. A little over 2,000,000 of the American people own all of the wealth that the workers have produced, having taken it from the producers through special privileges, secured by every conceivable species of chicanery, bribery and corruption. Whenever the masters meet an opponent who exposes their methods and practices, and protests against the present economic system, they first undertake to buy him by agreeing to divide with him the favors which they receive. Failing in that, they undertake to destroy him. No man can succeed for any length of time politically under our system if he exposes the methods of the corporations who own all of the great natural resources and artificial facilities of the United States.

Soon after the American Federation of Labor was organized and Mr. Gompers became its chief, the interests took him into "camp," as they express it, and formulated for him the arguments and program by which he was to handle the American Federation of Labor, so that it would be an adjunct of the present economic system. Of course strikes were permitted where the men represented by Gompers insisted upon having more pay than some of the employers were willing to give. Strikes like those of the steel workers in 1919-1920 might come and go. It was all one to the big fellows. But whenever the strike became so widespread as to seem dangerous, or when the demands of the men were so reasonable that they made a wide public appeal, the smallest possible concessions were made, generally through the leaders of the strikers to the men.

Before making concessions, however, the great combinations would undertake to bribe the leaders; would hire private detectives and use force, if necessary, to beat the strikers into submission. In order to justify the use of force in the eyes of the public, they would send their secret agents among the strikers, advocating some act of violence which they represented as dangerous to the welfare of the workers. They would talk violently and excite the men and advise bomb-throwing and even murder. Sometimes they even perpetrated such outrages. Generally the assaults were against property, and of course immediately the army or the police, or both, were called in to restore law and order.

From a close observation of the operations of the American Federation of Labor, as conducted by Mr. Gompers, I am satisfied that he was a party to the methods employed for breaking great strikes, and that the strikes advised by him were manipulated very much more in the interests of the capitalists than in the interests of labor. And that is why I wrote in a second letter to Mr. Gompers:

"The only way to make a Federation of Labor effective is to combine all those who are producers of wealth in a political organization and take charge of the Government, and then administer the Government in the interests of the rights of property and administered by the men who did not produce any of the property, but who have stolen it from those who did produce it."

Labor has no standing in Congress. Its acknowledged leaders — in conjunction with the masters of industry and finance — tie labor hand and foot. The American Federation of Labor has been in existence forty years (since 1881). During the period of its power the position of the American worker has become, on the whole, less, rather than more, advantageous. The big rewards, the great winnings have gone to the owners, while the workers have received only the crumbs.

Labor produces the world's wealth. The vast majority of the American people work for their living. Civilization is built upon labor, and labor is civilization. Yet the public life of the United States is so organized that the workers receive scant consideration, while every attention is paid to the owners of the property.

All our legislation has been aimed to increase the power and promote the interests of those who have, as against those who produce. The great question then that is presented to the laboring people of the United States is:

Shall the rights of man be superior to the rights of property?

Inasmuch as all property is created by labor, if the rights of man are safeguarded by legislation, no laws will be required to protect the rights of property in the hands of the men who produce it, but under our present system the laborer who produces the wealth has none of it. He is exploited out of it by the landlord, by the corporation which employs him, by the corporations which furnish him public utilities, by the insurance companies and trust companies which charge three times what it is worth to do the business, and by the general system of combinations of the parasites and idlers of society, who get away from the producers of wealth what their labor has created.

If forty laboring men were shipwrecked upon a distant island in the ocean, which was practically never" frequented by ships of commerce, and there were about one thousand acres of fertile land upon the island and only one spring of pure water, and one of their number should rush at once to the spring and the thousand acres of land and claim it as his property because he saw it first and insist that all the others should pay him a portion of their

70

products before they would be permitted to raise food upon the land or to drink water from the spring, the other thirty-nine people would be justified in taking it away from him, and proceeding to exercise their natural rights, giving, of course, the greedy usurper the same right which they all possessed — that of going to work and earning, with the rest of them, his own living.

Of course, the exploiters of labor are always talking about the dignity of labor and extolling the laborers, and the Labor Day orators — men who have never done a day's work in their life or produced a dollar's worth of wealth of the country — will speak of the laborers in the highest terms.

Why then should not the producers of wealth organize and take possession of the Government and run it in the interests of the workers rather than to have it run in the interest of the idle few, as at present?

It seems to me that it is about time we abandoned the barbarous doctrine of "the devil take the hindmost," and that, instead of universal selfishness and competition, we could found a civilization based upon the rights of man in the interest of the general welfare for all the people. Such a step would raise the mental, physical, and moral standard of the population, and would be the beginning of a new stage of civilization. This work must be done by the laboring classes. It will never be done by the beneficiaries of a special privilege economic system now existing in the United States.

[1] The bill was worded as follows: "An Act requiring common carriers engaged in interstate commerce to make full report of all accidents to the Interstate Commerce Commission.

"BE IT ENACTED BY THE SENATE AND HOUSE OF REPRESENTATIVES OF THE UNITED STATES OF AMERICA IN CONGRESS ASSEMBLED:

"It shall be the duty of the general manager, superintendent or other proper officer of common carrier engaged in interstate commerce by railroad to make to the Interstate Commerce Commission, at its office in Washington, District of Columbia, a monthly report, under oath, of all collisions of trains or where any train or part of a train accidentally leaves the track, and of accidents which may occur to its passengers or employees while in the service of such common carrier and actually on duty, which report shall state the nature and causes thereof, and the circumstances connected therewith.

"Sec. 2. That any common carrier failing to make such report within thirty days after the end of any month shall be deemed guilty of a misdemeanor and, upon conviction thereof by a court of competent jurisdiction, shall be punished by a fine of not more than one hundred dollars for each and every offense and for every day during which it shall fail to make such report after the time herein specified for making the same.

"Sec. 3. That neither said report nor any part thereof shall be admitted as evidence or used for any purpose against such railroad so making such report in any suit or action for damages growing out of any matter mentioned in said report.

"Sec. 4. That the Interstate Commerce Commission is authorized to prescribe for such common carriers a method and form for making the reports in the foregoing section provided.

"Approved March 3, 1901."

9. Plutocracy

Bit by bit the evidence accumulated under my eyes until it constituted a mountain of irrefutable proof — the public domain seized and exploited by the interests and for their private profit; the concentration of power in the hands of the bankers; their manipulation of money for their own benefit; the tariff, used as a favor granted by Congress for the few to plunder the many; the wanton and reckless creation of trusts and aggregations of capital; the vast strength of the railroads and other public utility monopolies; the ferocious indifference of these interests to the public welfare and to the well being of the masses of the people — as I surveyed this evidence I could form only one possible conclusion — that the power over American public life, whether economic, social or political, rested in the hands of the rich.

It is said that in the past, in the days of the Roman Empire, when a wealthy Roman wished to build a villa he purchased the right to tax and govern a conquered province in Asia, and returned to Rome to enjoy his fortune. But when an American millionaire wishes to build a villa, or buy a title in Europe, he purchases a tariff privilege from the Congress of the United States, or corrupts a legislature or a city council and secures a franchise, and proceeds to rob his neighbors.

I am of the opinion that the Roman way was the best

Plutocracy is a word that means rule by and for the rich. The United States is a country run by and for the rich. Therefore, it is a plutocracy.

The rich few own the United States. The rich few who own it direct its public policy. For years these facts have been apparent to the discerning. Today even the short-sighted may see them quite plainly.

Real the following letter which Lincoln wrote to William P. Elkin on November 21, 1864:

"I see in the near future a crisis approaching that unnerves me and causes me to tremble for the safety of my country. As a result of war, corporations have been enthroned, and an era of corruption in high places will follow, and the money power of the country will endeavor to prolong its reign by working upon the prejudices of the people until all the wealth is aggregated in a few hands and the republic is destroyed. I feel, at this moment, more anxiety for the safety of my country than ever before, even in the midst of war. God grant that my suspicions may prove groundless."

It has been well said by the famous English writer and philanthropist, Mr. Stead, that the modern business world has adopted a new Golden Rule as follows:

"Dollars and dimes, dollars and dimes;
To be without money is the worst of crimes.
To keep all you get, and get all you can.
Is the first and the last and the whole duty of man."

That this Golden Rule has been adopted by the so-called business men of the United States is evidenced by what has been accomplished in the distribution of the wealth produced by the great toiling masses of this country.

Recently it was announced that John D. Rockefeller had finally succeeded in accumulating one billion dollars, thus making him the richest man that ever lived.

The American people know how he succeeded in accumulating this vast sum. He produced none of it — he secured all of it by exploiting the American people who had produced it.

The most thrifty of the American people do well if they succeed in saving $300 a year above all their expenses, and they must he busy every day in the year in order to do that. To accumulate one billion dollars at the rate of $300 a year — a dollar a day for three hundred working days — a man would have to live and labor 3,383,333 years. He would have to be older than Methuselah — he would have to start when the world was hot no matter where he ended up.

But if he was cunning, unscrupulous and religious and followed Rockefeller's method of robbing his fellow-men, he could get the billion-dollar prize in fifty years.

One billion dollars is equivalent to the earnings of one hundred thousand men for twenty years, provided they earned $500 apiece each year, and during all that time leaving nothing out for sickness, death or accident. The fact that Rockefeller could appropriate the earnings of his fellow-men and the fact that he did do it is what has caused the social and economic protest against the existing system and the cry for justice.

This great and powerful force — the accumulated wealth of the United States — has taken over all the functions of Government, Congress, the issue of money, and banking and the army and navy in order to have a band of mercenaries to do their bidding and protect their stolen property.

Immediately after the announcement that Rockefeller was worth a billion dollars. Armour & Swift announced a dividend upon their capital stock of thirty-three and one-third per cent and each of these concerns increased their capital stock from twenty millions to one hundred millions.

It is safe to say that neither of these concerns had any capital stock for which they had paid a dollar. Their capital stock represented what they had stolen from the people of this country. Their working capital is represented by bonds. The eighty millions of stock which they have since added is also nothing but water and is issued so as to make the annual dividends appear smaller. The exploited people will object less to paying six or seven per cent on a hundred millions than to paying thirty-three and one-third per cent on twenty millions. It looks better in print.

How do Armour and Swift make their money? They are the great packers. They are in collusion. They fix the prices they pay the farmer for his hogs and cattle, and they fix the prices they will charge the consumer for their product. They are simply robbing the producer and the consumer, and their robbery is represented in their great wealth, which they did not produce but which they took from the people under the guise of law.

When the bill to take the census of 1890 was pending before Congress I secured an amendment requiring the enumerators to ascertain the distribution of wealth through an inquiry into farms, homes and mortgages.

Using the figures thus secured by the enumerators of the census of 1890, on June 10, 1898, I delivered a speech in the Senate of the United States on the subject of the distribution of wealth in the United States and, from the census of 1890, I showed that 52 per cent of the people of the United States owned $95.00 worth of property per capita, or $95.00 each of secondhand clothing and second-hand furniture, and that four thousand families owned twelve billions of the wealth, and that 6,640,000 families, or 52 per cent of the population, owned three billions of the wealth, or just five per cent of the total.

The facts, as ascertained by the census-takers in 1890, appear, summarized, in the following table:

Distribution of Wealth by Census 1890

Class	Families	Per Cent	Average Wealth	Aggregate Wealth	Per Cent
Millionaires	4,000	.03	$3,000,000	$12,000,000,000	20
Rich	1,139,000	8.97	27,000	30,600,000,000	51
Total Rich.......	1,143,000	9.00	37,358	42,600,000,000	71
Middle	4,953,000	39.00	2,907	14,400,000,000	24
Poor	6,604,000	52.00	454	3,000,000,000	5
Grand Total....	12,700,000	100.00	$ 4,725	$60,000,000,000	100

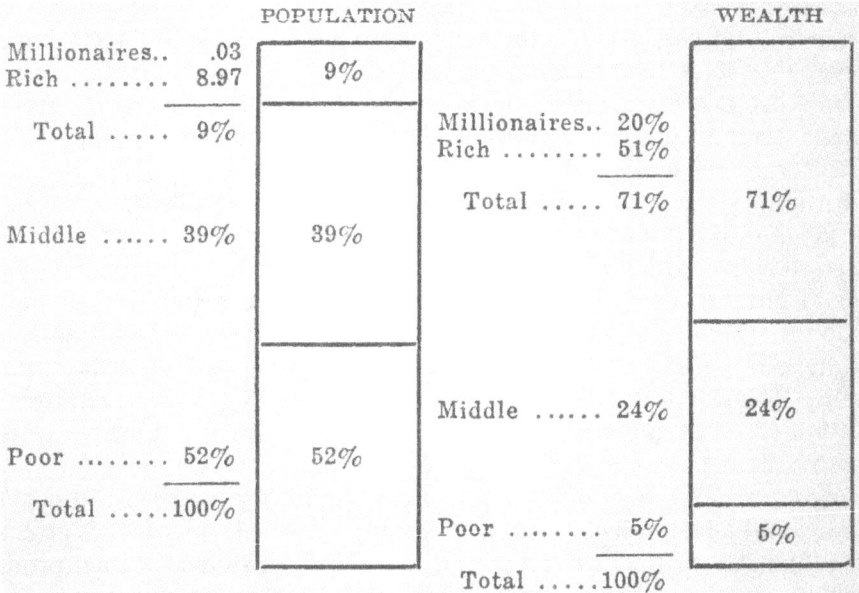

POPULATION

Millionaires.. .03
Rich 8.97   9%

Total 9%

Middle 39%   39%

Poor 52%   52%

Total 100%

WEALTH

Millionaires.. 20%
Rich 51%

Total 71%   71%

Middle 24%   24%

Poor 5%   5%

Total 100%

It will be seen from these tables, which are compiled from the census report of 1890, that 52 per cent of the people, or two per cent more than half of them, owned but five per cent of the accumulated wealth of the United States. The report of the Industrial Commission which thoroughly investigated the distribution of wealth in the United States discloses the fact that, after twenty-six years, covering half of the period in which Rockefeller and Armour and Swift and the other exploiters of the people have accumulated their vast fortunes, the number of people who participated in the five per cent of the wealth of the United States has increased from 52 per cent of our total population to 65 per cent.

I have prepared a diagram illustrating the conclusions reached by the experts of the Industrial Commission, which pictures the stupendous inequalities that have arisen in the United States during the past twenty-six years:

Distribution of Wealth, Report of Industrial Commission, 1915

Class	Number	Per Cent	Average Wealth	Aggregate Wealth	Per Cent
Rich	2,000,000	2%	$42,000	$ 84,000,000,000	60%
Middle	33,000,000	33%	1,480	49,000,000,000	35%
Poor	65,000,000	65%	107	7,000,000,000	5%
Grand Total..	100,000,000	100%	$ 1,400	$140,000,000,000	100%

Total Population of
Rich 2% or 2,000,000... 100,000,000

Total Wealth
$140,000,000,000

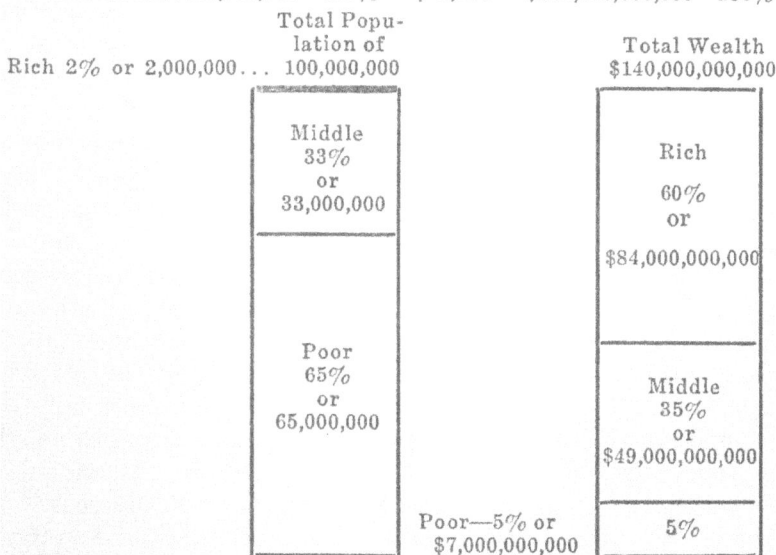

Middle
33%
or
33,000,000

Rich
60%
or
$84,000,000,000

Poor
65%
or
65,000,000

Middle
35%
or
$49,000,000,000

Poor—5% or
$7,000,000,000

5%

I wish a careful examination of these tables. You will see that sixty-five per cent of the people own five per cent of the wealth and that two per cent of the population — the little black line at the top of the diagram — own sixty per cent of the wealth. They did not produce the wealth. It was all produced by the sixty-five per cent of the population who have nothing. They were able to do it because they owned the Government and the courts and enacted the laws which made it possible. They have done it through manipulation, combination and exploitation. They have done it through corporations. They have done it because they own the railroads and the banks and all the public utilities, and used them all — all of these great important public service institutions in order to gather the products of everybody's toil into their own hands. In other words, they have stolen what others have produced.

These were the figures for 1916. Since that time there have come the war and the panic, with their huge crop of millionaires and their further concentration of wealth and of economic power.

But, you may ask, why is it necessary to turn to the figures of the Industrial Commission? Why not use the census figures? The answer is very simple. Since the publication of the 1890 figures, the plutocrats have decided that the facts regarding wealth distribution shall not be permitted to get into the hands of the American people.

When I entered the Senate I believed that the question of the distribution of wealth was one of the most important ones before the American people and one that was receiving no attention whatever. While I was in the House I had made the personal acquaintance of Senator Jones of Arkansas, who was on the Committee on Indian Affairs in the Senate, and Senator Berry of Arkansas, who was on the Committee on Public Lands in the Senate. So that, before the Senate convened in December, 1889 — when I took my seat in the Senate, I had talked with these two Senators about securing legislation to ascertain the distribution of wealth in the United States. They had entered heartily into the plan and we prepared a bill for that purpose, [1] which was introduced by Senator Berry as an amendment to the Census Bill of 1890. The bill attracted little attention and was passed practically without opposition, but I had great difficulty in getting the persons in charge of taking the census to go thoroughly into the question. Finally, under the head of "Farms, Homes and Mortgages," an investigation was made by Holmes and a report was issued, I think, about 1898. This report showed a remarkable economic condition in this country and disclosed the fact that 52 per cent of our population had five per cent of the wealth they had produced, and that nine per cent of our population had a majority of all the property in this country. I made a speech in the Senate upon this subject, going quite fully into the question, and in that speech I predicted that the number of people who had nothing would steadily increase under our system, and that the number of people who owned a majority of the wealth would steadily decrease.

I considered the question so important that I secured a place on the Senate Census Committee to prepare the bill for taking the census of 1900. In the committee I urged an amendment to the bill for taking the census which should go fully into the question of the distribution of wealth in this country, but the committee refused to adopt my amendment or to take any notice of the question whatever. Incidentally, the committee was composed of lawyers and a lawyer is trained to believe that it is the right of property in the hands of men who did not produce the property that is sacred, and not the rights of man. Or that society has any obligation whatever to those who toil. We bor-

76

rowed this from England and it is thoroughly inculcated into our whole system of educational and economic life that there is no question but that the lawyers honestly believe it to be true. After the Census Bill was reported to the Senate I offered my amendment under these circumstances:

(Congressional Record, 56th Congress, 1st Session, Jan. 11, 1900, vol. 331, p. 779.)

Mr. PETTIGREW: "I offer an amendment, which I send to the desk."

THE PRESIDENT PRO TEMPORE: "The amendment of the Senator from South Dakota will be stated."

THE SECRETARY: "It is proposed to add, as section 3, the following:

"Sec. 3. That the Director of the Census is hereby required to collect statistics relating to the indebtedness of individuals and corporations, public or private; also in relation to the distribution of wealth among the people of the United States; also statistics as to the displacement of labor by machinery, and the increase of the power of production by machinery in proportion to the number of laborers employed during the last thirty years. And for this purpose the Director of the Census may employ special agents, and such special agents shall receive such compensation as other special agents."

Mr. PETTIGREW: "Mr. President, this amendment is intended to secure statistics with regard to the distribution of wealth. It does not require the enumerators to gather the statistics on this subject, and therefore will not delay the purpose of the law which we have passed.

"We make the Census Bureau, as I understand, a perpetual bureau of statistics and information, and to fail to gather the information referred to in my amendment, it seems to me, would be a very serious mistake. The question as to what becomes of what the toilers of the land produce, whether it goes to them or is taken from them by special privileges, and accumulated in the hands of a very few people is a very important one and reaches ultimately the question of the preservation of free institutions.

'The other subject in my amendment is with regard to the displacement of labor by machinery and the increased power of production thereby. I desire this information for the reason that I believe man's power to produce, as the result of the adoption of machinery, has increased many times more than the increase of his wages, which should have occurred as a result of his increased powers of production; in other words, that the increased power of production is the result of machinery and has inured to the advantage of capital many times more than to the advantage of labor; that this has caused in a large degree the unequal distribution of wealth in this country; that the increased power of production, as the result of machinery, should go to the toiler in a much larger degree than to the capital employed; that the power to produce by machinery is a benefit to mankind if the increased power to produce goes to the toiler, because his power to consume is also increased, and thus the consumption and enjoyment of a greater measure of the luxuries and comforts of life must go to those who produce the wealth of the land.

"I therefore believe these two questions are exceedingly important; and I have asked that this information be collected by special agents rather than by the enumerators, so that it will not delay a single day or a single hour the securing of that information which seems to be the prime object of the bill.

"I hope the additional section I have offered will be adopted without objection."

(Jan. 11, 1900.)

Mr. TILLMAN: "I will say for the information of the Senator from Georgia that if it is not taken with the first census it cannot be taken at all, without an intolerable additional expense. It is for the Senate to determine whether it will enlarge the scope of the census. If we break down the barrier erected by the Census Committee, we simply, as we were notified by the Senator from Missouri (Mr. Cockrell) the other day, open up a flood of amendments concerning each special class of inquiry any senator may wish to have included."

Mr. PETTIGREW: "My amendment provides for nothing of the kind. It simply provides that this Census Bureau of statistics, which is perpetual, may, by special agents, not by enumerators, investigate this all-important subject. I think the census would be of very little value without it. It is not personal to myself, nor a subject that I am particularly or personally interested in, but it is a great public question. The question of the distribution of the wealth of this country is certainly a question of more importance than almost anything else that can be investigated. As the Senator from Colorado (Mr. Teller) has said, we have almost day by day a very accurate estimate of the population. We have very many other statistics which are constantly being produced by the statistical bureau, but the question of the distribution of the wealth of this country has never been adequately and fairly investigated. It ought to be.

"I do not propose to delay the taking of the census, and my amendment does not delay it at all. It simply provides an additional section for the doing of this additional work. If the schedules are all prepared and the work is disposed of, the enumerators can commence their operations; and therefore the Department will have the time to get out additional schedules for the special agents to do the work which I desire to have done. This work cannot commence until an appropriation is made. It is quite proper, then, that the amendment should be on this bill, because section 8 is in the original law, which provides a large amount of extra work to be done after the main census has been taken through the enumerators; and if it was a proper time to provide section 8 in the law when it passed last year, it is time now for my amendment to be placed on this bill. That is all I want. I do not care to discuss it further."

The reasons in favor of taking a wealth census seemed to me conclusive. Nevertheless, the amendment met with universal opposition, and it was rejected.

When the census bill was pending to take the census of 1910, I wrote to Senator LaFollette and urged him to secure an amendment with relation to the distribution of wealth in this country, but LaFollette is a lawyer and he did nothing. I also sent him a statement of the facts in connection with the matter and a copy of my speech delivered in 1898 on this subject, but I was unable to accomplish anything, as the Senate was still composed almost entirely of lawyers who had represented as attorneys, before they entered the Senate and who still continued to represent as attorneys after they entered the Senate, the great industrial, financial, transportation and exploiting interests.

While the census bill to provide for the census of 1920 was under consideration in both Houses, I went to Washington and personally went to the committee of both Houses and urged the importance of securing statistics with regard to the distribution of wealth in this country, but neither committee would entertain my proposed amendment or listen with patience to any argument.

In reply to my analyses of the situation, the members of the committees insisted that it was not true. "Why," said they, "look about you and see the prosperity everywhere. How can you say then that the wealth of the country is in the hands of the rich?"

"Well," I answered, "if it is not true, and if the Census of 1890, the Industrial Commission, and all of the rest of the authorities are wrong, the thing to do is to take another wealth census and disprove all of their false statements." Still, I could make no impression on the lawyers who made up both committees.

The Committees of Congress, having the censuses of 1910 and 1920 in charge, refused to include in the census bills a clause requiring the enumerators to ascertain the distribution of wealth, because they, as representatives of the plutocracy, did not desire the facts to be known. The bulk of the American people have little or no wealth; the economic power of the United States is concentrated in the hands of the few, and the few are determined to keep the many in ignorance as long as they possibly can.

I have gone into some detail with regard to this matter of the wealth census, not so much because of its intrinsic importance, but because of its relation to other and similar issues. Again and again, on other questions, the same men who refused to gather the evidence of wealth concentration have introduced and voted for the measures which were drawn up by the attorneys of the vested interests for the purpose of increasing wealth concentration.

The economic power of the United States has been concentrated in the hands of a very few, and they are the Government. They pass the laws that in their judgment will protect and defend the property upon which their power depends; they secure the appointment of judges who will interpret and who do interpret this legislation in the interest of the wealth-owning classes; control those who execute the laws, from the presidents down — indeed, for the most part, the presidents are lawyers, and either members of the plutocracy, or else paid retainers of the plutocracy; they control all of the channels of public opinion — the press, the schools, the church; they control the labor unions through the control of their leaders and of the policy that the leaders pursue; possessors of the land on which the farmer must work, of the mines and the machines with which the laborer must work, in order to live, the plutocracy — the wealth class — in the United States is supreme over the affairs of public life.

Today this economic power is not ashamed to show its head and take its place as the master of the American Government and as the overlord of the American people. They used to talk about the Invisible Government when I entered the Senate in 1890, but it is invisible no longer. The real government is not in Washington. Its attorneys are there, but its responsible directors are in New York and in the other great centers of commerce and industry. Wealth means power in an industrial civilization, and the few, owning the bulk of the wealth of the United States, exercise their plutocratic power over the lives of the American people, who are forced, whether they will or no, to do the bidding of their wealth lords. And therefore I say — Capital is stolen labor and its only function is to steal more labor.

[1] The bill was worded as follows:
"That a census of the population, wealth and industry of the United States shall be taken as of the date of June 1, 1890. Statutes of the U. S., p. 761, March 1, 1899."

10. Who Made the Constitution

I have written in some detail of the economic changes and of the changes in economic policy that have occurred in the United States during the past 50 years. The first year that I went to Washington (1870) the population of Chicago was 298,977; today (1920) it is 2,701,705; the population of Detroit was 79,577; today it is 993,739; the population of Minneapolis was 13,006; today it is 380,582; the population of Dakota was 14,181; today it is 1,281,569. I have watched the Middle West grow from a sparsely settled wilderness, the home of Indians and of buffaloes, to the greatest center of agriculture and of industry in the world. I have watched the public domain slip out of the hands of the people, and into the hands of speculators, of corporations and of monopolies. I have seen the bankers, the trust magnates and the masters of transportation and other forms of monopoly rise from obscurity to their present position of domination in public affairs. I have watched the growth of the plutocracy — the few who rule industry, the Government and the press because they are rich.

In the halls of the Capitol at Washington, I have watched these plutocrats, through their representatives on the floor of the Senate and the House, erect the governmental machinery that they required for the preservation of their power. Step by step and move by move I fought the system of imperialism which the McKinley administration enabled them to establish as the accepted policy of the country. The fight lasted twelve years. When it was over, the interests that I had opposed were the triumphant masters of the field.

When I entered the Senate, I did not understand what it was that I was facing. When I left the Senate, because Mark Hanna and the forces behind Mark Hanna willed that I should leave, I knew that the forms of our government and the machinery of its administration were established and maintained for the benefit of the class that held the economic and political power.

I realized that the machinery of government had been constructed by the ruling economic class to preserve and guarantee its own economic interests. Documents like the Constitution, which I, as a child, had been taught to regard as almost divine in their origin, stood before me for what they were — plans prepared by business men to stabilize business interests.

At the time that our Constitution was drawn up, Adam Smith wrote of the government in the "mother country" (Wealth of Nations, Book V., Ch. 1, published in 1776), "Civil government, so far as it is instituted for the security of property, is in reality instituted for the defense of the rich against the poor, or of those who have some property against those who have none at all." Again he stated (Book 1, Ch. 10), "Whenever the legislature attempts to regulate the differences between masters and their workmen, its counsellors are always the masters."

Concerning this same epoch a well-known modern historian writes: "During the period we are discussing (1760-1832)...the classes that possessed authority in the State, and the classes that had acquired the new wealth, landlords, churchmen, judges, manufacturers, one and all understood by government the protection of society from the fate that had overtaken the privileged classes in France." (The Town Laborer, J. L. & B. Hammond, N. Y. Longmans, 1917, p. 321). It was this government by landlords and manufacturers that the framers of the Constitution knew, and they knew no other. Their idea of government was the British idea — a machine for protecting the rich against the poor; a device for safeguarding and defending privilege against the clamorous and revolutionary demands of the populace. Their goal was the protection of the propertied interests and they drew the Constitution with that end in view.

Furthermore, it was the leading business men of the colonists, in their own persons, who drew up the Constitution and forced through its ratification. 'The movement for the Constitution," writes Charles A. Beard, the distinguished student of American Government, "was originated and carried through principally by four groups of personality interests, which had been adversely affected under the Articles of Confederation — money, public securities, manufacturers, and trade and shipping." (An Economic Interpretation of the Constitution, New York, MacMillan 1914, p. 324.) These events transpired nearly a century-and-a-half ago, and ever since that time we have been building up the kind of a government that bankers, manufacturers and merchants needed for their enrichment.

This point is so fundamental to a proper understanding of what I have to say about the machinery of American Government that I desire to emphasize it. School teachers talk to children and public men harangue their constituents as though the Constitution were a document drawn to establish human liberty. By these means our ideas as to the intention of the framers of the Constitution have been utterly distorted. Anyone who wishes to know the facts should examine the Journal of the Constitutional Convention. There the record is as plain as the road at noonday. The Constitution was not drawn up to safeguard liberty. Its framers had property rights in their minds' eye and property deeds in their pockets, and its most enthusiastic supporters were the leading bankers, manufacturers and traders of the Federated States.

The Constitution was made to protect the rights of property and not the rights of man.

These facts are neither secret nor hidden. They are a part of the public record that may be consulted in any first class library. Properly understood, they furnish the intellectual key that will open the mind to an appreciation of many of the most important events that have occurred in the United States during the past century.

The convention that framed the Constitution of the United States convened at Philadelphia in 1787 behind closed doors. All of the delegates were sworn to secrecy. Madison reported the proceedings of the convention in longhand and his notes were purchased in 1837 by Congress and published by the Government nearly half a century after the convention had finished its work. These notes disclose the forces that dominated the work of the convention and show that the object which the leaders of the convention had in view was not to create a democracy or a government of the people, but to establish a government by the property classes in the interests of the rights of property rather than the rights of man. All through the debates ran one theme: How to secure a government, not by the people and for the people, but by the classes and for the classes, with the lawyers in control.

Jefferson was not a member of the convention. As the author of the Declaration of Independence he was not wanted in the convention, and so he was sent to France on a diplomatic mission.

I will give two extracts from these proceedings to illustrate this point; they are typical, and are as follows:

Madison (p. 78) quotes Sherman of Connecticut as saying: "The people should have as little to do as may be about the Government. They want information and are constantly liable to be misled."

Again (p. 115) Mr. Gerry is quoted as follows:

"Hence in Massachusetts the worst men get into the legislature. Several members of that body had lately been convicted of infamous crimes. Men of indigence, ignorance and baseness, spare no pains, however dirty, to carry their point against men who are superior to the artifices practiced." This is the burden of the debates through page after page of the two volumes.

The chief contention in the Constitutional Convention was over representation in the United States Senate. The smaller states feared that they would be dominated by the larger ones and, after much debate, it was agreed that each state, no matter what its wealth or population, should have two votes in the Senate of the United States, while the House of Representatives should represent the people and the number of delegates from each state should be in proportion to the population. As a concession to the larger states, a provision was inserted requiring that all money bills should originate in the House of Representatives, and this was considered important, in view of the fact that the states of small area and small population, such as Delaware and Rhode Island, had an equal voice with large states like Virginia and Pennsylvania in the Senate of the United States.

The southern states believed they had obtained protection for their peculiar institution (slavery) by securing representation in the House of Representatives for the slave population. At the same time, the southern slaveholders and the northern slave-traders combined to secure the insertion of a clause (Article 1, Section IX, Clause 1) permitting the slave trade to continue until 1808.

At the time of framing the Constitution, and for many years thereafter, it was supposed and intended that the Senate should represent the states while the House represented the people. No vested interest ever thought of gaining control of the Senate for the purpose of advancing the commercial or financial position of any combination, corporation or individual. It was not until a third of a century after the adoption of the Constitution that the southern states began to look to the Senate for the protection of their interests and to insist upon the admission of a slave state whenever a free state asked for admission to the Union.

The immediate purpose behind the creation of a Senate that was not elected by the people, but that came from the state legislatures and thus spoke in name of states rather than of masses of citizens, was the protection of the small colonies against the large ones. The interests that dominated both the small and the large colonies, however, were the business interests. Therefore, this struggle between those who wanted one form of Senate and those who wanted another was a struggle between contending and competing business groups. It was not in any sense a struggle between the champions of liberty and the advocates of property rights.

This fact is made evident by an examination of the interests of these men who made up the Constitutional Convention of 1787. There were fifty-five delegates present in the Convention. A majority were lawyers; most of them came from towns; there was not one farmer, mechanic or laborer among them; five-sixths had property interests. Of the 55 members, 40 owned revolutionary scrip; 14 were land speculators; 24 were money-lenders; 11 were merchants; 15 were slaveholders. Washington, the big man of the Convention, was a slave-holder, land speculator and a large scrip owner.

Jefferson was in France!

The Constitution, as framed by the Convention, says nothing about the rights of man. It contains no guarantee of free speech, of free press, of free assemblage, or of religious liberty. It breathes no single hint of freedom. It was made by men who believed in the English theory, that all governments are created to protect the rights of property in the hands of those who do not produce it.

The revolutionary scrip-paper money, to finance the Revolutionary War, had been used to pay for supplies and to pay the wages of the men that did the fighting. In the years that followed the war, this scrip had been bought up by the financiers and great land-owners and their attorneys for about nine cents on the dollar. The Constitution, as adopted, made it worth one hundred cents on the dollar. This is but one of the many facts which prove that the Constitution, as drawn up by the Convention, was made to protect the rights of property rather than the rights of man.

Throughout the document the framers were careful to guard against too much democracy. The Government was erected in three parts— legislative, executive and judicial — each with a check on the other two. The House of Representatives alone was elected directly by the people, but all of its legislative acts were subject to revision or rejection by the Senate, the members of which were to be selected, not by popular vote but by the vote of the state legislatures. Thus, even the legislative branch of the Government did not represent the popular will. If the legislative branch had been responsible to the people, there were still the President, elected, not by the vote of the people, but by the vote of electors, who were elected by the people; and, last of all, and by no means the least, from the point of view of the vested interests, there was the Supreme Court — its members selected by the President, confirmed by the Senate, sitting for life. Over these supreme judges, the people could not exercise even an indirect control.

This was the Constitution drawn up while Thomas Jefferson was in France. It was submitted to the states for ratification and the states refused to accept it. In all probability it never would have been ratified had Thomas Jefferson not returned from France and thrown his great influence in favor of the first ten amendments — the Bill of Rights that was added to the Constitution by its business backers, as the necessary price of its adoption by the people. Article I of these Amendments reads:

"Congress shall make no law respecting an establishment of religion, or prohibiting the free exercise thereof; or abridging the freedom of speech or of the press; or the right of the people peaceably to assemble and to petition the Government for redress of grievances."

Article IV of the Amendments provides:

"The right of the people to be secure in their persons, houses, paper and effects, against unreasonable searches and seizures, shall not be violated; and no warrants shall issue but upon probable cause, supported by oath or affirmation, and particularly describing the place to be searched, and the persons or things to be seized."

These are the principal guarantees of liberty, inserted in the Constitution after the Convention of business men had finished its work, and inserted because the people insisted upon having them there.

Even at that, the Constitution is a lukewarm document. In it there are no such burning words as those written by Thomas Jefferson thirteen years earlier and published as the Declaration of Independence: "We hold these truths to be self-evident, that all men are created free and equal and are endowed by their Creator with certain inalienable rights; that among these are life, liberty and the pursuit of happiness. That to secure these rights, governments are instituted among men, deriving their just powers from the consent of the governed; that whenever any form of government becomes destructive of these ends it is the right of the people to alter or abolish it, and to institute a new government, laying its foundations on such principles and organizing its power in such form as shall seem to them most likely to effect their safety and happiness."

It was not until 1861, when Abraham Lincoln delivered his first inaugural address, that the right of revolution was definitely proclaimed by a responsible statesman, acting under the Constitution. "This country," Lincoln said on that occasion, "with its institutions belongs to the people who inhabit it. Whenever they shall grow weary of the existing government, they can exercise their constitutional right of amendment, or their revolutionary right to dismember or overthrow it."

That revolutionary right, so clearly proclaimed in the Declaration of Independence and so emphatically stated by Lincoln, remains today the avenue left to the American people as a means of escape from, the intolerable plutocratic tyranny that the Constitution has set up.

The Constitution is the fundamental law of the United States. It was drawn up 134 years ago by a convention consisting of business men and their lawyer-retainers. It was a document designed to protect property rights, and, through the century and a quarter that it has endured, it has served its purpose so well that it stands today, not only as the chief bulwark of American privilege and vested wrong, but as the greatest document ever designed by man for the safeguarding of the few in their work of exploiting and robbing the many.

11. Lawyers

The Constitution of the United States was made by business men. The work of managing and directing the government machinery that has been erected in pursuance of the Constitution has been placed almost exclusively in the hands of lawyers, who sit in the legislatures and make the laws; sit in the executive chairs and enforce the laws, and sit on the bench and interpret the laws.

Lawyers dominate the city, state and national governments to an astonishing degree. In one sense, they are the Government, at least in so far as manipulating its machinery is concerned. The lawyers have become a governing caste in the United States. Their official position is out of all proportion to their number.

The total number of "lawyers, judges and justices," as given in the census of 1910 (the latest one available at this writing) was 114,704. The same volume of the census reports that there were more than 38,167,000 gainfully occupied persons in the United States. That would make three lawyers for each 1,000 of the gainfully occupied population. Therefore, if the lawyers had their proportional share of the governing positions, they would get less than one-third of one per cent of the Government jobs.

The actual situation is far different. In the affairs of government — particularly of the Federal Government — the lawyer plays a leading part. He is only one one-three-hundredth of the gainfully occupied population, but he is the majority of those upon whom falls the duty of making and enforcing the laws.

Take the situation in the Federal Congress. There has never been a time during the fifty years that I have known Washington when the lawyers constituted less than half of the membership of both houses of Congress. Usually, they made up two-thirds of the membership. The proportion varies, but the principle holds. The present Congress (the 65th) reports in the House 263 lawyers out of a total of 388 who gave their occupations. (No occupations were given for 47.) In the Senate, there are 60 lawyers out of a total of 89 Senators who reported their occupations. The census shows that the lawyers constitute only three in every thousand of the gainful population. In the Senate, they are in the proportion of 674 per thousand; and in the House in the proportion of 677 in the thousand. Thus, two-thirds of our national lawmakers are lawyers.

The same thing holds true of our Presidents. Since the United States has become a government by the corporations, their presidential candidates have almost invariably been lawyers. Harrison, as President, was a a lawyer, and reputed to be a good one. He had been preceded in that high office by Grover Cleveland, a lawyer from Buffalo, New York. Harrison was followed by Cleveland. Cleveland was followed by another lawyer — McKinley, who was elected and assassinated, and thus Theodore Roosevelt, who was his Vice-President, and not a lawyer, accidentally became President. He was succeeded by another lawyer, Taft, who was not a good lawyer. He had neither the judgment nor the ability to make a good lawyer, and he was therefore a very satisfactory representative of the predatory and exploiting corporations which, during all of my time in public life, have been the real force in control of the Government. Taft was followed by Wilson, a lawyer, and after his eight years the people elected Harding, another lawyer — giving him a plurality of more than six million of votes.

There is no question of party politics involved. Of all the Presidents that I have known, two were Democrats (Cleveland and Wilson); the rest were Republicans. With the exception of Roosevelt, all of them since Garfield — and including Garfield — have been lawyers.

The lawyers have an even higher percentage among the successful presidential candidates than they have among the members of Congress.

When it comes to the courts, the whole field is in the possession of the lawyers, who have built up a system of exalting the law above everything else in the land — life, happiness and liberty included. They have worked out a "precedent" under which no one may become a judge unless he has previously been a lawyer. As a matter of practical fact, it is not necessary that a judge should be a lawyer. On the contrary, a lawyer trained under the present system is not fit to be a judge, but the thing has been worked out in such a way that all of the judges are lawyers.

The position of the lawyers in the Government is absurd in view of their small numerical importance. There are only a little more than a hundred thousand of them in a country of more than a hundred millions, yet they make up more than two-thirds of the membership of both houses of Congress; the majority of the state legislatures; most of the governors; all of the prosecuting attorneys; most of the Presidents, and all of the judges. The lawyers enact the laws; interpret the laws and enforce the laws. The Government is a lawyer-government, and we are a lawyer-ridden country.

Then there comes a question. If the business men of the United States run the Government, as I have asserted that they do, how comes it that they are willing to let the lawyers hold all of the important public positions?

The answer to that question is very simple: Because the lawyers do it so well!

If the lawyers failed to do what the business men want done, the business men would soon put an end to their domination of the political machinery. The lawyers know that as well as the business men. But the lawyers are kept in their present position because they are such splendid representatives of the predatory interests. A lawyer, by his training and by his practice, is calculated to serve the ruling class of the country, and, where the rulers can get able servants, there is no reason why they should do the work themselves. They have ample resources. They can afford to pay, and with the lawyers at hand to do their work they are as well served as though they served themselves. The lawyers are not experts in government, but in debauching and corrupting and crippling the Government in the interest of those who pay them their fees. So here they sit, in the legislatures, in the executive offices and on the bench, running the Government in the interest of those who are plundering the people.

Business interests support and finance their lawyer handy-men because these lawyers are able to do what the business world wants done. The lawyers have been developed into a class of professional manipulators and wreckers of Government machinery because they are trained from the outset to regard the interests of their clients as of greater moment than the public interest.

A man, to become a good lawyer, must have spent his life studying "precedent." What is precedent but the preservation of the status quo, and what is the status quo but the wisdom of yesterday? The good lawyer is therefore the lawyer who is able to preserve the shadow of yesterday and use it to darken the sunlight of today.

The good lawyer, to educate himself, pores over the Common Law of England. When his head is filled with seventeen hundred decisions handed down by judges who lived in the seventeenth century, before the American Colonies found the British rule intolerable, he fills up the chinks of his mind with Blackstone and with Kent's Commentaries. He then studies what the judges (lawyers) of the United States said during the past hundred years, and after that he is considered as prepared to defend the interests of the exploiters of America.

This precedent-fed human being is valuable to the great interests for three reasons:

First, because his study of precedent has rendered him incapable of thinking into the future and has thus made him a natural protector of things as they are; Second, because the tradition of property rights inherited from the past can best be preserved through such a class of "dead-hand" experts;

Third, because the lawyer, under the ethics of his profession, is the only man who can take a bribe and call it a fee.

The real work of the world is done by those who envisage the future and prepare for it. Such an ability is the first essential in a statesman, or in any other person who assumes to play a role in the direction of human affairs. The lawyer finds it virtually impossible to look ahead. He has been trained to move forward with his eyes over his shoulder.

Any ruling class, depending for its profits on some special privilege, like the ownership of land or of machinery, must see to it that these special privileges are not interfered with, otherwise its source of profit may be destroyed. At one time, under the Feudal System, it was the church that acted as the policeman for the landlord, keeping the tenants quiet with threats of dire punishment in the hereafter in case they interfered with the sacred person or with the still more sacred property of their overlords. That function, at the present time, has been taken over by the lawyers, who threaten the penalties of criminal codes and of Espionage Acts for those who transgress the sacred precincts in which the property of their clients is enclosed.

All of this work is done by the simple method of allowing one man for himself and for his heirs, forever, certain corner lots and choice quarter-sections without which his fellows cannot continue to make a living. The world marches by his door and, for the privilege of so doing, it pays the property-holder his rent.

The lawyer has studied the precedents established by the land-holding aristocracy of Great Britain. From them he has derived the "common law," and to that he has added tens of thousands of pages of statutes which are designed to perfect the system the landholding aristocracy of Great Britain has worked so hard to establish.

The traditions of English civilization are traditions of wealthy land-holders and manufacturers and bankers, on the one hand, and an overworked, exploited population of laborers on the other. No one who has seen the condition of the British workers can have any delusions as to the terrible way in which they have suffered under the "property-first" system of British society. It is this system that is being perpetuated in the United States, by means of the Constitution, the laws, the courts and the lawyers, who are the handymen of big business, in control of every important branch of the public service.

The lawyer makes a good servant of the ruling class because he spends his life making the world believe that the property rights are more important than the human rights. Again, he is useful because he may be bribed at almost any stage of his public career, and may accept the bribe without losing his professional self-respect.

During the twelve years that I was a member of the United States Senate, more than two-thirds of the members of both houses were lawyers, and those in the Senate were generally old lawyers who had spent their lives in the service of the great interests. So far as I know, these lawyers, in both Houses, never hesitated to take a fee from any interest that wished to employ them. They satisfied their consciences by assuring themselves and their friends that no matter what the size of the fee it did not influence their actions as lawmakers.

I know personally of one Senator who received a fee of $49,000 for representing one of the greatest of the industrial combinations in a case before a Federal court. This man was as honest a lawyer as I ever knew. His vote could not have been purchased for any consideration; yet after he had received the $49,000 fee, if a question had come up which involved the interests of that corporation, or which was in the nature of an attack upon it, it is useless to insist that the thought of the fee would not have had at least some influence in determining what he should do and how he should vote.

Senator Edmunds of Vermont was chairman of the Committee on the Judiciary during the twelve years that I was a member of the United States Senate. He reported the Sherman Anti-Trust Law from that Committee. Afterward, the United States Government began a suit against the Joint Traffic Association, which was a combination of thirty-two railroads running west from New York, on the ground that that combination was in violation of the Sherman Anti-Trust law, the suit having been started before Judge LaComb, the Circuit Judge of the District of New York. The judge announced from the bench that he was disqualified from hearing the case because he was the owner of the stocks and bonds of the defendant railroad, and he said, in open court, that he believed every judge in the circuit was suffering from a like disqualification. The railroads had put their attorneys on the bench. It was finally found that Judge Wheeler, just appointed through the influence of Senator Edmunds, from the State of Vermont, was not the owner of stocks and bonds in the defendant railroads, and the railroads thereupon employed

Edmunds to go before this judge — a creature of his — and tell the judge that the Sherman Anti-Trust Law was not being violated.

No one knows how big a fee Edmunds received, but it created no comment, for it is now well understood that a lawyer can be bought and call the purchase price of his opinions and convictions a fee.

In the case of Foraker, of Ohio, and Senator Bailey, of Texas, the amount of money paid them by the Standard Oil Company was so large, and the transaction was so under cover, that it excited no great amount of comment until the newspapers took it up, and then the matter became so scandalous that the public thought it best to call a halt.

These are only illustrations. It is a universal practice among the lawyers of both Houses to take a fee from the industrial combinations whenever they can get it, and they boast among their fellow members if the fee is big enough to be worth while.

This was the practice during the whole twelve years that I was in the Senate.

From what I have said about the training of lawyers it must be apparent that a lawyer cannot be a statesman. First, because he is trained to look backward rather than forward and, second, because in order to be a statesman it is necessary to have some appreciation of the general welfare, and the lawyer can only represent his clients and assist them to protect and defend property rights.

How is it possible to produce statesmen under the conditions that prevail in the United States, or in any of the other great capitalist countries for that matter? Under the system the land, the resources, the means of transportation and the money power are handed over to the favored few. They manipulate the Government, through their agents, the lawyers, and thus the machinery that should be employed to feed and care for the people is employed for the enrichment of the few at the expense of the many. It is the lawyers who have acted as the go-between. They have drawn the papers under which the riches of the nation have been placed in the hands of a few, who hold legal commissions that enable them to rob the many. Under these circumstances, it is not the general welfare that is uppermost in the minds of those responsible for the direction of public affairs, but the manipulation of public business in such a way as to add still more to the power of those who hold the special privileges of the nation.

It is only in England and in the United States that the people have been satisfied to build up a ruling class — the lawyers — and to put into their hands all branches of the Government.

The people of Russia have provided in their constitution that every person over eighteen years of age can vote if they are engaged in some useful employment, and have thus, in my opinion, disfranchised the lawyer, for a lawyer spends the first half of his life over the past, and the last half of his life trying to apply the past to the present, and lets the future go to hell; and I submit this is not a useful occupation.

90

Lawyers should be excluded from the bench and from every legislative assembly. A well-trained lawyer is unfitted for doing anything else except defending the cases that he is hired to defend, and he should be compelled to stick to that. Above all, he should not be entrusted with any share in the direction of public affairs.

12. Politics

Like most American boys I had been brought up to believe that the United States had a government of the people, by the people and for the people. My first real impressions to the contrary were obtained during my early experiences with Dakota politics. There I learned how the machinery of government is manipulated in the interest of those who are behind it and I learned something about the manipulators.

"Carpet-bag officials," as we used to call them, held the important offices in Dakota, while it was still a territory. The governors and other territorial officers were appointed by the President and confirmed by the Senate at Washington. Frequently these appointees lived thousands of miles from the territory in which they were appointed to serve and in many instances they had never set foot in these territories until they arrived to take up their official duties.

A territory is entitled to a "delegate" in the House of Representatives. The delegate has a seat, but no vote. He may sit on the floor; listen to the phrase-makers of the House; watch the proceedings; introduce bills; appear before committees to urge the interests of his territory and perform such committee work as the House may choose to assign. The delegate may also advise as to the appointment of local people such as postmasters and, in some instances, if he is in political sympathy with the President, he may secure the appointment of a citizen of the territory to a Federal post such as the land office. That, however, is very unusual.

In 1880 I was nominated for the position of delegate by the Republicans of the territory of Dakota, which at that time embraced what are now the two states of North and South Dakota. It had an area of about 150,000 square miles, with about 30,000 or 35,000 Indians included in its population. When I went to Dakota in 1869 there were only 14,000 people in the whole territory outside of the Indian population, but in 1880 railroads were building all over Dakota and the population was increasing with great rapidity. After my nomination, I entered actively into the campaign, visiting the small towns and making speeches.

Meanwhile President Hayes had appointed as governor of the Territory of Dakota a citizen of New Hampshire named N. G. Ordway. During the summer preceding the election, Ordway came out to Dakota and took possession of the office. Ordway had been for twenty-years Sergeant-at-Arms of the House of Representatives, but in 1878, when the Democrats got control of the

House, he was ousted from his position. Bill Chandler, who was factotum of the Republican Party for New Hampshire, secured Ordway's appointment as Governor of Dakota so that he might go out there, have the state admitted into the Union and then become one of the Senators. I watched the Governor's actions with a great deal of interest. His attitude towards the people of Dakota was extremely patronizing, and he talked about the people of Dakota as though, in his eyes, they were simply children entitled to his benevolent consideration. I soon found out that he was preparing to carry out the political program that had been mapped out for him. For example, he was reported as being engaged in filling a car with the products of Dakota with the idea of sending it through the eastern States as a means of inducing the emigrants or settlers to come out to Dakota and enter lands on the public domain.

Finally he announced that he had arranged with the railroads to carry this car without charge and had selected certain Dakota citizens to accompany it. It was also stated that the Governor had secured some of the very finest samples of corn, pumpkins, oats and other agricultural products from western Iowa and eastern Nebraska, placed them in the car and proposed to represent them as the products of Dakota. When questioned about this he said, "Of course, Dakota is new, and agriculture is not far advanced, but we all know that we can produce just such products, and therefore it is proper to represent that we have produced them, in order to induce the settlers to come to Dakota and enter land." And this episode disgusted me, and in some of my speeches I made fun of the Governor's antics and alluded to him as the "Siox Chief," because having pronounced the word "Sioux" as Siox, and alluded to the town in which I lived as "Siox Falls."

After the campaign was over I went to Yankton on some business, and Newton Edmunds, who had been Governor of Dakota before I went to the Territory, and who in 1880 was a banker at Yankton, called on me at my hotel and advised me to see Governor Ordway before I left town. Edmunds told me that the Governor was very much offended at the allusions I had made in my speeches, and had said that unless I came and apologized, he would not issue my certificate of election as a delegate in Congress.

I immediately told ex-Governor Edmunds, — he was a man of excellent parts, of fair ability and strict integrity, — that if that was Ordway's attitude I would rather reaffirm what I had said about him, and that under no circumstances would I call upon him, but would leave it for him to decide whether to perform his duty as Governor and issue the certificate of election, or to betray his office in order to punish a political rival. I added that I rather thought his failure to perform his duty would not keep me from getting my seat in the House of Representatives. Before the 4th of the following March, when I would take my seat in the House, I received my certificate of Election from the Governor without comment, but I was told by friends in Yankton that the Governor remarked when he issued the certificate that he guessed I might as well have it, as I would not amount to anything in Washington; I would be nothing but a wall flower, he said, while he would control the patronage ordinarily granted to a delegate from a territory. When I finally reached Washington, I found that South Dakota Post Office appointments were being made on the Governor's recommendation. At least one had been confirmed at an Indian Agency. I at once insisted that the Postmaster General remove Ordway's appointee and put in his place a man whom I recommended. The Postmaster General was reluctant to do this because Ordway had been very prominent in republican politics and knew all of the leading men in the nation. He had also been the representative of the predatory interests, the railroads, the public utilities generally, the contractors, etc., about Washington, and he had acted, while Sergeant-at-Arms, as their go-between in the purchase of votes and the control of the lawyers who made up the bulk of members in the House of Representatives. Of course, the "bribe" always took the form of a "fee." Because of his intimate acquaintance with their deals, Ordway was feared by the politicians, and the Postmaster General finally refused to comply with my request.

The Post Office Department relies upon a delegate to recommend certain things that should be done in the territory that he represents, and I told the Postmaster General that I certainly would take no part whatever in trying to promote and protect the interests of the Government with regard to mail routes, etc., or ever visit his department again unless I was accorded the full recognition which belonged to a delegate, and so the matter rested until Congress convened. When Congress met I went to Senator Piatt, of New York, with whom I was well acquainted, told him of the controversy that had arisen over South Dakota patronage between N. G. Ordway, as governor and me as delegate and asked him to have the Postmaster General recognize me as the Representative of Dakota instead of N. G. Ordway. Piatt at once said, "Yes, you are entitled to that recognition. The Postmaster General is from my State. I suppose I endorsed him for the position, but Ordway has been to see me about this matter and he is a very powerful factor in Republican politics, besides being very competent as a political manipulator. Now, you are a young man and he is a man of great experience; why don't you get together?" I told Senator Piatt that was very difficult because of the Governor's statement that he would not issue my certificate of election unless I would apologize to him for what I had said about him, my reply was that I would never do it.

In a day or two, however. Senator Piatt asked if I would receive and talk with the Governor if he called upon me. I told him I would, and thereupon I made an appointment through Senator Piatt for Ordway to see me at my hotel the next evening.

The Governor arrived in due time, I took him to my room and he opened the conversation by saying that he was an old and experienced politician and had been in public life for many years; that I was a young man just starting out, but that I gave great promise for the future, and that he was anxious to form a political alliance with me to take control of the political affairs of the Territory of Dakota. He then proceeded, by way of argument and advice, to say that if I would consult him about all my appointments as delegate he would consult with me about his appointments as governor, and that by thus combining our influence and working in harmony, we could become so strong and influential as to elect each other to the United States Senate, when the territory of Dakota was admitted as a state.

After he had completed his argument I said, "Governor, this is the first time I have ever met you. I was not impressed by what I knew of you before this meeting. We are here with the idea of perfecting some kind of an alliance by which we can work in political harmony. As things stand now, that would be very difficult. I have a suggestion, however. Suppose you go back to Dakota and attend to your duties as governor, while I look after the duties of my office here, in such a way as to promote the welfare of the people of Dakota. If you will do that, and use your office to promote the interests of South Dakota and its people, without consulting me at all, you will become so popular with the people and so strong politically that you will easily be the most prominent man in the territory. If you make a good, honest and capable Governor, and I make a good, honest and capable delegate in Congress, the time will not be distant when we will naturally work together, — our common purpose being the welfare of the people."

The governor did not take to that advice. He had never done anything that way and probably did not understand what I meant. He seemed to conclude that I talked that way because I wanted to make money, so he started on another tack.

"You know," said Ordway, "I, as Governor, have the right to appoint the Commissioners of every new county that is organized. These commissioners can locate the county seat of the county, and therefore there is always great competition among the citizens of a county to secure these appointments so that they can locate the county-seat town. You know there are a great number of new counties being organized every year all over Dakota. Now, if you and I will go in together, we can so manipulate the organization of these counties as to get part of the land upon which the county-seat is located, or else we can make the people pay high who have land on which they want the county seat located.

"Besides that, there is something even bigger. People want a new capitol city for the territory. By uniting together we might easily arrange to move the capitol from its present location at Yanktown to some more central location, and make a fortune out of building the new city."

I let the Governor go on developing his whole scheme, together with his method of achieving it. He seemed very enthusiastic and acted as though he were well satisfied with himself and with the impressions that he had made. But when he had finished, I said: "The Territory of Dakota is about 400 miles square, but it is altogether too small for both of us. Either you will have to get out of it or I will. I will never have anything to do with you but will fight you as long as you remain in the territory. You are the most miserable corrupt scamp that in my brief career I have ever come in contact with."

The next morning I called on Senator Piatt and told him, in detail, just what had occurred. Piatt made no comment except to say that he would have the Postmaster removed that Ordway had had appointed, and would ask the Postmaster General to put in whomever I recommended.

Upon inquiring with regard to the Governor and his career as Sergeant-at-Arms at the House, I found that when the Democrats had got control in 1878 and had removed Ordway from the position as Sergeant-at-Arms, they had appointed a Committee to investigate the conduct of the office of Sergeant-at-Arms under Ordway's regime. The conduct of the investigation was in the hands of Glover, who, I think, was from Missouri. I thereupon secured from Glover a copy of the testimony taken by the Committee and of the report that the Committee had made to the House. The testimony showed that Ordway was the person who carried the funds that were used to persuade the members of the House to grant privileges to the few in order that they might rob the many. That custom has been continued ever since at Washington in both Houses of Congress. While I was in the Senate, Aldrich of Rhode Island, who was Senator, held this important post. He died worth, I believe, twenty millions. Others have done similar work. There always are in Washington certain agents of big business, employed to look after the attorneys in both houses who are there to represent the great industrial, financial, and transportation corporations — the real government.

I also wrote the Chairman of the House Committee that investigated Ordway and he sent me the following letter which I published with a copy of the testimony taken by the Committee:

"La Grange, Mo., July 24, 1881.

"Hon. R. F. Pettigrew, M. C.

"My Dear Sir:

"Your letter of the 17th came duly to hand. You refer to N. G. Ordway, ex-sergeant-at-arms of the house of representatives, and at present governor of Dakota territory, and ask, 'has he ever answered the damaging evidence taken before your (my) committee to your (my) satisfaction.' I answer emphatically. No! It was impossible for him to make satisfactory answer. I have no hesitancy in giving it as my opinion, in view of all the evidence developed against him, that he is one of the most *corrupt* and *unprincipled* men that ever *disgraced* and *degraded* the public service of this country. I am convinced that he never sought or held an office with a view of being satisfied with its honors and its legitimate emoluments, but to *prostrate* it to the worst *jobbery* and *fraud* for money making. "It would seem simply impossible for N. G. Ordway to hold an official position and not *taint* and *disgrace* it. He belongs to a class of office seekers that infest this country now by thousands, that should be *doomed* to *destruction* by the efforts of all honest men of all parties. I am, sir, very respectfully your obedient servant,

"J. M. GLOVER."

Had the Republicans continued in power, Ordway would have continued to operate in the House. When the Democrats came in, they decided to have one of their own men do his work. Consequently they staged an investigation which cost Ordway his job in the House, but which, far from destroying his public career, left him free to launch new schemes among the men on the frontier.

After our meeting in Washington Ordway went back to Dakota and tried his hand at being governor. He entered into a scheme to move the capitol, and secured the passage through the Legislature of a bill establishing a Capitol Commission to go about and receive bids for the location of the capitol and its removal from Yankton. His purpose, of course, was to locate the capitol somewhere in about the center of the southern half of Dakota. Alexander McKinsey, who lived in Bismarck, in the center of the north half of the Territory, was a person having very many times the ability of Ordway and was far his superior in integrity, — a man of very many powerful parts. He had managed to capture Ordway's Capitol Commission and to locate the capitol at Bismarck, which is now the capitol of North Dakota.

Ordway got nothing out of that scheme, but he was actively organizing new counties all over Dakota and the air was full of rumors of scandals. Finally, he received $10,000 in money to appoint a Commissioner in a county where the county-seat location was of considerable importance. This performance was so scandalous and barefaced that he was indicted for bribery and corruption by a Grand Jury of one of the counties, and his case came up before Territorial Judge Edgerton, who had been appointed through the influence of Senator Davis of Minnesota. Edgerton was an honest man — more honest than is the rule among lawyers. I do not believe he could have been persuaded by money to violate his judicial oath or do any act not in strict accordance with the duties of his office.

The Governor was evidently very much alarmed. He employed Senator Davis, of Minnesota, who had been responsible for having Edgerton appointed judge, to defend him. Davis was not a criminal lawyer, but in those days the fee of $10,000, which Ordway offered Davis, was rather tempting, so Davis went out to Dakota when the case was called, and told the judge that it should be dismissed because the only punishment that could be meted out for crimes committed by a Governor was an impeachment and removal from office. The judge ruled that such was the law and the case against Ordway was dismissed. The episode convinced Ordway that even 160,000 square miles of territory was too small an area for both of us to live on and so he left Dakota and came back to Washington.

However, in 1882 Ordway made the greatest fight of his life to defeat me for the Republican nomination for delegate in Congress. North and South Dakota were already divided as the people of each half had come to believe that when Dakota ceased to be a territory it would be admitted as two separate states into the Union. In this campaign North Dakota put up a candidate, John B. Raymond, who was the United States Marshal, a young man of excellent principles, who had been appointed by the President and sent out from some eastern state. Raymond carried most of the Counties of North Dakota, and they endorsed him for my position.

In South Dakota Ordway put up George B. Hand, from Yankton, who had been Secretary of the Territory. He was a man of ordinary intelligence, but he always agreed with everybody and was affable and suave. Hand made a poor showing. I carried almo.st every county in South Dakota and I had an overwhelming majority of the whole territory, but Ordway contested nearly every county that I carried. He did not try to contest the county in which I lived or the adjoining counties east and west of where I lived. He contested Moody County where my brother lived, although there were not over three members of the county convention against me, but those three felt that they had been beaten by fraud. The same practice was pursued in almost all the counties of South Dakota, so that the uncontested delegates from South Dakota, who were controlled by Ordway, united with those which Raymond had from North Dakota and made a majority in the preliminary organization of the Convention. They then selected a committee on credentials, a majority of whose members were my political enemies. That committee proceeded to seat all of the contesting Ordway delegates, knowing that my delegates would immediately form another convention and nominate me. This would have split the Republican party of the Territory into three parts and would have resulted in the selection of a Democrat.

I went to their candidate, John B. Raymond, from North Dakota, and said to him, "You know that Ordway is not a friend of yours, and that if he gets control of this convention he will not nominate you, although you have united with him against me as a common enemy. Now if you will agree to have the Committee on Credentials seat the delegates who are elected and were fraudulently contested, I will go into the convention and withdraw as a candidate in your favor."

'If I do," Raymond replied, "you will have a majority of the whole convention and can proceed to nominate yourself." "Of course," I said, "you will have to take my word for that."

"Well," said Raymond, "if you will have McKinsey guarantee that you will do as you say — and McKinsey is the most prominent man in Republican politics in North Dakota and is my friend — I will take your promise and McKinsey's guarantee and do as you request."

McKinsey promptly agreed to the arrangement and I then assembled all of my delegates in a room at Grand Forks, a little town in North Dakota where the Convention was held, and told them what I had offered to do.

"In the interests of harmony," I told them, "and for the purpose of rebuking this corrupt carpet-bag Governor, I think it is the wise thing to do."

They were unanimous in accepting my view of the matter.

"All of you who were contested will be seated," I said, "and we will take control of the party machinery, but the success of the scheme depends upon our keeping it to ourselves. Now, there are 140 of you fellows. I don't believe there is a man among you who will tell."

They promised that they would not say anything and that they would carry it out.

The Committee on Credentials submitted their report to the Convention, with a minority report, in favor of seating my delegates. When the vote was taken, the North Dakota delegates voted unanimously in favor of the minority report. County after county, as the roll was called, voted this way. Ordway himself came into the Convention, in great excitement, and rushed among the delegates, exclaiming, "You are voting wrong; you don't understand what you are doing; you are voting for the wrong report." But he made no impression.

After the vote was announced, I arose in the Convention and said, "In the interests of harmony and to prevent the disrupting of the Republican party in Dakota, I conclude that it is best for me to withdraw from the contest. I therefore do so and I nominate John B. Raymond as delegate to Congress and thus rebuke the miserable, contemptible and fraudulent scheme which had been perpetrated by our carpet-bag Governor, the 'Siox Chief.'"

The plan worked perfectly. Not a single one of the hundred and forty delegates had told what was to be done, and the Ordway crowd had no chance to prepare a counter offensive. Raymond was almost unanimously nominated as territorial delegate to Congress. Of course, a majority of my friends were placed on each of the party committees selected for the Country, and my friends were selected as chairmen in all cases. Ordway had had some measure of revenge. I lost my place in Congress, but gained control of the Party. The episode lost him both standing and popularity.

This story of political intrigue in a sparsely settled mid-western territory is not unique. It could be matched, in every essential detail, out of the political experiences of men in every state of the Union. That is why I tell it — because it is so general in its application. But more important than that, I tell it because it reveals some of the forces that were at work underneath the surface of the machinery of government.

There was ambition, of course, and trickery, and jealousy, and revenge; but beneath and beyond these personal traits there were the economic forces that have played so large a part in shaping the Government of the United States. The men who exhibited the greatest abilities and who displayed the most faculties were selected and used as the tools and spokesmen of big business. Bribery and corruption were not crimes — unless they became too blatant. Ordinarily they were businesses in which the capital was furnished by the "interests" and the work was performed by officials sworn to uphold and defend the Constitution of the United States.

Later in my political experience I was to learn that the whole structure of our government, from the Constitution onward, had been framed by business men to further business ends; that the laws had been passed by the legislatures and interpreted by the courts with this end in view; that the execution of the laws was placed in the hands of executives known to be safe and that these things were more true of the national than they were of local and state political machinery.

13. The United States Supreme Court

The Convention of 1787 that framed the Constitution of the United States was dominated by lawyers, money-lenders and land owners. It did its work behind closed doors, all members being sworn not to disclose any of the proceedings.

Madison reported the proceedings in long-hand; his notes were purchased by Congress and published in 1837, nearly half a century after the convention had finished its work. These published notes disclose the forces that dominated the work of the convention. All through the debates ran one theme: how to secure a government, not by the people for the people, but by the classes for the classes, with the lawyers in control. This was the burden of the debates, page after page, through all of the 760 pages of the two volumes of Madison Notes.

The Constitution thus framed did not create a government of the people; its whole purpose was to promote and protect the rights of property more than the rights of man. Two extracts from those proceedings illustrate this point; they are typical, and are as follows:

P. 78. Sherman of Connecticut said: "The people should have as little to do as may be about the Government. They want information and are constantly liable to be misled."

Gerry, of Massachusetts: "The evil we experience flows from the excess of democracy."

P. 115. Mr. Gerry: "Hence in Massachusetts the worst men get into the legislature. Several members of that body had lately been convicted of infamous crimes. Men of indigence, ignorance and baseness spare no pains, however dirty; to carry their point against men who are superior to the artifices practiced."

Jefferson was not a member of the convention. He was the author of the Declaration of Independence; he was not wanted, so he was sent to France.

There were 55 delegates in that convention. Let us see who they were: A majority were lawyers; most of them came from towns; not one farmer, mechanic or laborer; five-sixths had property interests. Of the 55 members, 40 owned Revolutionary scrip; 14 were land speculators; 24 were money-lenders; 11 were merchants; 15 were slave-holders. Washington was a slave-holder, a large land-owner, and a holder of much Revolutionary scrip.

What The Constitution Does Not Contain

It is not strange that the Constitution as framed by that convention said nothing about the rights of man. It was made by men who believed in the English theory of government — that all governments are created to protect the rights of property in the hands of those who do not produce the property.

Revolutionary scrip was issued to finance the Revolution, and used to pay for supplies and the wages of the men who did the fighting; it had been bought up by the financiers and great land-owners and their attorneys for about nine cents on the dollar. When the Constitution was adopted, it was made, at once, worth one hundred cents on the dollar.

Thus a Constitution was made, by property interests, for property interests alone. The great "Bill of Rights" had been thrown into the wastebasket.

Jefferson was in France.

The Ten Amendments To The Constitution

Against the Constitution, as thus framed, seven of the thirteen states protested, but five of them were finally induced to ratify in reliance upon the "Bill of Rights" being promptly added by amendments. The first eight amendments were speedily formulated and soon the ninth and tenth were added, to be submitted by the first Congress to the States, and that was promptly done. It is certain that the Constitution could never have been adopted without these amendments for the protection of fundamental human rights.

Thomas Jefferson had returned from France.

AMENDMENT I.

The First Amendment is as follows:

"Congress shall make no law respecting an establishment of religion, or prohibiting free exercise thereof; or abridging the freedom of speech, or of the press, or of the right of the people peaceably to assemble, and to petition the Government for a redress of grievances."

It is amazing that this great basic principle of civil and religious liberty should have been left out of the Constitution as framed by the convention. It could not have been overlooked or omitted by accident; it is obvious that it was done deliberately.

AMENDMENTS II.-VIII.

The next seven amendments protect the people against military rule in defiance of civil authority; against the search or seizure of their persons, homes, papers, etc., except by authority of a warrant duly issued under proper legal restrictions; against being put in jeopardy of trial and conviction; without the alleged charge being investigated and approved by a grand jury, or the taking of life, liberty, or property without due process of law; against trial and conviction except by an impartial jury where the alleged crime was committed, with information as to the cause and nature of the offence, faced by accusing witnesses, and the right of counsel for defense; against the courts overturning a jury's verdict; against excessive bail, or "cruel and unusual punishments."

Jefferson had returned, and his tongue and pen were in action; the priceless Bill of Rights was thus saved and made a part of our organic law. But Jefferson, with foresighted wisdom, based on a deep knowledge of men and things, knew that it was necessary to protect liberty and all human rights by clear and positive safeguards; therefore, the ninth and tenth amendments were added for this purpose. The Ninth Amendment was as follows:

AMENDMENT IX.

"The enumeration in the Constitution of certain rights shall not be construed to deny or disparage others retained by the people."

A wonderfully wise provision; a recognition and declaration of the great fundamental fact that all rights and power are inherent in the people themselves, and are not derived as concessions from usurpers masquerading under the "Divine rights of Kings." But the enemies of human freedom in high places have often betrayed this trust and ignored and trampled under foot this great basic principle of the divine right of the people, as I will show below.

Jefferson also foresaw that the time would come when an ambitious Federal executive, a usurping Federal court, or a reckless Congress would take the position that the people and the States had no power or rights which were not subordinate to the Federal power and authority. He knew that when that time came our great representative Democracy, created by the amended Constitution, would be dead, and that on its grave there would rule, with a tyrant's hand, the worst autocracy of plutocracy that the world has ever seen. To prevent such usurpation, the Tenth Amendment was submitted and adopted along with the other amendments. It is worded as follows:

AMENDMENT X.

"The powers not delegated to the United States by the Constitution, nor prohibited by it to the States, are reserved to the States respectively or to the people."

This amendment, in such clear and concise language, was the greatest possible victory for preventing encroachments on the reserved rights and liberties of the people and the independence of the States necessary for State sovereignty. It made our Federal Government one of defined, expressed powers, limited definitely to the powers enumerated and granted. One of the great dangers which Jefferson feared, and which he was sure had been forever killed by this amendment, as shown by his later writings, was the usurpation by the Supreme Court of the power to supervise the Executive Department or to declare a law enacted by Congress unconstitutional, or to construe the Constitution so as to take from or add to the powers granted by the States and the people. He knew no such power had been granted to the Judiciary Department and, on the other hand, he knew (though Madison's notes had not then been published) that every effort made by the enemies of Democracy in the Constitutional Convention to get such a dangerous provision in the Constitution had been defeated: yet he determined to affirmatively deny that power and every other power not expressly delegated to each of the three departments respectively of the Federal Government, and this was done by the plain and precise words of the Tenth Amendment.

In this connection, I call attention to Madison's Notes, p. 533, which show that the proposition to confer upon the Supreme Court the power to declare an Act of Congress void was squarely at issue; and that Maryland, Delaware and Virginia voted aye; while Massachusetts, New Hampshire, Pennsylvania,

Connecticut, New Jersey, North Carolina, South Carolina and Georgia voted nay. The proposition was brought up in the convention on several other occasions, but was each time decisively defeated.

While the members of the Constitutional Convention were ultra-conservative, serving property rights with a contempt for human rights, and always trying to hobble and gag the rule of the people, yet they were familiar with the fact that when an English court, about three hundred years before, held an Act of Parliament void, the Chief Justice, Trassillian, had been hanged and his associates on the bench had been banished from the country. They also knew that since that time no English court had dared to usurp such unconstitutional authority. It was this fact, no doubt, which deterred such a Constitutional Convention from conferring upon the Supreme Court the power to declare an Act of Congress unconstitutional.

With the Constitution thus amended, Jefferson declared that the Bill of Rights, buttressed by the Tenth Amendment, were the "two sheet anchors of our Union." He felt sure that a government of, for, and by the people was assured for all time." He saw a great representative Democracy launched, with every delegated power necessary for national purposes, and the rights and liberties of the people enthroned and safe beyond successful attack or encroachment. But he soon had a rude awakening.

The First Act of Judicial Usurpation

Chief Justice Marshall, who was an Englishman, in the case of Marbury vs. Madison, usurped the power to interpret the Constitution and to instruct another coequal and co-sovereign department of the Government as to its powers and duties.

Jefferson denounced that decision as a bald usurpation and a glaring unconstitutional encroachment on the powers and duties of another independent department of the Government. He lamented the failure of the House of Representatives to bring the Court to trial under impeachment proceedings. In a letter to Judge Spencer Roane, under date of September 6, 1819, he said:

"In denying the right they usurp of exclusively explaining the Constitution, I go further than you do, if I understand rightly your quotation, from the Federalist, of an opinion that the 'judiciary is the last resort in relation to the other departments of the Government, but not in relation to the rights of the parties to the compact under which the judiciary is derived.' If this opinion be sound, then indeed is our Constitution a complete **felo de se.** For intending to establish three departments, co-ordinate and independent, that they might check and balance one another, it has given, according to this opinion, to one of them alone, the right to prescribe rules for the government of the others, and to that one too which is unelected by, and independent of the nation. For experience has already shown that the impeachment it has provided is not even a scarecrow... The Constitution, on this hypothesis, **is a mere thing of wax** in the hands of the judiciary, **which they may twist and shape into any form they please.** It should be remembered, as an axiom of eternal truth in politics, that whatever power in any government is independent is absolute also; in theory only, at first, while the spirit of the people is up, but in practice, as fast as that relaxes. **Independence can be trusted nowhere but with the people in mass. They are inherently independent of all but moral law.** My construction of the Constitution is very different from that you quote. It is that each department is truly independent of the others, and has an equal right to decide for itself what is the meaning of the Constitution in the cases submitted to its action; and especially where it is to act ultimately and without appeal."

In a letter to Judge William Johnson, under date of June 12, 1823, commenting on the same decision, he said:

"But the Chief Justice says, 'there must be an ultimate arbiter somewhere.' True, there must; but does that prove it is either party? The ultimate arbiter is the people of the Union, assembled by their deputies in convention, at the call of Congress, or of two-thirds of the States. Let them decide to which they mean to give an authority claimed by two of their organs. And it has been the peculiar wisdom and felicity of our Constitution to have provided this peaceable appeal, where that of other nations is at once to force."

In a letter to William Charles Jarvis, under date of September 28, 1820, reviewing a book which attempted to defend this court usurpation of power, he said;

"You seem, in pages 84 to 148, to consider the judges as the ultimate arbiter of all constitutional questions — a very dangerous doctrine indeed and one which would place us under the despotism of an oligarchy. Our judges are as honest as other men and not more so. They have, with others, the same passion for party, for power and the privilege of their corps. Their maxim is **'bon judicis est amplaire jurisdictionem,'** and their power is the more dangerous as they are not responsible, as the other functionaries are, to the effective control. The Constitution has created no such single tribunal, knowing that to whatever hands confided, with the corruptions of time and party, its members would become despots. It has more wisely made all the departments co-equal and co-sovereign with themselves."

No one ever has or ever can question the truth of this statement that "the Constitution has erected no such single tribunal" to supervise and to veto the acts of the other two "co-equal and co-sovereign departments of our government; therefore Congress inertly surrendered its co-equal and co-sovereign powers when it failed to impeach the Judicial Department of the Government for this contemptuous usurpation of powers, over which the people reserved to themselves elective control.

Further on in the same letter, Jefferson says:

"The Constitution, in keeping three departments distinct and independent, restrains the authority of the judges to judiciary organs, as it does the executive and legislative to executive and legislative organs. The judges certainly have more frequent occasion to act on constitutional questions, because the laws of meum and tuum and of criminal action, forming the great mass of the system of law, constitute their particular department. When the legislative or executive functionaries act unconstitutionally, they are responsible to the people in their

103

elective capacity. The exemption of the judges from that is quite dangerous enough. I know no safe depository of the ultimate powers of the society but the people themselves; and if we think them not enlightened enough to exercise THEIR CONTROL WITH A WHOLESOME DISCRETION, THE REMEDY IS NOT TO TAKE IT FROM THEM, BUT TO INFORM THEIR DISCRETION BY EDUCATION. THIS IS THE TRUE CORRECTIVE OF ABUSES OF CONSTITUTIONAL POWER. PARDON ME, SIR, FOR THIS DIFFERENCE OF OPINION. MY PERSONAL INTEREST IN SUCH QUESTIONS IS ENTIRELY EXTINCT, BUT NOT MY WISHES FOR THE LONGEST POSSIBLE CONTINUANCE OF OUR GOVERNMENT ON ITS PURE PRINCIPLES: IF THE THREE POWERS MAINTAIN THEIR MUTUAL INDEPENDENCE ON EACH OTHER IT MAY LAST LONG, BUT NOT SO IF EITHER CAN ASSUME THE AUTHORITIES OF THE OTHER."

I have already shown that the Constitution confers no power on the Judiciary Department of the Government to question the legality of an Act of Congress, and that every time the conferring of such dangerous powers on that department was proposed in the convention it was voted down. I have also shown that the states would not, even then, accept the Constitution until the ten amendments were formulated and satisfactory assurances were made that they would be at once submitted for adoption; and also that these amendments, after including the great Bill of Rights, concluded with the most important Tenth Amendment, which affirmatively and positively reserved to the people and to the states all powers and rights not expressly granted to the Federal Government, and which expressly inhibits the taking away of or the adding of any powers by construction or by implication. On these clear and concise reasons, Jefferson correctly asserts that the power to determine the constitutionality of a law is reserved to the people. They, and they alone, have the power to pass on the legality of any law of Congress, and they can use that power at any and every election.

This is the plain truth of the whole matter.

In another letter, under date of December 25, 1820, to Thomas Richie, commenting on a book by Colonel Taylor, which vigorously criticized the extravagance of the Government and the greatly increased appropriations and taxes called for by the Treasury Department, Jefferson said:

"If there be anything amiss, therefore, in the present state of our affairs, as the formidable deficit lately unfolded to us indicates, I ascribe it to the inattention of Congress to their duties, to their unwise dissipation and waste of the public contributions. They seemed, some little while ago, to be at a loss for objects whereon to throw away the supposed fathomless funds of the Treasury... The deficit produced, and a heavy tax to supply it, will, I trust, bring both to their sober senses.

"But it is not from this branch of government we have most to fear. Taxes and short elections will keep them right. The Judiciary of the United States is the subtle corps of sappers and miners constantly working underground to undermine the foundations of our confederated fabric. They are construing our Constitution from a coordination of a general and special government to a general and supreme one alone. This will lay all things at their feet, and they are too well versed in English law to forget the maxim, **boni judicis est amplaire jurisdictionem.** We shall see if they are bold enough to take the daring stride their five lawyers have lately taken. If they do, then, with the editor of our book, in his address to the public, I will say that against this every man should raise his voice,' and more, **should uplift his arm...** That pen should go on, lay bare these wounds of our Constitution, expose the decisions seriatim, and arouse, as it is able, the attention of the nation to these bold speculators on its patience. Having found, from experience, that impeachment is an impracticable thing, a mere scarecrow, they consider themselves secure for life; they skulk from responsibility to public opinion, the only remaining hold on them, under a practice first introduced into England by Lord Mansfield. An opinion is huddled up in conclave, perhaps by a majority of one, delivered as if unanimous, and with the silent acquiescence of lax or timid associates, by a crafty Chief Judge who sophisticates the law to his mind by the turn of his own reasoning. A judiciary law was once reported by the Attorney General to Congress, requiring each judge to deliver his opinion seriatim and openly, and then to give it in writing to the clerk to be entered in the record. A judiciary independent of a king or executive alone is a good thing; but independence of the will of the nation is a solecism, at least in a republican government."

Such criticism of this startling usurpation by the Judiciary Department and talk of the impeachment of the judges were effective to prevent the court from again usurping the power to declare an Act of Congress void for over fifty years.

The Second Act of Usurpation

It was not long, however, before this same court overstepped its defined powers and, in defiance of every principle of law, equity and morals, rendered the notorious Dartmouth College decision, in which it was held that property interests, past, present and future, had vested rights, under a special privilege granted in a private charter, which it was impossible for the people, through legislation, to change, no matter how injurious to the public interests the terms of the charter might be. It has been claimed, in excuse for the Court, that it was hypnotized by the overpowering but false reasoning of Daniel Webster; but, let that be as it may, it is gratifying that such an unsound doctrine, based on such a decision, has been repudiated by nearly every state in the Union, and by nearly every civilized country in the world.

A Bald Defiance of Congress by the Judiciary

In 1857 Judge Taney, for a majority of the court, held an Act of Congress in the Missouri Compromise case unconstitutional. There was, however, no indignation or threat of impeachment of the court for this bold usurpation, so ever since the Supreme Court has made a plaything of the acts of Congress as often as it has pleased them so to do. This is what Jefferson said they would soon become bold enough to do if they were not called to account for usurpation of power. It was against the first usurpation by the court that Jefferson said: "I will say that "against this every man should raise his voice, and more, should uplift his arm.""

The Supreme Court Destroys The Tenth Amendment

The pitiable surrender by Congress to its "co-equal and co-sovereign powers" has emboldened the Supreme Court not only to continue to declare Acts of Congress unconstitutional, but also to go further and wipe out completely the Tenth Amendment to the Constitution. This has been done not only to give to the Federal Government powers never granted by the people or by the states, but also to take from the Federal Government powers clearly granted, when necessary to do so in order to confer special privileges on big property interests. A striking example is the famous, or rather infamous, income tax decisions. In the case of Pollock vs. Farmers Loan & Trust Company, the Supreme Court, after one of its judges, Shiras, had changed his opinion overnight, decided, by a majority of one, that the constitutional power to levy a fair and just tax on incomes, which Congress has exercised for a hundred years, was unconstitutional. This startling decision did not arouse Congress to its duty to impeach the court; but it so aroused the people everywhere that a movement was at once started all over the country which resulted in the adoption of the Sixteenth Amendment to the Constitution.

Judge Shiras was a Pennsylvania lawyer and had for years, so I am informed, been the attorney of many of the chief beneficiaries of his change of position as a judge on this question; but I know a lawyer is the only person who can legally take a bribe — he calls it a fee.

This amendment again conferred upon Congress the power which the Court, by an unconstitutional and revolutionary decision, had attempted to take away. Under the broad terms of this Sixteenth Amendment, which, in specific language, makes all incomes from whatever source derived, liable for an income tax, Congress passed another income tax law. The court, not daring to again declare an income tax unconstitutional, then proceeded to render a legislative decision in which it holds that an income received in the form of a "stock dividend" is not liable for a tax on such income. This opened the way to relieve all the largest incomes in this country from any tax whatever. All the big corporations at once began declaring stock dividends instead of cash dividends, and thus they are robbing the Treasury of the United States annually of hundreds of millions of dollars, which must be made up and paid by the people of less means and less capacity to pay.

This monstrous decision was rammed through the court by a majority of one, four of the justices dissenting; Mr. Justice Brandeis, in his dissenting opinion, said:

"If stock dividends representing profits are held exempt from taxation under the Sixteenth Amendment, the owners of the most successful business in America will, as the facts in this case illustrate, be able to escape taxation on a large part of what is actually their income."

How quickly this prophecy was fulfilled is indicated by the volume of stock dividends that have been declared since the court delivered this opinion. Mr. Justice Brandeis, in the same dissenting opinion, adds: "That such a result was intended by the people of the United States when adopting the Sixteenth Amendment is inconceivable."

The same conviction is expressed with pungency by Mr. Justice Holmes in his dissenting opinion in the same case, in which he says:

"I think that the word incomes in the Sixteenth Amendment should be read in 'a sense most obvious to the common understanding at the time of its adoption,'...for it was for public adoption that it was proposed...The known purpose of this amendment was to get rid of nice questions as to what might be direct taxes, and I cannot doubt that most people, not lawyers, would suppose when they voted for it that they put a question like the present one to rest."

This is a strong and timely indictment of such judicial usurpation.

A Most Brazen Decision

The Supreme Court, by this decision, had protected their rich friends from paying an income tax, but had not protected themselves, since their salaries from the Government were paid in cash, and not in stock dividends; so another decision was rendered, declaring the income tax law unconstitutional as far as it requires the judges and the President to pay an income tax. This raw personal decision was rendered by Judge Van Devender, a sage-brush lawyer from the cowboy country of Wyoming, who was appointed by Roosevelt, and whose only qualification seems to be that he had been an attorney for the Union Pacific Railroad. I have seen no reputable citizen who has attempted to defend this outrageous decision, rendered in the interests of their own personal pockets.

The Judiciary Drunk With Power

In short, the court, having become drunk with unrestrained power, has boldly entered the field of legislation, and now does not hesitate to alter, amend, or repeal any act of Congress. The court could not find any grounds on which to declare the Anti-Trust law unconstitutional, so it proceeded to amend the law. The act makes unlawful "a conspiracy in restraint of trade"; but the court amended it by inserting the word "unreasonable," so restraint of trade is no longer unlawful unless it is "unreasonable" restraint. Highway robbery is no longer a crime unless it is "unreasonable" robbery.

The cases of such judicial juggling with legislation are too numerous to mention; but I will cite one other case which caps the climax of flagrant usurpation — the notorious Steel Trust case. The Steel Trust was indicted and tried for violation of the Anti-Trust law. The evidence of guilt was overwhelming and conclusive. The court admitted it was clear that the Steel Trust had been violating the law in a wholesale manner; yet it held that it was not committing any new acts of lawlessness just at that time, and, therefore, that no good purpose would seem to be served in now punishing the trust for past gross violations of law.

I quote the following from the decision of the court in that case:

"A holding corporation which by its formation united under one control competing companies in the steel industry, but which did not achieve monopoly, and only attempted to fix prices through occasional appeals to and confederation with competitors, whatever there was of wrongful intent not having been executed, and whatever there was of evil effect having been discontinued before suit was brought, should not be dissolved nor be separated from some of its subsidiaries at the suit of the Government, asserting violations of the Sherman Anti-Trust Act — especially where the court cannot see that the public interest will be served by yielding to the Government's demand, and does see in so yielding a risk of injury to the public interest, including a material disturbance of, and, perhaps, serious detriment to, the foreign trade.

"In conclusion, we are unable to see that the public interest will be served by yielding to the contention of the Government respecting the dissolution of the company or the separation from it of some of its subsidiaries; and we do see in a contrary conclusion a risk of injury to the public interest, including a material disturbance of, and, it may be serious detriment to, the foreign trade. And, in submission to the policy of the law, and its fortifying prohibitions, the public interest is of paramount regard."

But you must remember the judges are lawyers, and a lawyer is the only person who can legally take a bribe — he calls it a fee.

So the public has been robbed in a wholesale manner, but, inasmuch as the robbers are not just now doing any stealing, and they promise to use some of their stolen money for charity, it is not deemed to be in the public interests to punish them; they are allowed to go scot-free with their ill-gotten gains, and not even put under bond not to violate the law again.

Of course, a court that will render such a line of decisions could be depended on to declare unconstitutional the law passed by Congress making "profiteering" illegal during the war, which thing the court has just done; and now all the profiteers, big and little, who have been indicted for most treasonable profiteering on the Government, contributing to the suffering and death of thousands of soldiers, whose lives otherwise would have been saved, are discharged with honor and are permitted to go scot-free with their blood-money fortunes.

Jefferson is dead; and Congress is composed of lawyers.

How All The Ten Amendments Are Being Destroyed

These cases illustrate how the Federal courts have usurped powers in order to shield and confer special privileges on big property interests, in flagrant violation of the Tenth Amendment to the Constitution. But the courts have gone further, and have attempted to destroy all the ten amendments, which were put into the Constitution to safeguard and protect human rights.

In the Abrams case, recently decided by the Supreme Court, it was held that Mollie Steiner and Abrams and two others were guilty of violating the Espionage Act because they circulated in New York a pamphlet urging the raising of the blockade against Russia. The lower court had sentenced Mollie Steiner to prison for fifteen years — a mere slip of a girl, a little over twenty years of age — and the three men, who had also circulated this petition protesting against the blockade, for twenty years each to the Federal penitentiary. This monstrous decision, which is clearly in violation of the First Amendment — guaranteeing freedom of speech and of the press — and which is also squarely in defiance of the Eighth Amendment, which provided that cruel and unusual punishments shall not be inflicted, was affirmed by a majority of the Supreme Court of the United States. I quote from the dissenting opinion of the court rendered by Justice Holmes and concurred in by Justice Brandeis:

"To hold such publications can be suppressed as false reports, subjects to new perils the constitutional liberty of the press, already seriously curtailed in practice under powers assumed to have been conferred upon the postal authorities. Nor will this grave danger end with the passing of the war. The constitutional right of free speech has been declared to be the same in peace and in war. In peace, too, men may differ as to what loyalty to our country demands, and an intolerant majority, swayed by passion or by fear, may be prone in the future, as it has often been in the past, to stamp as disloyal opinions with which it disagrees. Convictions such as these, besides abridging freedom of speech, threaten freedom of thought and of belief.... In this case, sentences of twenty years' imprisonment have been imposed for the publishing of two leaflets that I believe the defendants had as much right to publish as the Government has to publish the Constitution of the United States now vainly invoked by them."

Such an infamous and inhuman decision requires no further comment from me.

Similar cases are so numerous in the recent decisions of the Supreme Court that it is astonishing that Congress has not acted to call the offending members of the court to accountability for such flagrant usurpations, in violation of the basic rights of a free people guaranteed by the first and other amendments to the Constitution. The President of the United States should have removed these offending judges for want of "good behavior," which is the constitutional qualification for a Federal judge. A judge should not be permitted to remain on the bench until he commits offenses so great as to make him guilty of the grave crimes named by the Constitution for impeachment. But the offenses here cited amount to "high crimes and misdemeanors," and also to "treason" against free government, and therefore call loudly to Congress to apply the impeachment remedy of the Constitution, since the President has failed to remove them for want of "good behavior."

I will mention one more case: In the Gilbert case from Minnesota, the Supreme Court held outright that the expression of opinion is a crime. In that case, the speaker had simply stated that the people had no voice, really, in the selection of any of their officers, but that they were selected for them; that voting was no particular remedy for any of the evils of which we complain, because the candidates and the platform were prepared in advance by big business interests; and that people could vote or not vote, just as they chose, it making no difference in the result.

The indictment in that case charged that Gilbert in time of war used the following language in a public speech in the State of Minnesota:

"We are going over to Europe to make the world safe for democracy, but I tell you we had better make America safe for democracy first. You say, 'What is the matter with our democracy? I tell you what is the matter with it: Have you had anything to say as to who should be President? Have you had anything to say as to who should be Governor of this state? Have you had anything to say as to whether we would go into this war? You know you have not. If this is such a good democracy, for Heaven's sake why should we not vote on conscription of men? We were stampeded into this war by newspaper rot to pull England's chestnuts out of the fire for her. I tell you if they conscripted wealth like they have conscripted men, this war would not last over forty-eight hours..."

It was for expressing these opinions that he was sent to jail for three years and fined five hundred dollars.

What has become of the Bill of Rights guaranteeing "freedom of speech"?

Let us read again the First Amendment to the Constitution:

First Amendment

"Congress shall make no law respecting an establishment of religion, or prohibiting the free exercise thereof; or abridging the freedom of speech, or of the press, or of the right of the people peaceably to assemble, and to petition the Government for a redress of grievances."

When the court convicted Gilbert for the expression of such an opinion, it repealed, by judicial fiat, this amendment to the Constitution.

Hear Judge McKenna roar, and hear the other little judges join in the chorus:

"...The war...was not declared in aggression, but in defense, in defense of our national honor, in vindication of the most sacred rights of our nation and our people." (Words of President Wilson in his War Message to Congress, April 2, 1917.)

"This was known to Gilbert, for he was informed in affairs and the operations of the Government, and every word that he uttered in denunciation of the war was false, was deliberate misrepresentation of the motives which impelled it, and the objects for which it was prosecuted. He could have had no purpose other than that of which he was charged. It would be a tragedy on the constitutional privilege he invokes to assign him its protection."

This language of the court needs no comment, because it shows on its face utter want of judicial reasoning; it is not expressive of any legal principle; it is an assertion of naked power, avowedly guided by emotion.

Here is a court — the Supreme Court — the court of last resort, depriving an American citizen of his liberty, and founding their opinion on emotion and hysteria; on instinct without logic, without sense or reason, overturning the Constitution and violating their oath of office, while Congress fails to act because it is composed of lawyers.

It is needless to cite or examine other decisions of a court which has become so irresponsibly drunk with usurped power as to render two such monstrous decisions. They are flagrant violations of the basic guarantees of the Bill of Rights and the ten amendments, and are revolutionary in the extreme. It is such treasonable judicial tyranny as this that breeds anarchy.

Let us read again the earnest and warning words of Jefferson:

"The judiciary of the United States is the subtle corps of sappers and miners constantly working underground to undermine the foundations of our confederated fabric.... I will say, that against this every man should raise his voice, and, more, should uplift his arm."

But Jefferson is dead, and Congress is composed of lawyers who are the attorneys of big business. A lawyer is the only person, whether a judge or Congressman, who can legally take a bribe — he calls it a fee.

Against this ugly and most dangerous thing, I, as one American citizen of this generation, have been and will continue to raise my voice. It must stop; if neither the President nor Congress will exercise their constitutional power and duty to remove such judges for such inhuman usurpations, the people will uplift their arm.

What Is The Matter With The U. S. Courts?

In answer to that question, Jefferson said that the judges of the United States courts "are as honest as other men, but not more so"; that they have the same passions for party and for power; that their power is all the more dangerous because the}" are appointed and are not responsible, as the officials of the legislative and executive departments are, to elective control; that, when on the bench they become indoctrinated with the false and dangerous English doctrine, that "it is the part of a good judge to enlarge his jurisdiction," which is squarely prohibited by our Constitution. JEFFERSON FURTHER POINTED OUT THAT SUCH JUDGES, AS SOON AS THEY SHALL FEEL THAT THERE IS NO DANGER OF IMPEACHMENT BY CONGRESS, "WILL BECOME BOLD ENOUGH TO USURP POWER AND BECOME DESPOTS TO DESTROY OUR LIBERTIES." IT WAS FOR THESE REASONS THAT JEFFERSON WARNED THE PEOPLE OF OUR COUNTRY THAT "THE JUDICIARY OF THE UNITED STATES IS A SUBTLE CORPS OF SAPPERS AND MINERS CONSTANTLY WORKING TO UNDERMINE THE FOUNDATIONS OF OUR CONFEDERATED FABRIC."

These were Jefferson's fears after he saw the Supreme Court, composed of men of average ability and honesty, usurp power for the first time to wipe out the Tenth Amendment to the Constitution. What would he say if he could see the kind of men who now fill most of the Federal Judiciary, and the flagrant lengths of usurpation and despotism to which they have gone to serve mammon and to trample upon the rights and liberties of the people?

I am of the opinion that the Supreme Court of the United States, by a long line of decisions, has become ridiculous, absurd and contemptible. They cannot go to any greater length and, if Congress was not composed of lawyers, the Supreme Court would be abolished at once. They should be impeached for high crimes and misdemeanors, and banished from official life forever. If the present court is impeached it will not remedy the evil. The only remedy is to abolish the courts created by Congress and thus reduce the Supreme Court to impotency.

One of the additional things which is the matter with the Federal courts is an evil which has developed under our modern reign of plutocracy in the selection of attorneys of corporations and special privilege, who are obviously disqualified to be judges because they are necessarily prejudiced in favor of the ever-increasing selfish demands of big business and, therefore, prejudiced against the rights and welfare of the general public. In fact, as a rule, corporation lawyers who have spent their lives conniving with cunning skill to enable the great combinations to evade the law of the land, alone are selected to be judges of the United States courts.

The judges of the United States courts are advanced in years before they are appointed, having spent their lives in the employ of the exploiters of the people of the United States. They all believe that property rights are sacred and not human rights.

A concrete illustration of this state of affairs arose in New York in 1895. The General Traffic Association, which was a combination of all the railroads between New York and Chicago, was attacked by the United States District Attorney for the Southern District of New York on the ground that it was a combination in violation of the Sherman Anti-Trust Law. Mr. McFarland, the United States Attorney for the Southern District of New York, appeared before the Interstate Commerce Committee of the United States Senate and, under oath, made the following statement:

"When the case came up, Judge LaCombs stated in his opinion he was disqualified to hear the case, or any proceedings in it, as at that time he owned bonds or stocks in some one of the railroads, and he also stated that he understood that most, if not all, of the judges of that circuit were under the same disqualification."

It was finally decided that Judge Wheeler, the District Judge of the Vermont District, was apparently the only judge in the circuit who was not under a disqualification similar to that which Judge LaCombs had stated he was under, namely, the holding of some bonds or stock of the railroads. The case was finally tried before Judge Wheeler, and as he was a creature of the political system then in vogue, that is, had been appointed through the influence of the senators from Vermont, one of those senators — Edmunds, of Vermont — was employed by the railroads as one of their attorneys and filed a brief in the case.

Judge Wheeler decided the case in favor of the railroads. An appeal was taken by the United States to the Circuit Court, and then Judge LaCombs stated, from the bench, that he was now qualified to try the case because he had disposed of his stocks and bonds in the defendant railroads. He thereupon affirmed the decision rendered by Judge Wheeler and the case went to the Supreme Court. of the United States. The Supreme Court reversed the decision, but, as several years had elapsed since the case was commenced, the railroads had found out another way to do it, so it created no embarrassment for them whatever.

Very prominent lawyers in more than one circuit have told me that when a circuit or district United States judge had a son, who had been graduated and was ready to practice law, it was quite common for the judge to call upon some law firm employed by some trust or combination and say that his son was now ready to enter upon the practice of law, and ask if they knew of an opening, and of course the answer was:

"Send him right over here - we have been looking for just such a man."

So, in many cases, the United States judge sits upon the bench, himself having been graduated from the office of attorney for some great industrial combination, and listens to the reading of a brief, prepared by his own son, in the interest of the corporation for whom the judge has served before he went upon the bench.

Thus we see today a Federal judiciary is composed, very largely, of corporation lawyers, who have spent their lives conniving in the interests of the great corporations whose attorneys they were, and who without scruple have done whatever their clients demanded in order to carry their point and more successfully exploit the people of the United States. When such lawyers get upon the bench their former practice and training asserts itself in every act. Such men are disqualified to sit on a jury, and all the more are they disqualified to sit on the bench. Chief Justice White is a man of little ability and no genius. He was a Louisiana lawyer and attorney for the sugar interests; he was elected to the U. S. Senate in 1890 and was assigned to the Committee on Public Lands. I was a member of that committee, so I became very well acquainted with White as a senator. He was a man of very ordinary capacity and in no way qualified for the Supreme bench, and indeed so much so that I was very much surprised when Cleveland even made him Associate Justice of the Supreme Court in 1894.

The lawyers who serve monopoly and special privilege try to create the impression that the Supreme Court is infallible; that its decisions are the final law of the land, even when in violation of the Constitution, and that no one must criticize or question the sanctity of the court. Yet the present Supreme Court of the United States is a most ordinary body of men. No matter who their predecessors were, they certainly were not selected because of their wisdom, genius or learning. They are a long way from being infallible. In fact, the records of the Supreme Court show that they are exceedingly and wilfully fallible. In all our history, no judge ever voted **other than with the political**

party from which he came.

In short, the obvious and ugly truth is that the United States courts have become the greatest enemy to justice, and the greatest menace to a free government.

The Remedy For Judicial Usurpation and Tyranny

The time has come when this growing and overshadowing evil must be checked. There are today but two checks on the Federal judges. First, the power of impeachment, which the Constitution vests in Congress; second, the power of removal, which the Constitution vests in the President, by and with the advice and consent of the Senate.

To impeach a judge and remove him from the bench by that means makes it necessary for the House of Representatives to formulate and present impeachment charges, and to convict the judge of treason or of high crimes and misdemeanors, and by a two-thirds vote of the Senate. Congress has never exercised that constitutional power and duty, and probably never will, unless there shall be a revolution at the polls, on that specific issue, against some judge or judges, whose corruption and guilt are known to all men.

The other check, the power of the President to remove a judge by and with the advice of the Senate, would be very effective if we had a President who would exercise the power when and where it is needed.

It is a common error that Federal judges are appointed for life. The words of the Constitution are that the President, by and with the advice and consent of the Senate, has the power to appoint judges "who shall hold their offices during good behavior"; the commission which every judge holds today so reads.

Thus the Constitution clearly puts the Federal judges in a class by themselves, and requires of them a higher degree of accountability than is required of other Government officials. Other public officials, from the President down, cannot be removed from office until they can be convicted, by a two-thirds vote of the Senate, of being guilty of the "high crimes" which are prescribed for impeachment. But a Federal judge may not stay on the bench until he has reached that degree of known unfitness; he must live and act on the bench, and off, up to the high standard of "good behavior" which he was deemed to possess by the President and the Senate when he was appointed and confirmed. When a judge ceases to be a man of "good behavior," such as he was required to possess to qualify him for appointment as judge, he at once becomes disqualified, under the Constitution, to serve longer on the bench. Since the Constitution does not prescribe some other way of determining want of "good behavior," that power remains inherently in the appointing powers, and Congress may, by law, define what is bad behavior, if Congress chooses to do so. Therefore, the President, by and with the advice and consent of the Senate, has vested in him primarily the constitutional power and duty to determine when a Federal judge becomes disqualified to

114

serve for want of "good behavior." The procedure is simple: The President, having determined that a certain judge no longer measures up to the standard of "good behavior," so informs the Senate, when nominating his successor. If the Senate concurs and confirms the nomination, then the judge in question is pro-tanto removed for want of "good behavior," and the new judge takes the office thus vacated. It is most remarkable that no President has, so far, ever exercised this plain constitutional power when the frequent occasion for its exercise has made it a most vital presidential duty.

If we can ever elect a President who will remove judges who shall fall below the standard of "good behavior," which the Constitution makes an essential qualification for a man to continue to serve as judge, then the people will be able to exert at each presidential election their reserved power for the correction of judicial usurpation and abuses.

When neither of these constitutional checks on the judiciary is exercised, then the Federal judges, realizing that they are free from any kind of check or restraint, and responsible to no one, boldly usurp power and become despots of the most vicious and dangerous kind. This is the condition today, and this is what is the matter with the Federal judiciary.

There is a growing popular demand for an amendment to the Constitution to make the judiciary department of the Government responsible to the people, as are the executive and legislative departments. But that is a slow and uncertain remedy.

An Immediate Remedy That Will Be Efficient

There is, however, an immediate remedy before us, without amending the Constitution, which shall be effective to check and cure most of the evils and abuses from which we now suffer. It is simply to repeal the act of Congress creating all United States courts inferior to the Supreme Court, thus abolishing all Federal courts inferior to the Supreme Court, and thus confining the operations of the Supreme Court to its original jurisdiction, as clearly defined by the Constitution. The language of the Constitution is as follows:

"The judicial powers of the United States shall be vested in one Supreme Court and in such inferior courts as the Congress may from time to time ordain and establish...In all cases affecting ambassadors, other public ministers and consuls, and those in which the State shall be a party, the Supreme Court shall have original jurisdiction. In all other cases before mentioned, the Supreme Court shall have appellate jurisdiction both as to law and facts, with such exceptions, and under such regulations as the Congress shall make."

It is clear that if Congress will repeal the act creating the United States courts inferior to the Supreme Court, then the Supreme Court will be at once stripped of all appellate jurisdiction from the circuit and district courts. This will leave in the State courts the constitutional jurisdiction which Congress has conferred upon the inferior United States courts. This will take from the Supreme Court the opportunity to use the judicial legerdemain by which it has contrived to usurp the power to declare acts of Congress unconstitutional and to render legislative decisions. There will then be no hocus-pocus by which the court can get an act of Congress, before it to be repealed, amended or juggled. This will be perfectly safe, and is indeed the only way to safety; because if Congress shall make a mistake about the Constitution, the people can correct it at the next election; but if the Supreme Court makes a mistake, or is corrupt as it surely must have been in the cases herein cited — the income tax and in many other grievous cases — then the unanimous vote of the whole electorate is powerless to correct it until the Constitution is amended. It took the people twenty years to do that in the income tax case, and now the Supreme Court has attacked and tried to destroy the Income Tax Amendment to the Constitution. Such usurpation will never stop unless this remedy is applied.

Last April I sent the following letter to every member of Congress and to every judge of the Supreme Court:

"Washington, D. C, April 10, 1920.

"I enclose a pamphlet which I prepared some years ago with regard to the United States courts. I will be much pleased if you can find time to read it. You know the Supreme Court of the United States is provided for in the Constitution, but its original jurisdiction is limited to controversies between states and to the consular and diplomatic service, though Congress may provide certain appellate jurisdiction; and that afterwards Congress, by an act, provided for the United States Circuit and District Courts. It is through this congressional act that constitutional questions have been raised so as to reach the Supreme Court.

"The framers of the Constitution never intended that the courts should have power to nullify an act of Congress, by declaring it unconstitutional. That was supposed to be the only ground for veto by the President. But the courts have usurped this authority and in the recent decisions they have nullified the Constitution and usurped legislative functions by declaring that it is not expedient to dissolve the steel trust, although its conduct is in plain violation of the statutes; and in the Abraham case they have sent three men to prison for twenty years for doing what the minority opinion of the court says they had a perfect right to do. As a result of these decisions, Senator LaFollette and perhaps others have proposed an amendment to the Constitution of the United States changing the method of selecting our United States judges. I submit that an amendment to the Constitution is not necessary. Besides, that method of securing relief from such obvious usurpations of power is slow, difficult and possibly impossible of accomplishment. Now, what I propose and all that is necessary, is that Congress repeal the law creating United States district and circuit courts, and leaving the cases hereafter that arise between citizens of the United States to the courts of the various states for final decision. This will leave the Supreme Court clothed simply with authority and jurisdiction given them by the Constitution.

"Courts of the various states are elected by the people. There is no place in a democracy for officials appointed for life; and when they usurp power and authority and violate the Constitution and assume legislative powers, it becomes intolerable.

The Supreme Court, as I have shown, was created by the Constitution, while the United States circuit and district courts have been created by an act of Congress.

These inferior courts were established by Congress upon the theory that a citizen of one state could not get justice in the courts of another state. We all know that a citizen of Massachusetts can secure justice in the courts of Illinois. If a citizen of the United States goes to a foreign country, he and his property submit to the courts and laws of the country where he happens temporarily to reside, and, therefore, there is no reason why these United States courts should exist.

These courts do not properly belong to our system of Government. There is no place in a representative republic for an officer who can usurp power and become a despot. Therefore, these courts should be instantly abolished, and in their place courts substituted that are elected by the people subject to recall; that is, courts of the several states.

If the people are capable of enacting laws, they are capable of saying what they meant by those laws when they enacted them; and the right to recall an unfaithful servant ought to be as great on the part of the people as upon the part of an individual.

Abraham Lincoln, in a speech at Cincinnati, on September 15, 1859, declared:

"The people of these United States are the rightful masters of both Congress and the courts, not to overthrow the Constitution, but to overthrow the men who pervert the Constitution."

Lincoln said, in his first inaugural address, March 4, 1861:

"This country with its institutions belongs to the people who inhabit it. "WHEN EVER THEY SHALL GROW WEARY OF THE EXISTING GOVERNMENT, THEY CAN EXERCISE THEIR CONSTITUTIONAL RIGHT OF AMENDMENT, OR THEIR REVOLUTIONARY RIGHT TO DISMEMBER OR OVERTHROW IT."

The Federal courts are perverting the Constitution; they are undermining the foundations of free government; these usurpations and despotism must be stopped. This question is so important and so fundamental that immediate action, in my opinion, must be had to take the Government out of the hands of the lawyers and the judges, and restore it to the people, if we wish to prevent a revolution in this country.

The United States courts, created by act of Congress, can and should be abolished by act of Congress.

They do not belong to democratic institutions.

14. Senates and Senators

The control of the machinery of the Government by the business interests of the United States is nowhere better exemplified than in the Senate of the United States. I was a member of the Senate for twelve years. During that time the Senate never legislated for the American people and had not the slightest regard for their interests. I was intimately acquainted with many of the Senators. I came into daily contact with them, until I learned how they acted, under a given set of circumstances, and why.

During my term of service in the Senate, lawyers always made up the majority of the senators. At times as many as three-quarters were lawyers. Hence follows that everything I have said about lawyers applies generally to United States senators. Indeed, it was my two terms in the Senate that helped me to form my opinion of lawyers and their practices.

The representatives of business, who held seats in the Senate, were not satisfied to pass the laws that their clients demanded. They went out of their way to attacked any other senator who held a brief for the interests of the American people. After I had gained the reputation of being anti-privilege and in favor of human rights above property rights, they came at me again and again.

From the moment that I took sides against the railroads, the trusts and other forces of imperialism, I was a marked man. Senator after senator felt it his duty to go on record against me personally, as well as everything that I stood for. Depew, representing the New York Central; Lodge, representing the conservative propertied interests of New England; Wolcott, representing every interest that would buy him, and David B. Hill, a representative of the New York business interests, scored and denounced me.

Chauncey Depew, as one of his first acts in the Senate, delivered a speech (February 7, 1900, p. 1602), in which he denounced my attitude toward the Philippines.

Even more personal and vindictive was the attack of Senator Wolcott (January 15, 1900, pp. 810-12).

In reply, I merely said:

"Mr. President, the senator from Colorado says that I never speak a kind word of my fellow-senators. I am not going to dispute that assertion except to say that my relations are most pleasant with almost all of my fellow-senators, and I hope he will not undertake to hide the whole Senate behind his large personality. I have not spent much time in laudation of him because I never saw anything in his public career or private life worthy of praise; but I will confess one thing, and that now, which ought to be his praise and his advantage — he has a loud voice. It seems to me that his attack upon me is not worthy of a reply, and I shall not reply to it."

With most of these men, personally, I was on good terms, but when it came to political and economic views, we were enemies. Probably under such circumstances I may judge the Senate and the senators more harshly than they deserve. At the same time, I do not see how it would be possible to exaggerate their utter fealty to business, and their supreme failure to do anything or even think of anything that was in the public interest.

Naturally, to such a generalization, there were a number of honorable exceptions as, for example, that furnished by Senator John P. Jones, of Nevada, and Senator Butler, of North Carolina.

Marion Butler was elected to the Senate of the United States in 1894 and took his seat in 1895, which was the beginning of my second term. So he served with me for six full years. He was elected on the people's ticket as a Populist. He was but 30 years of age, a lawyer by profession, having graduated from the University of Virginia, and was the youngest man in the Senate at that time.

Butler was a man of very decided ability and of strict integrity. He discharged the duties of his office with great credit to himself and to the state that he represented. He voted with me on almost every question, always against the predatory interests. He made really the most brilliant career of any man I ever knew in the Senate during his first term. He was the author of the Rural Free Delivery service of the Post Office Department, which he secured; also the appropriation for the building of the first submarine. He attacked and exposed the infamy of Cleveland's administration, and his bond sales, and also assisted me in the fight with regard to the railway mail pay, and in the armor-plate controversy he showed up many remarkable and startling facts. He was a member of the Committee on Naval Affairs, and was a sturdy opponent of graft and extravagance.

John P. Jones was one of the American delegates to the "International Monetary Conference," held at Brussels in 1892. His fellow-commissioners were James B. McCreary, Henry W. Cannon, president of the Chase National Bank of New York, and E. Benjamin Andrews. These gentlemen knew more or less about money and finance, and they signed the report. There were other members of the commission, among them Senator Allison of Iowa. He did not sign the report. If he attended the Brussels Conference it must have been as an onlooker, for, if he had undertaken to discuss the question, he certainly would have been the laughing stock of the financiers of Europe.

The great speech of that conference was made by John P. Jones of Nevada, who was the ablest man in the Senate of the United States during the twelve years that I was there. He was a careful student, had a great intellect, and understood the science of political economy and the money question. His speech in the Senate of the United States, delivered in October, 1893, is by all odds the greatest contribution to the science of political economy now in print. He was seven days delivering that speech, which is a marvel of eloquence, composition and logic, and yet there were never more than three or four senators listening to it. As soon as Jones arose to speak, everyone would leave the Senate chamber in order to be sure not to possess any knowledge upon the question which he was presenting. Statesmen or scholars are rare in the Senate of the United States and when, by accident, one does get in there he is treated like a pariah. He is "not their kind" to the rest of the senators who are typical products of a political system under which it is impossible to produce scholars, for the senators, as the representatives of the great industrial and financial combinations who own and run the Government entirely, are expected to have, not scholarship, but facility in managing public affairs in the interests of the classes. The rights of the people are never considered. Few senators ever stop to ask the question, "What is the public welfare?" Rather, they ask, "What does my client want?"

Senator Jones was brought up on a farm near Cleveland, Ohio. When about twenty years of age he joined with others, secured a sailing vessel of 250 tons, sailed down Lake Erie through the Welland Canal, across Lake Ontario, and out into the ocean through the St. Lawrence River, and went around the south end of South America to California in search of gold.

It was fortunate that Jones did not have a college education; he had less to forget. Our colleges do not develop to any great degree the only human faculty that distinguishes men from the animals — the power to reason. On the contrary, the college cultivates the memory and develops a veneration for the past. Jones attended the "University of Hard Knocks," which is a pretty good school for a man who possesses any genius, because his mind is not filled up with the doings of the dead past, and he has not learned to venerate war by reading Caesar until he thinks that war is the only road to fame. Jones was a self-made man if ever there was one, and he surely did an excellent job.

After the bill had passed, authorizing the sending of commissioners to the Brussels Monetary Conference, I was in New York and the president of the Chase National Bank, Mr. Cannon, whom I had known in the West, told me that President Harrison had offered to appoint him one of the commissioners to the Brussels Monetary Conference. He wanted to consult with me as to whether he could afford to lower his dignity by accepting the appointment in view of the fact that "the cowboy senator from Nevada" (Jones) was to be one of the commissioners. In reply I told Cannon that he would do' well, before going to Brussels, to read Jones' report on the Brussels Monetary Conference of 1876. This, I told him, would give him some information on the subject. If he could not find time to read that report, I advised him to make the acquaintance of Jones at the earliest moment and to talk with him all he possibly could on the trip, so that he would not make himself ridiculous when he came to speak at the conference. I told him, further, that Jones knew far more about the subject than any other man in the United States, and that he could express what he knew more logically than anybody else.

I did not tell Senator Jones until after he had returned to this country what Cannon had said, because I wanted to give Cannon a show, but, after our commissioners had returned and had made their report (and the report was written by Jones), I asked the senator one day what he thought of Cannon.

"Well," he replied, "Cannon, you know, like all bankers, has no knowledge of the subject of money; but then I got along all right."

120

Then I told Jones that Cannon had consulted with me before they went to Brussels as to whether it would comport with his position as president of the Chase National Bank to accept an appointment as a commissioner to the Brussels conference in company with the cowboy senator from Nevada.

Jones simply smiled. "Well," said he, "you know a banker has no time to spend informing himself on the money question. Cannon probably went into a bank when he was a boy and grew up there. He learned, or knew as much about the money question, as the average banker, but he is not to blame for that." Jones chuckled, and then added: "A little incident occurred after we returned to London, at the close of the Brussels conference, which, in this connection, might amuse you. Rothschild, the great London banker, was a delegate to the conference, listened to my speech and, immediately upon our return to London, gave a dinner in my honor. The guests were the great financiers and economists of England — and Cannon was not invited. In introducing me at the dinner, Rothschild referred to my speech on the money question at the Brussels Monetary Conference as "the greatest recent contribution to the science of political economy."'

The next time I saw Cannon I questioned him about the Brussels conference and his relations with Jones. He said that Jones was a very pleasant and agreeable gentleman, but that he was of the opinion that there were other men at the conference far better informed upon the question than Jones. I finally said: "By the way. Cannon, did you attend the dinner given by Rothschild in London to Jones, at which he, in introducing Jones to the guests, said that Jones' speech was the greatest recent contribution to the science of political economy?"

"Why, no," answered Cannon, "I didn't know there was such a dinner."

I relate this incident to show that even in the United States Senate there are men whose attainments can command respect in the capitals of Europe. But such men are as rare as genius. The rank and file members of the Senate are such stuff as political bosses and political henchmen are made of. Of this Knute Nelson, of Minnesota, is an excellent example.

Knute Nelson was elected to the United States Senate from a country town of Minnesota, where he was practicing law and earning about $500 a year by patching out with insurance and writing deeds. He took his seat in 1895 at the commencement of my second term in that body.

Since he arrived in the Senate he has been a subservient tool of the exploiters, never failing to vote in their interest. He is a representative of the two per cent of our population who own sixty per cent of the wealth. Needless to say, he has done better in the Senate than he did practicing law in the Minnesota village.

In 1897, when the McKinley tariff was under consideration in the Senate, I introduced an amendment providing for the admission, free of duty, of all articles that competed with trust-made products. This amendment was printed and laid upon the tables of the senators to be called up at the proper time. About a week afterwards, Knute Nelson introduced an amendment of the same import as my amendment, and had it printed and laid upon the tables. He waited for a few days and then came over to my seat and said that he would like to have me withdraw my amendment and have the vote taken on his amendment.

"Nelson," I said, "why not let my amendment be voted down, for it surely will be, and then call up yours, and I shall surely vote for it."

"But I want you to withdraw yours so that I can have the credit of this effort to break the trust."

I looked at him for a moment and said: "Nelson, I would withdraw my amendment if I felt certain that after I had done so, you would ever offer yours or bring it up for consideration."

He seemed offended at this and turned away.

When the time came to call up my amendment there was a long discussion on the whole question of tariffs and protection. During this discussion I showed that the duty in the McKinley bill on oil and sugar was a special duty intended to raise the price of both of these commodities in the interest of the trust magnates. I read from Havemeyer's testimony passages showing that they controlled the price completely. I also showed that the oil trust was in the same situation, and I charged that these two trusts received the special fostering care of the Republican party because of their large campaign contributions and because of the fact that their stocks could be manipulated to buy the votes of the lawyers in the Senate.

My amendment to the McKinley Tariff Bill finally came up for a vote and was defeated and Nelson voted against my amendment. I then went to Nelson and asked him if he was going to offer his amendment. I stated that I would like to have him do so and I would like to discuss it and urge its adoption, but he would give me no answer; I waited until the next day and then I offered Nelson's amendment.

Nelson voted against his own amendment and it also was defeated.

It was as I had suspected. He offered his amendment as a means of getting me to withdraw mine. He had no intention of fighting any trust. On the contrary, he was as favorably inclined toward them as any one I ever knew.

During the same debate on the tariff, ex-Governor Grier, of Iowa, showed himself a special champion of the sugar-oil combination. He was outshone, however, in this role, by Senator Wolcott, of Colorado, a lawyer with little knowledge of the law and a great reputation as a phrase-maker. Wolcott was also a special champion of all railroads.

Wolcott entered the Senate without property. He had extravagant tastes and habits. His salary was far less than enough to pay his current bills. Yet, when he died, he left a large fortune.

I was on the committee charged with deciding the membership of the committees of the Senate. Senator Teller, of Colorado, an old senator and a man of integrity and character, came to me and insisted upon having Wolcott placed upon the Committee on Finance, which was the most important committee in the Senate for a lawyer wishing to make a fortune. Although Wolcott had just entered the Senate, I knew something of his character and caliber and I told Teller that I would not put him on that committee, because I believed that he would use that position for corrupt purposes. I stated that I should be very much pleased to put him (Teller) on the committee, but that Wolcott should not go on. But Teller insisted, explaining that he was a candidate for re-election and that Wolcott would help him, and that he vouched for his character and integrity.

As a result of Teller's guarantee, Wolcott went on the Interstate Commerce Committee and the Finance Committee, which possibly accounts for the great fortune he accumulated while he was in the Senate.

Nelson and Wolcott were individuals. Their treason to the best interests of the American people was not confined to them. It was a part of the atmosphere in which senators lived.

The disgraceful lengths to which the Senate was used as a bulwark of the vested interests is well illustrated in the fight over the ratification of the Spanish Peace Treaty.

While the Spanish treaty was pending, there was bitter opposition to it because, under it, we were to acquire the Philippine Islands. So strong was the protest against annexing the Philippines that the administration leaders were unable to round up the two-thirds vote necessary to pass the treaty.

I, as leader of the opposition, had canvassed the field thoroughly, and knew that they would have to use some means to secure votes in order to pass the bill. Aldrich, who was paymaster of the financial combinations, the trusts and the railroads, was exceedingly active, moving around among the senators and talking to them at their desks.

One day Senator Hoar of Massachusetts, a lawyer, came to me and said that he thought we had better ratify the treaty and then we could give the Philippines their independence afterwards. He had made a speech against the treaty and had promised to fight it to the end. John Spooner, of Wisconsin, had made speeches against the treaty and promised to help me fight it to the bitter end, and even to filibuster if that proved necessary. He voted for the treaty. When his term expired, he went to New York and began the practice of law. The next time he appeared in Washington it was as the attorney for J. Pierpont Morgan & Co.

Senator Hoar voted against ratifying the treaty with Spain after everybody knew that Aldrich had votes enough to pass the treaty. In order to give Hoar an excuse for voting against the treaty, it was agreed that he should offer an amendment to the treaty which would be rejected, and then he could vote against the treaty because of the rejection of this amendment. In pursuance of this agreement. Hoar offered an inconsequential amendment which was rejected by the Senate without debate or even a roll call. Immediately thereafter the vote was taken on the treaty and Hoar voted against the treaty and gave as his reason that his amendment had been rejected.

Billy Mason, of Illinois, and McLaurin, of South Carolina, had both made long speeches against the ratification of the treaty. Both of them finally voted in favor of it. Aldrich used to go and talk with them over their desks and he evidently succeeded in convincing them. The day before the vote was taken on the ratification of the treaty, I went to Davis, who was chairman of the Committee on Foreign Affairs, and who had represented the United States at Paris when the treaty was drawn up. Of course, he was pushing for the ratification of his work.

"Davis," I said to him over his desk in the Senate, "you are going to ratify this treaty, but it is the most terrible thing I have seen in my twelve years' service in this body."

"What do you mean?" he asked.

"I mean," I replied, "the open purchase of votes to ratify this treaty right on the floor of the Senate and before the eyes of the senators and all the world."

Davis became decidedly serious. He looked at me and said in a steady voice, "They came into my office and tried to tell me about it and I said, 'Gentlemen, get out of here. You cannot open your stinkpot in my presence.'"

"Well," I said, "I can guess who came to your room and whom you ordered out. It was Aldrich, of Rhode Island."

To this Davis did not reply. The next day the treaty was ratified by a majority of one.

Great crises like this one seldom arise in the Senate, but when they do there are always enough lawyers on hand to do the work that the corporations want done. Spooner, Mason, McLaurin were all of them lawyers.

The Senate is as safe for plutocracy and imperialism on small issues as it is on big ones — even to the alteration of the record of official and Senate proceedings.

In February, 1901, Queen Victoria died. When the news was transmitted officially to the Senate of the United States, Senator Cockrell, of Missouri, a member of the Committee on Foreign Relations, came to me with the following resolution:

"RESOLVED, That the death of her Royal and Imperial Majesty Queen Victoria, of noble virtue and great renown, is sincerely deplored by the Senate of the United States."

I read the resolution and then told Cockrell that I certainly did object to it. I added that if it were offered I would tell the whole story of the opium war and all its infamies on the floor of the Senate. I proposed to show how the English Government had forced opium upon China at the point of the cannon; had bombarded and captured her ports and murdered her people, in order to compel the Chinese Government to allow the English Government opium monopoly to carry on its nefarious business among the Chinese people. I proposed to show, further, that every package of opium had upon it the coat of arms of Victoria, Queen of England. In consequence of this opposition, the resolution was not presented by the Committee on Foreign Relations and never was passed, at least as long as I was a member of that body.

However, the following appears in the Congressional Record of January 28, 1901 (p. 1288):

"Death of Queen Victoria."

Mr. ALLISON: "Mr. President, I offer a resolution and ask unanimous consent for its immediate consideration. The resolution will be read."

The secretary read as follows:

"RESOLVED, That the death of Her Royal and Imperial Majesty, of noble virtue and great renown, is sincerely deplored by the Senate of the United States of America."

THE PRESIDENT PRO TEMPORE: 'Is there objection to the present consideration of the resolution? The Chair hears none. The question is on agreeing to the resolution.

Mr. Allison submitted the following resolution which was considered by unanimous consent and agreed to.

"RESOLVED, That the President pro tempore of the Senate causes to be conveyed to the Prime Minister of Great Britain a suitably engrossed and duly authenticated copy of the foregoing resolution."

The above proceedings never occurred in the Senate and Allison never asked or received unanimous consent to pass the above resolution in relation to Queen Victoria. The Senate had a practice of allowing any member to make any correction in the record, which he might desire to make, at any time within three days, and the bound volumes or permanent record are made up from this corrected record. Allison, of Iowa, who was known as a "pussyfoot" among his fellow-senators, evidently had that item put into the permanent record in this way, and then notified the English Government that we had passed the above resolution in relation to the death of Queen Victoria, and thus prevented me from exposing to the world her infamy and the infamy of the British Empire.

These are but instances of the manipulation that I have witnessed in the Senate. I have seen senators change long-held convictions over night; I have seen men enter the Senate poor and leave it rich; I have seen situations saved by money, and imperialism protected by an altered record. Each time that these changes of mind have occurred over some momentous issue, the change has taken place in the direction of the wealth owners and other interests. Not once was the public weal ever so much as an alleged cause of action.

The Senate is declining in importance. It can now be ignored by business, whereas, twenty years ago, it had to be reckoned with. It had become a sort of storage plant for the preservation of mediocre intellects and threadbare reputations. The senators themselves proclaim this. I quote from the official record of a United States Senate Committee:

SENATOR OVERMAN: "The Committee will come to order. Miss Bryant, do you believe in God and in the sanctity of the oath?"

Miss BRYANT: "Certainly, I believe in the sanctity of the oath."

SENATOR KING: "Do you believe in God?"

Miss BRYANT: "I suppose there is a God. There is no way of knowing."

SENATOR NELSON: "Do you believe in the Christian religion?"

Miss BRYANT: "I believe all people should have any sort of religion they wish."

SENATOR NELSON: "You are not a Christian, then?"

Miss BRYANT: "I was christened in the Catholic Church."

SENATOR NELSON: "What are you now— a Christian?"

Miss BRYANT: "Yes, I suppose I am."

SENATOR NELSON: "And do you believe in Christ?"

Miss BRYANT: "I believe in the teachings of Christ."

SENATOR OVERMAN: "Do you believe in God?"

Miss BRYANT: "Yes, I will concede that I believe in God, Senator Overman."

SENATOR KING: "This is important, because a person who has no conception of God does not have an idea of the sanctity of the oath, and the oath would be meaningless."

SENATOR WOLCOTT: "Do you believe in a punishment hereafter and a reward for duty?"

Miss BRYANT: "It seems to me as if I were being tried for witchcraft."

SENATOR OVERMAN: "That is not so at all."

Miss BRYANT: "Very well, I will concede even that there is a hell."

SENATOR OVERMAN: "Now, I want to find out about matters in Russia and what you have observed there. What is your name? Where have you been living since you have been in Washington?"

Miss BRYANT: "I stopped for a while at the National Woman's Party Headquarters..."

SENATOR NELSON: "Did you belong to the picket squad?"

Miss BRYANT: "I do not know what that had to do with Russia, but I did. I believe in equality for women as well as for men, even in my own country."

SENATOR NELSON: "Did you participate in the burning of the President's message?"

Miss BRYANT: "I DID."

SENATOR NELSON: "Did you participate in the burning of the effigy?"

Miss BRYANT: "I did, and went on a hunger strike."

SENATOR OVERMAN: "What do you mean by that?"

(The Senators are told just what a hunger-strike is.)

SENATOR KING: "Where did you live before you lived in New York? You lived in Oregon, did you not?"

Miss BRYANT: "Yes, sir, but I do wish you would let me tell you something about Russia."

SENATOR KING: "And your husband and Mr. Rhys Williams were on the staff of the Bolsheviki for the purpose of preparing propaganda for..."

Miss BRYANT: "A revolution in Germany."

SENATOR KING (Shouting): "For the Bolsheviki!"

Miss BRYANT: "No, for a revolution in Germany.... If you will allow me, I will show you the kind of papers they printed there. There has never been any secret about this propaganda. For instance..."

SENATOR NELSON: "We do not care about that."

Miss BRYANT: "You do not care about it?"

SENATOR NELSON: "About those papers. We want facts!"

Miss BRYANT: "These papers are facts and you must admit the facts. Here is an illustrated paper in German prepared for sending into the German lines in order to make."

SENATOR NELSON: "Don't be so impertinent."

Woodrow Wilson must have had episodes like this in mind when, on his return from Paris in the spring of 1919, he said: "The senators of the United States have no use for their heads except to serve as a knot to keep their bodies from unraveling."

During the winter of 1918 I went upon the floor of the Senate, and Lodge, of Massachusetts, who had served with me in the Senate for several years, got up from his seat and came over and shook hands with me.

"Pettigrew," he said, "I wish you were here."

"What for?" I asked.

"Why," he answered, "I would like to have you here to shake up this rotten and contemptible Democratic administration."

That rather amused me, because I was not prepared to hear so emphatic and pronounced an expression from the historian of Harvard.

A few minutes afterwards I went over to the Democratic side to shake hands with Senator Tillman, of South Carolina, who had also served several years with me in the Senate. Tillman was at that time an invalid and unable to stand upon his feet. When I shook hands with him he pulled me down near to him and said: "Pettigrew, I wish you were back here."

"What for?" I asked.

"We need you to shake up this rotten and corrupt Republican party in the Senate," he replied.

Then I went over to Lodge and brought him to Tillman's chair. First I told Lodge what Tillman had said to me and then I told Tillman what Lodge had said to me. "Gentlemen," I concluded, "if I were back here I am sure you would both be entirely satisfied."

Perhaps I can best conclude what I have to say about the United States Senate by quoting an item from the Washington "Post" of May 29, 1902:

"SENATE PASSES WATER POWER BILL WITH 25 MILLION LOCAL ITEM OMITTED

The Senate yesterday approved the conference report on the water power bill without the appropriation for $25,000,000 for the development of the Great Falls water power project. The conference report, however, carries $25,000 for further investigation of the project. The vote was 45 to 21. The measure now goes to the President."

A determined, though futile, attempt was made by Senator Norris to have the Great Falls item restored in the conference report. He said that since 1894 eleven investigations had been made, the most comprehensive by

Colonel Langfitt, now General, in 1913, and, in his opinion. Congress should authorize the development of the project at once.

Senator Norris said that, with the development of the Great Falls project, there would be twice as much power as would be needed to light every home and turn every wheel in the District of Columbia. He added that there should have been no coal shortage during the war or last winter, nor would there have been a water shortage if the work recommended in 1913 had been pushed.

At this juncture of his speech, Senator Norris was interrupted by Senator Nugent, who asked why Colonel Langfitt's report had not been followed.

"In my opinion, the first reason is the Potomac Electric Power Company," replied Senator Norris. "The second reason is the Potom.ac Electric Power Company, and the third reason is the Potomac Electric Power Company. There were certain other outside interests opposed to it also."

Senator Nugent then asked if it was not a fact that the Washington Railway and Electric Company and its allied corporation, the power company, have blocked every effort of Congress to develop the Great Falls project.

"Yes, that is my opinion," replied Senator Norris.

It is the old story. The august Senate of the United States in leading-strings to a public utility company that has held its grip on the city of Washington for a generation. In this little thing, as in many a greater thing, the Senate of the United States has proved itself a faithful servant of predatory wealth.

Charles Francis Adams had some experience with the United States Senate, as he was elected president of the Union Pacific Railroad by the Goulds and other gamblers who controlled the road in 1884. These men chose Adams to go to Washington and make a settlement with the Government for the second mortgage which the Government held on the road. Ames had been in Washington before and had organized the Credit Mobilier and had bought both the House and Senate when the bill was passed giving the Union Pacific Road the land grant and the money to build the road, and so it would not do for Ames to go to Washington.

The Goulds, who owned the road with Ames, were the most disreputable gamblers in the United States. They could do nothing in Washington, so the scamps — these leading financiers — selected Charles Francis Adams to go to Washington and see what could be done.

Adams failed because he refused to corrupt the Houses of Congress or the members thereof, and because he would not do their kind of work. He was at once removed as president of the Union Pacific Railroad.

I quote from page 192 of Charles Francis Adams' autobiography:

"I was sent over to Washington to avert the threatened action of the Government, and then and there I had my first experience in the most hopeless and repulsive work in which I ever was engaged — transacting business with the United States Government and trying to accomplish something through congressional action. My initial episode was with a prominent member of the United States Senate. This senator is still (1912) alive, though long retired.

He had a great reputation for ability and a certain reputation, somewhat fly-blown, it is true, for rugged honesty. I can only say that I found him an ill-mannered bully and by all odds the most covertly and dangerously corrupt man I ever had opportunity and occasion carefully to observe in public life. His grudge against the Union Pacific was that it had not retained him. While he took excellent care of those competing concerns which had been wiser in this respect, he never lost an opportunity of posing as the fearless antagonist of corporations when the Union Pacific came to the front. For that man, on good and sufficient grounds, I entertained a deep dislike. He was distinctly dishonest — a senatorial bribe-taker."

I have tried to decide who this senator was and I am of the opinion it was Edmunds of Vermont. Adams should have given the name of the man, but I do Edmunds no injustice by stating that, in my opinion, he was the man, although there were many other lawyers in the Senate at that time that would answer Adams' description, and would do just what Adams describes — and I know them all personally.

Marion Butler was elected to the Senate of the United States in 1894 and took his seat in 1895, which was the beginning of my second term. So he served with me for six full years. He was elected on the people's ticket as a Populist. He was but 30 years of age, a lawyer by profession, having graduated from the University of Virginia, and was the youngest man in the Senate at that time.

Butler was a man of very decided ability and of strict integrity. He discharged the duties of his office with great credit to himself and to the state that he represented. He voted with me on almost every question, always against the predatory interests. He made really the most brilliant career of any man I ever knew in the Senate during his first term. He was the author of the Rural Free Delivery service of the Post Office Department; he secured the appropriation for the building of the first submarine. He attacked and exposed the infamy of Cleveland's administration, and his bond sales, and also assisted me in the fight with regard to the railway mail pay, and in the armor-plate controversy he showed up many remarkable and startling facts. He was a member of the Committee on Naval Affairs, and was a sturdy opponent of graft and extravagance.

15. Ten Presidents

I have been personally acquainted with every president of the United States from Andrew Johnson to Woodrow Wilson. With some of them my acquaintance was very slight. Others I knew intimately for many years. I saw enough of all of them to form a pretty definite idea of their qualities.

These ten presidents were not brainy men. They were not men of robust character. They were pliable men, safe men, conservative men. Many of them were usable men, who served faithfully the business interests that stood behind them. All but two of them were lawyers, and they took into the presidency the peculiar limitations under which lawyers suffer.

I met Grant first in his first term — in the winter of 1871-1872 — and our acquaintance lasted as long as he lived. Grant was a soldier — not a president — but he filled the office as acceptably as a general could be expected to do.

Among the ten presidents, I am of the opinion that William H. Harrison was pre-eminent in ability and character. He was elected in 1888, beating Cleveland, who was then a candidate for a second term. Although Harrison was a strong man, he was not a leader. He misjudged the political machinery of the Republican party and had a reputation of being the most ungrateful person that ever occupied the White House. At the outset he proclaimed his opposition to bosses and to machine control in the Republican party. As soon as he was elected president, he began to build up a machine of his own, using his patronage as a bait and a whip, and disregarding the leaders and bosses entirely.

Soon after I came to the Senate, in December, 1889, I went to see the President about some of the appointments in the State of South Dakota, which had just been admitted into the Union. The President immediately gave me to understand that he thought I was the political boss of Dakota and that he would have to look into the recommendations which I made. I do not think he ever appointed anyone to any political position because of my endorsement. I am informed that he treated the leaders in the other states in the same manner.

Any sort of president, Republican or Democrat, can renominate himself for a second term. The power that he holds through his patronage and his veto enables him to appeal to the personal interest of a large number of influential men and thus to compel their support.

The Republican leaders were strongly opposed to Harrison and to his re-election. Quay and Cameron, of Pennsylvania, Farwell, of Chicago, Tom Piatt, of New York, and a large number of others held conference after conference with a view to choosing his successor. They knew the power of the machine that the President had built up and knew it was difficult to accomplish their purpose, but, after much consideration, they finally decided, at a meeting which I attended, to persuade Blaine to be a candidate.

It had been the ambition of Blaine's life to be president, and we had hoped to get him into the field as the only person who could beat Harrison. He was at that time a member of Harrison's Cabinet and Secretary of State. I was delegated to see Blaine and to report on his attitude. I went to Blaine's house on McPherson Square, in front of the White House, and had several conversations with him. In every instance he said that he would accept the nomination but that he would not seek it, nor would he be a candidate. At the last interview, just before we went to Minneapolis for the National Convention, he told me that, in his opinion, if he were nominated he would not live through the campaign, because of the bad state of his health.   Therefore, he was resolved to do nothing to aid in securing his nomination.

When we arrived at the convention we found everything cut and dried for Harrison's renomination, and he was nominated almost immediately. After the nomination had been made, a committee of his followers came to us — by "us" I mean the political managers of the Republican Party in the various states of that date — and wanted us to name the vice-president. We replied that we would do nothing of the kind. It was their ticket, nominated without even consulting us, and it was their job to elect it.

Levi P. Morton was Vice-President and President of the Senate during Harrison's first term. He was a capable and cordial gentleman of whom we were all very fond, and we supposed, of course, that he would be nominated by Harrison's crowd, but he was passed over and WHITELAW REID was nominated in his place.

There was a great deal of discussion over the matter and reporters tried to interview us on the outcome of the convention. We all refused to be interviewed but one reporter did get into Quay's room, and asked him what he thought of the ticket put up at Minneapolis. Quay gazed out of the window, and in his quaint way said, 'It looks as though it might snow!"

I returned to Washington before any of the other senators and the moment I went upon the floor of the Senate, Morton, who was in the chair, came over to where I was sitting and, in a very hurt tone of voice, wanted to know why he was not nominated with Harrison. I told him the facts — that Harrison's followers had sent a delegation to us asking us to name the vice-president; that we told them it was their ticket; and that they would have to elect it and, therefore, they should designate Harrison's running male. I added, "We supposed of course that they would nominate you, but we also believe that Harrison will be defeated and, therefore, we did not wish to participate in the nomination."

Harrison selected, for the important post of Chairman of the Republican National Committee, Senator Carter, of Montana. Tom Carter was a bright man. He was a lawyer of considerable ability and had a wide knowledge of the law, but he was ignorant of the methods employed by the Republican Party machine to win a campaign.

Carter did not know how to go about reaching the bankers, the railroad financiers, the trust magnates and the other exploiters who controlled the surplus of American wealth. He did secure a contribution of $400,000 from Cramp, the shipbuilder, by telling Cramp that if he put up $400,000 it would, beyond a doubt, elect Harrison. He also told Cramp where the money would be laid out in order to secure this result, and assured him that he would see that Cramp got the money back out of building ships for the Government as soon as Harrison took office.

Campaign funds were not usually raised in this rough fashion. Instead, the campaign managers went to the real government, the managers of railroads, the great industrial, financial and transportation interests, and secured their contribution without any direct promise as to the method of using the funds, leaving that to come along as a matter of course in case of success.

Had the Republican managers been in control of the campaign, none of these sources would have been neglected. As it was, while Tom Carter's crowd was fooling around, these sources of funds were pre-empted by Grover Cleveland, who was the Democratic candidate against Harrison. As a result of this mismanagement, Harrison was badly beaten at the polls and Grover Cleveland was elected in his place.

Never do I hope to deal with a more difficult human being than Grover Cleveland. His naturally perverse disposition was supplemented by personal habits that made it next to impossible for anyone to work with him.

In the Senate of the United States, on June 3, 1896, I made a speech on the River and Harbor Bill that was then under consideration. Cleveland had vetoed the bill, and while I was opposed to it I felt bound to vote for its passage over the veto, because I believed that the President had violated his oath of office by vetoing the bill. I believe that the veto power was never intended by the Constitution or its framers to be used as a legislating instrument. In that speech I referred to Grover Cleveland as follows:

"The present occupant of the White House is not content with the violation of the Constitution by the exercise of the veto power alone, but with an utter disregard of his sacred oath of office, as well as the Constitution, he overrides the laws, influences congressmen with patronage, enriches his favorites at the public expense — in fact, permits no restraint but his imperial will. I think he might fairly be charged with high crimes and misdemeanors. He has exercised the veto power in direct violation of the Constitution. He has appointed men to office without the advice and consent of the Senate. He has defied the Senate and the Constitution alike by appointing men to official positions after the Senate has twice refused its consent, and still retains them in office.

"During his first term he openly used his appointing power to intimidate members of Congress, and during his second term he had given appointments to members of Congress for the purpose of securing their votes upon measures pending in the two Houses. "On his own motion he has undertaken to overthrow the Hawaiian Government, doing acts in direct violation of the Constitution. He has borrowed money in violation of the law for ordinary expenses of the Government, and then falsified the facts in relation thereto in a message to Congress. He has refused to remit taxes as required by law, and has collected taxes unlawfully. He has refused to enforce the laws of Congress so often that the list of violations is next only to the list of his vetoes. He has sold bonds at private sale to his favorites and former associates upon terms and at a price many millions of dollars below the market price of the bonds on the day of such private sales. In view of these facts it is time for Congress to give some attention to these usurpations. If this Government is to survive, we can no longer look with indifference upon the shameful autocracy of Grover Cleveland."

In this connection, I referred to his veto record as unparalleled in our history, and showed that he had vetoed up to the first of May, 1896, 551 bills in his two terms as President, while all the other Presidents of the United States together had vetoed but 109 bills passed by Congress.

Cleveland was reputed to have certain rugged virtues. The only one that I remember his friends boasting about was that he should do as he agreed. He continued his career as a vetoer until the end of his term, or, rather, until the end of January, 1897. During February he was reported to be so drunk that he was incapacitated from public business. A prominent Democratic member of Congress told me, at that time, that he went to the White House to see the President and found Cleveland lying on the floor in a rather hilarious state of intoxication. Many other stories of a similar character — many of them worse — came to our ears during the last days of this disgraceful administration.

Most of the great appropriation bills are passed during the closing days of Congress. An act of Congress, having been sent to the President, must be vetoed by him within ten days, otherwise it becomes a law without his signature if Congress is in session. If Congress expires during the ten days, the unsigned bill is not a law, and this is called a pocket veto. Cleveland thus vetoed all of the bills which were sent to him during the last ten days of Congress. Thus he made it necessary for his successor, McKinley, to call an extra session of Congress immediately, in order to pass the appropriation bills and thus secure sufficient funds for the running of the Government.

On the 4th of March, Grover Cleveland came to the Senate, as is the custom, to see his successor inaugurated. My seat was the first seat on the main aisle. Grover Cleveland was brought in by two or three men and placed in a chair right across the aisle from me. He was still stupidly intoxicated, his face was bloated, and he was a sight to behold. He did not seem to know what was occurring, but looked like a great lump of discolored flesh. When McKinley had delivered his address and had taken his oath of office, Cleveland was carried out of the Senate by the men who brought him in, and I understand was loaded into a carriage and taken to the wharf in Washington and there loaded on a yacht — and I think it was Benedict's yacht (he was a very wealthy man, a citizen of New York, and was one of the chief factors in running Cleveland's administration in the interests of big business). The yacht sailed down the Potomac with Cleveland for a few weeks so that he could wind up his spree.

I have not written about Grover Cleveland for the purpose of attacking him or his private life, or from any feeling of personal animosity or ill-will, but because these things are a part, and a vital part, of his public and official life as President of the United States, and account for his erratic conduct as chief executive of this great nation, and no accurate history of his career as President can be written and fail to consider the two Clevelands — drunk and sober. His ultimatum to England in the Venezuela affair; his conduct with regard to Hawaii, and his hundreds of vetoes and his bond sales, in violation of his oath, and of the Constitution, can in this way only be accounted for.

None of his successors approached Cleveland in personal uncleanliness, but the political records of some of them were far from enviable.

I took my seat in the Senate in December, 1889. During that session of Congress the McKinley Tariff Bill was under discussion in the House of Representatives, and I think the only thing for which I was interested in having tariff protection was metallic tin cacitevite. I interviewed members of the House Committee, of which William McKinley was chairman, and asked that a certain duty be placed on metallic tin.

LaFollette, of Wisconsin (now Senator LaFollette), was a member of this committee. I had known him from boyhood and we were good friends; consequently, he promised to attend to the matter of the tariff on tin for me. However, I saw nearly every member of the committee, including the chairman, Mr. McKinley, and I got from McKinley a definite promise that he would do all he could to secure the tariff I wanted on metallic tin.

Dalzell, of Pennsylvania, was a member of the committee from Pittsburgh, where they made tin plate. His clients wanted a very high tariff on tin plate but wanted the metallic tin to come in free of duty so that the manufacturers of the black plates might make an added profit. Dalzell told me that he was opposed to any tariff upon metallic tin, which made me still more active until I thought I had the promise of the majority of the committee to stand for a tariff on metallic tin.

When the matter came up for a vote in the committee (I think the whole committee was present), the vote on the tin schedule was a tie. The chairman, McKinley, was compelled to cast the deciding vote, and he voted against the duty and against what he had specifically promised me. LaFollette immediately wrote down the names of the committee members who had voted for and against the tariff on tin and also the fact that McKinley had cast the deciding vote against me, and sent it by a page over to the Senate.

I went over to the House of Representatives and, as I went upon the floor of the House in the direction of McKinley's seat, I met McKinley in the aisle coming from the session of the tariff committee.

"McKinley," I said, "how are you getting along with the duty on metallic tin?"

He was very patronizing and conciliating. "Well, Senator," he said, "I do not believe we can get it through my committee."

"How in the devil do you expect to get it through your committee," I replied, "when you vote against it yourself?"

He shrank a little under my remark, then he rallied and said: "Well, I concluded that it was not best to put a duty on metallic tin."

"If you had told me that in the first place," I answered, "instead of lying to me about it, I would have some respect for you. That would have given me a chance to have worked a little harder and to find someone on the committee that would tell the truth."

The incident gave me an insight into McKinley's character and may possibly have had something to do, in addition to other things, with my walking

134

out of the St. Louis Convention in 1896, after McKinley's nomination. I always had the impression that the course pursued by McKinley in the committee of the House was characteristic of the man, and I am still of the opinion that as President he continued the same practices.

There is nothing that better illustrates President William McKinley than his agreement with the Sultan of Sulu, and his double dealing in connection with the same. I quote from the Congressional Record of January 21, 1900.

"Manilla special, July 12, 1899.

"General Bates, in the capacity of agent of the United States Government, sailed for Jolo this morning to negotiate with the Sultan of Jolo regarding the future relations of the Jolo (or Sulu) Archipelago, including the Basilians, as a naval station. The Sultan assumes that the Jolos reverted to him, the evacuation of the Spaniards nullifying the treaty of 1878. General Bates will explain to the Sultan that the Americans succeeded the Spaniards in the treaty assuming its obligations and continuing the annuities it provides for. He will also present to the Sultan $10,000 in Mexican money as an evidence of good will. The local administration of the Jolos will remain unchanged. The Sultan will enforce the law, and will also be expected to fly the American flag continuously and co-operate with America to maintain order and suppress piracy.

"General Bates then entered into the following agreement:

"'Agreement between Brig. Gen. John C. Bates, representing the United States, of the one part, and His Highness, the Sultan of Sulu; it being understood that this agreement will be in full force only when confirmed by the President of the United States, and will be subject to future modifications by the mutual consent of the parties in interest.'

"I deem it proper to state that this agreement has been confirmed by the President of the United States in a letter transmitting the treaty to the Senate. However, this is a treaty apparently with a quasi-sovereign power, over which the Senate, according to our new doctrine of imperialism, has no other authority and no control, and it requires no ratification by the Senate and no consideration on our part.

"'Article 1. The sovereignty of the United States over the whole archipelago of Sulu and its dependencies is declared and acknowledged.

"'Article 2. The United States flag will be used in the archipelago of Sulu and its dependencies on land and sea.

"'Article 3. The rights and dignities of his highness the Sultan and his datos shall be fully respected; all their religious customs shall be respected, and no one shall be persecuted on account of his religion.

"'Article 4. While the United States may occupy and control such points in the archipelago of Sulu as public interests seem to demand, encroachment will not be made upon the lands immediately about the residence of his highness the Sultan unless military necessity require such occupation in case of war with a foreign power, and where the property of individuals is taken, due compensation will be made in each case.

"'Article 10. Any slave in the archipelago of Sulu shall have the right to purchase freedom by paying to the master the usual market value.

"'Article 12. At present Americans or foreigners wishing to go into the country should state their wishes to the Moro authorities and ask for an escort, but it is hoped this will become unnecessary as we know each other better.

"'Article 13. The United States will give full protection to the Sultan and his subjects in case any foreign nation shall attempt to impose upon them.

"'Article 14. The United States will not sell the island of Sulu or any other island of the Sulu Archipelago to any foreign nation without the consent of the Sultan of Sulu.

"'Article 15. The United States Government will pay the following monthly salaries: "To the Sultan, $250; to Dato Muda, $75; to Datto Attik, $60; to Dato Calbe, $75; to Dato Joakanain, $75; to Dato Puyo, $60; to Dato Amir Haissin, $60; to Habji Buter, $50; to Habib Mura, $40; to Serif Saguin, $15.

"'Signed in triplicate, in English and Sulu, at Jolo, this 20th day of August, A. D., 1899 (13th Arakuil Akil 1317).

"The SULTAN SULU
Dato RAJAH HUDA
Dato ATTIK
Dato CALBE
Dato JOAKANAIN

"'Signed: J. C. BATES,
Brigadier-General, U. S. V.'

"The annual aggregate of these salaries is $9,120. The Spanish agreement was for $6,300 a year. This agreement was one we offered to the Sultan, not one that he insisted upon. It is our own proposition that we are to maintain slavery in the Sulu Islands.

"Farther than that, Mr. President, an investigation would show that, although this agreement was made on the 20th day of August, it was not possible to secure from the State Department a copy of the agreement until after the election in Ohio.

"I say this agreement, when the Associated Press tried to get a copy of it before the Senate convened, was furnished in Arabic, and an Arabic used in the Sulu Islands. Therefore it was not possible to have it translated in the United States, and we only got this copy which I have read after Congress convened and after the elections last fall were over. This is on a par and in line with the whole business of concealing from the American people the facts in regard to our maiden foreign venture. We are unable to procure the truth through General Otis. Mr. Collins, of the Associated Press, says the censor told him he was to send nothing and they were going to allow nothing to be sent that would injure the Administration or help Mr. Bryan.

"Here is an agreement by which we are to maintain not only slavery, but polygamy in the Sulu Islands. Here is an agreement by which our flag is made to float over two crimes; and we further solemnly agree that no nation in the world shall be permitted to interfere. It is the chief part of the business of the Sultan of Sulu to get into quarrels with the natives of the interior in the island of Mindanao; then to declare that they are in revolt against his authority. Upon this pretext he takes prisoners and sells them into slavery, the planters of Borneo being the purchasers. That has been his business heretofore whenever he needed money. We now propose to maintain that sort of thing under the flag of the United States, and we stipulate, and the stipulation is approved by the President, that no foreign nation shall be permitted to interfere."

MR. SPOONER: "Does the Senator wish to be understood as asserting that the President approved article 10 of this agreement, which refers to slavery in the archipelago of Sulu?"

MR. PETTIGREW: "I do."

MR. SPOONER: "Well, the President says in his message — and if the Senator will permit me I will read it—

"'I have confirmed said agreement, subject to the action of the Congress, and with the reservation, which I have directed shall be communicated to the Sultan of Jolo, that this agreement is not to be deemed in any way to authorize or give the consent of the United States to the existence of slavery in the Sulu Archipelago. I communicate these facts to the Congress for its information and action.'"

BY MR. PETTIGREW: "The President approver of an agreement which provides that the slave may purchase his liberty at the usual market price, and according to the first paragraph of the agreement it goes in full force upon the approval of the President and cannot after that be altered except by another agreement. This transaction is on a par with all the other inconsistencies attached to this miserable business. He then says that he wants the Sultan to understand that he does not authorize slavery; though he has approved the agreement which ratifies slavery. How could he transmit the agreement to us with his approval and then send back word to the Sultan that he did not wish to be understood as approving slavery? Who knows whether or not the word will ever get to the Sultan?

"Almost everything we receive here in regard to this matter is on a par with the transmittal to the Associated Press of a copy of the Sulu agreement in Sulu Arabic to conceal the infamy until after the elections were over last fall. It is on a par with the statement of the commissioners who made this agreement, which I shall proceed to read. Mr. Schurman in an interview says:

"'It seems to me that were it not for the ignorance displayed the present hue and cry about polygamy and slavery in these islands would be absolutely criminal.'

"If it were not for the ignorance displayed, the present hue and cry about polygamy and slavery would be absolutely criminal I suppose the hue and cry about slavery before our civil war was criminal. Many people so asserted, many people honestly so believed, and I presume that Mr. Schurman honestly believes that the hue and cry about polygamy and slavery again existing under the flag of the United States would be criminal but for the ignorance of the people who cause it.

"In taking over the Sulu group we have acquired no rights of any sort there except those bequeathed us by Spain.

137

"And yet the President, time and again during last fall in his speeches everywhere made to the people, asserted that the flag meant the same thing everywhere, meant the same here, in the Sulu group, and in Hawaii; that it meant in every place the same, and that its presence conferred liberty and happiness upon the people under it.

"She was bound by her agreement with the Sultan not to interfere with the religion or customs of the islands, and it would be most unwise for us to attempt this by force when it can be ultimately accomplished by the slower method of civilization and education.

"Mr. President, we tried the slower method of disposing of slavery and polygamy in the United States, also the slower method of civilization, but finally we resorted to war — the greatest war in modern times — and thereby succeeded in destroying slavery under our flag. It has been restored by the act of a President elected by the Republican party. How will it strike the veterans of that war to annex slavery after all these sacrifices and then propose to abolish it when the slaveholders conclude it is wrong and give their consent?"

"The Sulu group proper contains about 100,000 inhabitants. They are all Mohammedans. To attempt to interfere with the religion of these people would precipitate one of the bloodiest wars in which this country has ever been engaged. They are religious fanatics of the most pronounced type, who care nothing for death and believe that the road to heaven can be attained by killing Christians. Polygamy is a part of their religion, and slavery, about which so much is being said just now, is a mild type of feudal homage. The Sultan believes from what he has seen of Americans that they are ready to be friendly and deal honestly by him.

"Mr. President, I will show what kind of feudal homage this slavery in the Philippines is. Owing to the fact that those people will fight, we prefer to enforce slavery and polygamy, and we attack the Christians in the island of Luzon and compel them to surrender — what? Surrender their desire for a government of their own. We prefer to turn from polygamy and slavery and endorse them, put our flag over them, and declare that nobody shall interfere with them, and then turn our armies and our navies to the destruction of the independence and freedom of a Christian population, which we also purchased from Spain.

"I will read from the second edition of Mr. Foreman's book, which was published in 1899, and brought up to date. He says:

"The Sultanate is hereditary under the Salic law. The Sultan is supported by three ministers, one of whom acts as regent in his absence (for he might have to go to Mecca, if he had not previously done so), the other is minister of war, and the third is minister of justice and master of the ceremonies.

"'Slavery exists in a most ample sense. There are slaves by birth and others by conquest, such as prisoners of war, insolvent debtors, and those seized by piratical expeditions to other islands. A Creole friend of mine, Don A. M. was one of these last. He had commenced clearing an estate for cane growing on the Negros coast some years ago, when he was seized and carried off to Sulu Island. In a few

138

years he was ransomed and returned to Negros, where he formed one of the finest sugar haciendas and factories in the colony.'

"I now read from Social History of the Races of Mankind, by Featherman:

"'Slavery exists on Sulu Island, and the slaves, who were formerly brought from the Philippines, are not well treated, for their masters exercise the power of life and death over them, and sometimes kill them for trifling offenses. The datos frequently punish a disobedient or fugitive slave by drawing their campilan or kris and cutting off his head at one strike without process of law.' "And this is the mild form of feudal homage Schurman would have us believe should enjoy the protection of our flag until we can persuade the slaveholders that it is wrong.

"Why did Schurman make this statement? The reason is plain. He did it just before the elections; about the time the State Department gave out the Sulu copy of the treaty for the information of the people of the United States. I contend that after this statement, made at the time it was made by Mr. Schurman with an evident purpose to deceive, he has forfeited all right to be believed by anybody hereafter, and that his statements on all subjects in relation to the Philippines are not worthy of credence.

"I read also from St. John's Far East, volume 2, page 192, as follows:

"'The slaves are collected from all parts of the archipelago, from Acheen Head in New Guinea, and from the south of Siam to the most northern parts of the Philippines. It is a regular slave market.'

"Then he describes the people. Not only have the slaveholders the right of life and death over their slaves, but the monarch himself has complete and full right to take the life of any of his subjects whenever he chooses. There is no restraint upon him."

I was intimately acquainted with Roosevelt for a great many years, having met him first at Bismarck, in 1884 and 1885.

About 1909 I was the guest of Robert Hunter at a dinner at the Alden Club in New York City. At this dinner, Arthur Brisbane, Morris Hilquit, Professor Giddings, of Columbia University, and others were present. After discussing many questions with these radicals and socialists — questions that covered a wide range of socialism, imperialism and social and economic justice — Professor Giddings turned to me abruptly and asked, "What do you think of Roosevelt?" I replied that I had known him intimately for years and that when I was with him he made me believe that he was sincere and honest in his expression of his views as to what should be done and what he wanted to do, but that when I was away from his presence he did or said something that made me doubt. Thereupon Professor Giddings replied that he had known Roosevelt from boyhood and watched him from every position and that when he was with him and talked with him face to face he always came away convinced that Roosevelt was the greatest faker in the world, but that when he was not present with him, Roosevelt did or said something that made him doubt.

We continued to talk about Roosevelt and I finally told the company that I had just been to Washington at Roosevelt's request, he having written me that he was very anxious to see me. On arriving in Washington I went to the White House and called upon Roosevelt, and as I came in he rushed across the room, extending both hands, and said at once that he wanted me to secure Democratic votes enough to pass the Hepburn Railroad Bill through the Senate. He said that Aldrich was opposing it and trying to amend it so that it would amount to nothing.

I immediately replied that I was not in favor of the Hepburn Bill in any form, that the only remedy was the Government ownership of the railroads — that the railroads were the highways of the nation, and should be operated for the benefit of the whole people of the United States and not for private profit. Roosevelt immediately said: "I have the bill here at the White House which you introduced for the Government ownership of the railroads; also the argument you made in support of the same." And he went and brought out both the argument and the bill. Then he said: "We cannot pass a bill for Government ownership at the present time and I am therefore very anxious to try regulating the railroads."

I replied that regulation was entirely futile and useless for the reason that, if the power to regulate the railroads and to fix the rate were placed in the hands of any commission, the railroads would at once own the commission — that a railroad man, J. Lowery Bell, who was receiving $12,000 a year as superintendent of a railroad, was the second assistant Postmaster General at $4,000 a year, in charge of the Railway Mail Service of the Post office Department during the whole twelve years that I was in the Senate, and therefore it was perfectly idle to try to regulate the railroads and their rates through any commission, no matter who selected it, for it would ultimately be selected by the railroads themselves.

I said, "Do you know the Hepburn Bill cuts off broad court review and only allows the courts to review as to the law but not as to the facts? The Hepburn Bill also empowers the Interstate Commerce Commission to make rates; in fact, to initiate rates." And I added, "Do you want these two things? Are they what you desire?"

Roosevelt jumped up and said, "Yes, that is just what I want."

"Well," I said, "if you will stand for that I will see what can be done."

The next day I took two senators to the White House — two Democrats — and told Roosevelt that these two men would assist him in getting others, and that they could furnish votes enough to put the bill through in spite of Mr. Aldrich. But I added — "Roosevelt, you are so partisan a Republican that I feel that we run great risk in dealing with you at all, because you are liable, after you see you can pass the bill, to make a deal with Aldrich and abandon your democratic allies m the interests of party harmony." He thereupon pounded the table and declared he would never surrender, but would stand to the end.

When I had finished this statement. Professor Giddings remarked that he knew Roosevelt far better than I did, and that Roosevelt would sell me out together with the democratic senators and make a deal with Aldrich, and pass the bill in the form which would be satisfactory to the railroads. That is exactly what Roosevelt did.

This episode convinced me of what I had before suspected — that Roosevelt never stood for anything that was against the settled interests of those who were exploiting the American people.

After Taft had been nominated, in 1912, Roosevelt asked me to come to his home at Oyster Bay on Long Island, as he wished to talk with me about the political situation. Accordingly I went to Oyster Bay and spent the day with him.

When I went into the library at Oyster Bay, Roosevelt rushed across the room, put out both hands and said: "Pettigrew, you were right about Taft. Are you going to support me?"

"I said, "Why, Roosevelt, I didn't know you were running for anything."

He said: "I am going to run as an independent candidate for President."

I said, "Well, I don't think I will support you; there is no sense in your running — all you can accomplish is to elect Woodrow Wilson, and that will be a national disaster."

He said: "Oh, well, we might as well suffer four years under Wilson as four years more under Taft."

I said, "No, there is a great difference. Taft is amiable imbecility. Wilson is wilful and malicious imbecility and I prefer Taft."

Roosevelt then said: "Pettigrew, you know the two old parties are just alike. They are both controlled by the same influences, and I am going to organize a new party — a new political party — in this country based upon progressive principles. We won't win this year, but four years from now we will elect the President, and you are going to support me."

I said, "Roosevelt, if you mean that you will stand for a new party — I recognize the great necessity of it — the two old parties are absolutely dominated by the predatory interests, and if your platform suits me I will certainly support you."

Roosevelt then said, "What do you want in that platform?" And I began to tell him that I wanted government ownership of the railroads; I wanted a reformation of the financial system by which money would be issued by the Government and the Government alone, and many other radical things. In fact, Roosevelt and I sat down that afternoon and drew the platform. When we had finished, Roosevelt said:

"Now are you going to support me?"

And I said: "If your convention adopts that platform I will support you, and when the convention afterward adopted the platform I wrote Roosevelt I would give him my hearty support; and I did, and I carried South Dakota for him in the election.

I told him that I considered the issue and the control of money of great and vital importance, and we finally agreed on the plank that appeared in his platform, i.e., that the issue of money should not be subject to private manipulation, but should be controlled absolutely by the Government in the interests of the people.

We then talked about the labor planks as related to men, women and children.

After the convention had adopted a platform and nominated Roosevelt as a Progressive, I received a letter from him asking me if I intended to support him and if the platform was satisfactory. I answered briefly that I would support him because of his statement to me that he would organize a permanent party in the interests of social and economic justice, and because of the progressive principles that he had placed in his platform.

I am now convinced that he never had any real intention of organizing a permanent progressive party. As an egoist his chief interest centered around his own personality; the nomination of Taft was so sharp a blow to his self-love that there was nothing for him to do except to throw himself into the limelight in another direction. His over-regard for himself, which had grown so rapidly during his later years, tended to make him, par excellence, the monumental faker of the world. In playing this role, he was simply following out the line of conduct established during his early years in public life.

When the battleship MAINE was blown up in Havana Harbor, just previous to the war with Spain, Col. Melvin Grigsby was at Fort Pierre, S. D. Fort Pierre is on the west side of the Missouri River and in the very heart of the greatest cattle range in America. Here it was that Catlin met the Sioux chiefs and thousands of Indians in 1832. In this country were the greatest buffalo pastures in the world.

Col. Grigsby was a veteran of the Civil War, having seen four years of service — a man of great courage and superior intelligence. And from Fort Pierre he telegraphed President McKinley that the sinking of the MAINE meant war, and that the best soldiers that could be secured on short notice for the war with Spain were the cowboys of the plains. He offered his service in this connection. Shortly afterward. Col. Grigsby came to Washington and secured an amendment to the bill, which had already passed the House, authorizing the raising of volunteers for the Spanish War, which provided that 3,000 men of special fitness might be recruited independently, the officers to be appointed by the President.

At this time, Theodore Roosevelt was Assistant Secretary of the Navy. Leonard Wood was a contract surgeon in the army of the United States, located at Washington and detailed to attend to Mrs. McKinley. He applied to be appointed one of the colonels of one of the Rough Rider regiments of cowboys, and Theodore Roosevelt applied to be appointed Lieutenant Colonel of the same regiment. These two doughty soldiers, with no experience except Mr. Roosevelt's experience as a cowboy one season on the little Missouri River, and Wood's experience as a contract surgeon, received their respective appointments. They raised a regiment of so-called cowboys in the eastern states and went to Florida.

From Florida they embarked for Cuba, leaving their horses behind. They landed east of Santiago and started through the jungle for San Juan Hill, General Wood being colonel of the regiment and Mr. Roosevelt acting as lieutenant colonel.

About ten miles from San Juan Hill, they were ambushed by the Spaniards and some of the Rough Riders were wounded in what was called the El Caney fight. They would have been cut to pieces, but General _____, in command of some regiments of Negro troops, rushed in these colored regulars and rescued Wood and his doughty lieutenant-colonel from the hands of the Spaniards.

The Rough Riders — all on foot, for they had left their horses back in Florida — then proceeded to a field near the foot of Kettle Hill, which blanketed San Juan Hill, and remained there until General _____ and his colored troops took San Juan Hill from the Spaniards.

After San Juan Hill had been captured. Col. Wood and Lieutenant Colonel Roosevelt charged up Kettle Hill, where there was nothing but an old kettle which had been used for evaporating sugar cane juice. There were no fortifications or trenches or blockhouses, or Spaniards, dead or alive, on Kettle Hill. Yet Roosevelt, in his book "History of the Spanish War," says that he charged up San Juan Hill and found the trenches full of dead Spaniards with little holes in their foreheads, and that two Spaniards jumped up and ran away, and that he missed one of them but killed the other with a shot in the back from his revolver.

I refer to the records of the War Department, which show that Roosevelt had nothing to do with the taking of San Juan Hill. I refer also to a pamphlet by Colonel Bacon, of Brooklyn, in which he says that he secured affidavits of one hundred soldiers and officers who were in the campaign to take Santiago, and that all of them testified that Roosevelt was not in the battle of San Juan Hill, or, in fact, in any other battle except the ambush at El Caney.

Afterwards, when Roosevelt became President of the United States, he posed on horseback at Fort Meyer, and had his picture painted by a famous German artist, charging up San Juan Hill.

After the Spanish War was over, Mr. Roosevelt located in the city of Washington, and, having inherited a fortune, the tax assessor of New York placed him on the tax list for a large sum as resident of New York State. Mr. Roosevelt thereupon swore off his taxes, swearing that he was not a resident of the State of New York, but of the city of Washington, and, not being a citizen of New York, was not liable to taxes under the laws of that state.

Shortly after taking this oath. Boss Piatt called upon Mr. Roosevelt and proposed that he should be a candidate for Governor of New York. Roosevelt promptly replied that he could not run for Governor as he was not a citizen of New York, and related the incident of his swearing off his taxes. Piatt thereupon remarked: "Is the hero of San Juan Hill going to show the white feather?"

143

Mr. Roosevelt answered, in his dramatic and eloquent way, that he was no coward, and would be a candidate.

After election, when he came to take the oath of office as Governor of New York, he had to swear that he was a citizen of the State of New York. But sufficient time had not elapsed for him to acquire citizenship since he had sworn that he was not a citizen of the state. The difficulty was overcome by Elihu Root's statement that domicile in Washington for the purpose of escaping taxes in the State of New York was not a sufficient loss of citizenship to disqualify Roosevelt for governor. Root was afterwards much pampered and petted by Roosevelt when he became President of the United States.

Having by accident become President, Roosevelt served out McKinley's term and was then nominated and elected. At the end of four years more, having named Taft as his successor, Roosevelt concluded to emulate the exploits of the Romans and add Africanus to his name. Scipio had conquered provinces in Africa and led their kings and princes and potentates in triumph. Roosevelt's triumph was graced with elephants' feet and leopards' tails, and, on his way back to his own country to enjoy his triumph, he stopped in Paris long enough to address the great literary and scientific society founded by Voltaire, whose president was Pasteur, the discoverer of many scientific marvels. And to this body of students of science and biology and literature Teddy delivered his oration of thirty minutes in length, advising them to raise babies!

And this was not the end of his achievements. He examined the map of South America and found a strip of country marked upon all the geographies as unknown or unexplored — a little west of and south of the mouth of the Madeira River. He went in by way of Paraguay, and striking this unknown region at its southern extremity passed down through the tropical jungle of this country to the mouth, and announced to the world that he had discovered a new river of great importance — a new and unknown river, thus adding to his exploits as a conqueror in Africa the proud name of discoverer. But, after he had announced to the world his great discovery, it was found that at the mouth of this river there was a small Spanish town which had existed for two centuries and that for over a hundred and fifty years the river had been navigated to the first falls by the Spanish gatherers of rubber.

Roosevelt was a dramatic artist first and a president afterwards. All of his actions were strongly colored by his love for effect. He posed. That was his life. Of his successor, Taft, nothing need be added to the characterization — "an amiable man weighing 250 pounds."

Woodrow Wilson was not a Democrat after 1896. In that year he left the party for the same reason that I joined it. He came back and voted for Parker in 1904, and for the same reason that led me not to vote for Parker. Wilson did not support Bryan in 1908. At no time was he an advocate of the principles of progressive democracy.

I first met Woodrow Wilson the year before he was nominated. It was in August, 1911, that I received a letter from him saying that he would like to see me. He was residing at the Governor's summer home on the Atlantic coast of New Jersey, about eighty miles from New York. A friend of mine — I think it was ex-Senator Towne, had been down to see him and had told Wilson that I was in New York. Wilson thereupon wrote me that he was very anxious to meet me, and that, if I could not come down to his home, he would come to New York. So I went down to see him.

I went early and remained all day, and we talked on very many subjects. He told me that he was an active candidate for the Democratic nomination for President of the United States and, thereupon, I began discussing public questions with him, for I was prejudiced against him because of his attitude in the Bryan campaigns.

Late in the afternoon of my visit, Wilson asked me if I would support him for the Democratic nomination and take charge of his campaign in the West. I said that I did not know; that I had come down there prejudiced against him; but that he had said things during the day that interested me very much, and that if he would send me all of his recent speeches and every one of his veto messages, so I could study his attitude of mind upon public questions, in about a month I could tell him whether I could support him or not.

In our conversation I had discovered that Wilson knew nothing about the practical working of the Government. He had boasted that he was educated and trained as a lawyer and had practiced in his native state, Alabama, and this did not leave a good impression upon my mind, because any man well learned in the law has come honestly to believe that the rights of property and not human rights are sacred and is, therefore, unfitted to serve the interests of the people. But Wilson had declared for the public ownership of public resources — that is, iron and oil, and had suggested the single tax as a method of taking the raw material from the trusts and combinations, such as the iron, oil, etc.

I left the Governor's house after dinner, and as I reached the door Tumulty — he was then the Governor's secretary — was at the door with an automobile and said that the Governor wished him to talk with me and that, if I would permit him, he would take me back to New York. I therefore got into the automobile, and he took me back to Newark. We discussed the same questions I discussed with the Governor, and he said that the Governor wanted my support, and wished me to take charge of his campaign in the West.

About the time the thirty days had expired, I received a letter from Tumulty saying that the Governor was anxious to know what my decision was, and I promptly replied that I had read all of the Governor's recent speeches and his veto messages, and most of his works, and after carefully considering the same I was of the opinion that he was the worst Tory in the United States and that he used camouflage to conceal his settled opinion, and that I would not support him for the office of President even if no one else was a candidate.

I had many reasons for taking this stand. For example, in a speech which was carefully prepared and delivered before the Society of Virginians in New York City in 1904, he had made the following statement:

"The real opportunity of the South is of another sort. It had now a unique opportunity to perform a great national service. As the only remaining part of the Democratic party that can command a majority of its votes in its constituency, let the South demand a rehabilitation of the Democratic party on the only lines that restore it to dignity and power.

"Since 1896 the Democratic party had permitted its name to be used by men who ought never to have been admitted to its councils — men who held principles and professed purposes which it had always hitherto repudiated.

"There is no longer any Democratic party either in the South or in any northern state which the discredited radicals can use. The great body of one-time Democrats that musters strong enough to win elections had revolted and will act with no organization that harbors the radicals — as the radicals did not in fact act with the organization they themselves had discredited in the recent campaign when the whole country felt that the Democratic party was still without definite character and makeup.

"The country, as it moves forward in its material progress, needs and will tolerate no party of discontent or radical experiment, but it does need a party of conservative reform, acting in the spirit of the law and ancient institutions."

I wish to call especial attention to the fact that Wilson wished to throw the Populists and Silver Republicans and radicals out of the party; and to this paragraph:

"The country, as it moves forward to its progress, needs and will tolerate no party of discontent or radical experiment, but it does need a party of conservative reform, acting in the spirit of the law and ancient institutions."

This is Woodrow Wilson's whole political creed.

His position with regard to labor is well expressed in his baccalaureate address of June 13, 1909:

"You know what the usual standard of the employee is in our day. It is to give as little as he may for his wages. In some trades and handicrafts no one is suffered to do more than the least skilful of his fellows can do within the hours allotted to a day's labor. It is so unprofitable that in some trades it will presently not be worth while to attempt at all. He had better stop altogether than operate at an invariable loss. The labor of America is rapidly becoming unprofitable under its present regulation by those who have determined to reduce it to a minimum. Our economic supremacy may be lost because the country grows more and more full of unprofitable servants."

And he was reported in the New York "World" as saying:

"We speak too exclusively of the capitalist class. There is another as formidable an enemy to equality and freedom of opportunity as it is, and that is the class formed by the labor organization and leaders of the country, the class representing only a small minority of the laboring men of the country,

146

quite as monopolistic in spirit as the capitalist, and quite as apt to corrupt and ruin our industries by their monopoly."

One of the veto messages which he sent me revealed the true Wilson point of view. He wrote a long message in vetoing the bill to eliminate grade crossings on the railroads of New Jersey. The bill by the New Jersey legislature had provided that every railroad in the state should eliminate one grade crossing for each thirty miles of track each year until they were all eliminated. Wilson vetoed this bill on the ground that it would be a hardship for the railroads to comply with the provisions. In the state of New Jersey at that time the railroads ran through the main streets of the principal towns — right on the surface — and large numbers of people were killed and injured at grade crossings. The bill was a mild and "evolutionary" method of eliminating the crossings — it permitted the killings to continue for many years before the last grade of crossing was eliminated. Even that mild provision proved to be too strong for Wilson who, true to his lawyer training, and his attitude of mind where the question of property rights was involved, vetoed the bill because it involved a hardship on the shareholders.

These and many other facts which I had discovered in my study of his writings and his speeches led me to write, early in the campaign of 1912:

"If Mr. Wilson becomes President he will oppose any legislation that interferes with big property or in any way curtails its profits. He has behind him an ancestry of slave-holders and he has no sympathy with labor. He thinks the Chinese are much better than the European immigrants that come crowding in from Europe.

"He is bitterly and sneeringly opposed to every man who toils and to every progressive principle; he knows little or nothing about the purposes of socialism, does not comprehend the great revolution going on in the minds of men which must shake to the very foundation our social and economic structure. His effort will be to check, to turn aside and to neutralize this movement, and he will do it all in the interests of the capitalistic classes.

"He will undertake some reforms. He will rail about the bosses; he will talk about purity, but he is absolutely owned by the great moneyed interests of the country who paid the expenses of his campaign for the nomination and will now furnish the funds for the election. No progressive Democrat should vote for him under any circumstances."

Wilson was nominated by the usual influences that control a Democratic convention. He had almost a solid South at his back. The South is behind the world in ordinary civilization, in social and economic thought. This mass of ignorance and barbarism joined with the corrupt exploiting bosses of the North and brought about Woodrow Wilson's nomination. Murphy, the exploiter of vice in New York; Sullivan, the exploiter of the people of Chicago, through the gas franchise; Ryan, the exploiter of the street railway franchise of New York, and Taggart, who for years ran a gambling house at French Lick, Indiana, and Bryan, of Nebraska, were all actively at work to bring about Woodrow Wilson's nomination.

Wilson, as President, more than fulfilled the promise of Wilson as Governor. His first public surrender to the interests came in the passage of the Federal Reserve Act. His real abdication accompanied his declaration of war with Germany.

On the 26th of February, 1917, President Wilson, in an address to Congress, said:

"I am not now proposing or contemplating war, or any steps that may lead to it."

The President made this declaration eleven days after the Advisory Council of Big Business, appointed by him, had in its secret sessions, as now disclosed by an examination of the records of the meetings, discussed the exclusion of labor from military service, and discussed the draft law months before it had been intimated to Congress or the country that we were to raise an army by draft to fight a foreign war.

William J. Graham, of the Select Committee of the House of Representatives at Washington on Expenditures in the War Department, examined the minutes of the meetings of the Council of Defense. He made copious extracts from these minutes. Based upon that investigation, Chairman Graham reported to the full committee as follows:

"An examination of these minutes discloses the fact that a commission of seven men chosen by the President seems to have devised the entire system of purchasing war supplies, planned a press censorship, designed a system of food control, and selected Herbert Hoover as its director, determined on a daylight saving scheme and, in a word, designed practically every war measure which Congress subsequently enacted — and did all this, behind closed doors, weeks and even months before the Congress of the United States declared war against Germany."

For months before the United States declared war, Wilson was planning war with a secret committee of New York representatives of Big Business that he, Wilson, had appointed for that purpose.

W. P. G. Harding, president of the Federal Reserve Board, gives the reason why the United States went to war in a statement published on March 22, 1917:

"As banker and creditor, the United States would have a place at the peace conference table, and be in a much better position to resist any proposed repudiation of debts, for it might as well be remembered that we will be forced to take up the cudgels for any of our citizens owning bonds that might be repudiated."

Harding, as a representative of the New York bankers, knew what the secret committee was doing with the President at its head. He could, with perfect confidence say, weeks before the United States went into the war, "It might as well be remembered that we will be forced to take up the cudgels for any of our citizens owning bonds that might be repudiated."

Wilson went to Paris as the representative of the New York banks. That he was their representative and consulted with them all through the conference is proven by the fact that Thomas W. Lamont (of J. P. Morgan & Co.) was chief financial adviser in Paris, and that the New York banks had a copy of the treaty weeks before the United States Senate received its copy.

It is not an inspiring record — this story of ten presidents — all of them actively or passively serving the interests that have been plundering the American people. Very few Americans now living have known ten presidents. Very few have had my opportunity for observation. If they had, I think they would be compelled to agree with me that the control of the American plutocracy is exercised as directly and as effectively over and through the Presidents of the United States as over any other department of American Government.

16. Political Parties

In these descriptions of the relation between business and Government in the United States, I have not tried to draw any sharp distinctions between the Republican and the Democratic parties. Indeed, such an effort would be quite futile, since no real distinction between them exists. Historically, the two parties represent varying points of view as to the best method of robbing the workers. The Democrats favored slavery as a method. The Republicans preferred the wage system. But those differences were ironed out during the Civil War. During more than half a century both parties have accepted the system of wage labor as the most practical and remunerative system of exploitation. Today Republicans and Democrats are alike the spokesmen of big business. This assertion I can make without the slightest fear of contradiction, as I have known the leaders of both parties for fifty years and have worked in the inner circles of both party machines.

I was elected to the United States Senate as a Republican when the state of South Dakota was admitted to the Union. I was re-elected in 1894, also as a Republican. I listened to the debates in 1890 on the Anti-Trust Law which was presented by Senator Sherman, of Ohio. The trusts were at that time beginning to show great strength and both parties had declared against them in their platforms. The Sherman law was a Republican measure, but I observed to my great surprise that the leaders of the Republican party were very careful not to include anything in the bill that would interfere with big business. Indeed, the anti-trust legislation was so framed as to encourage rather than discourage combinations in restraint of trade; I also observed that those amendments which were offered to the Sherman Anti-Trust Law in order to make it effective by preventing combinations in restraint of trade, were promptly defeated by a solid Republican vote. This opened my eyes, and I began to wonder if I was really a Republican. Out on the prairies of Dakota there was a strong protest against the exploitation of the people by eastern bankers and railroad operators, and I had never for one moment supposed that the Republican party which always claimed to be the opponent of slavery and the champion of freedom was presenting a united front to any measures looking to a diminution of this exploitation.

In 1896 I was elected as a delegate to the Republican National Convention which assembled at St. Louis for the purpose of adopting a platform and of nominating a presidential candidate. After the St. Louis platform had been adopted, twenty-two of the delegates, I among the number, left the convention and the Republican party. Our reasons for leaving were, first, that the party, in its platform, declared for a very high protective tariff and made no pronouncement against trusts and combinations in restraint of trade, but left out the plank on that subject which it had included in every National convention for at least eight years previously. The tariff wall for which the platform provided was so high as to make the trusts absolutely secure against foreign competition, which was the only competition they had to fear. The convention also declared for the gold standard and at every opportunity announced that it was in favor of the great industrial combinations, whose attorneys not only dominated the convention, but made up two-thirds of both Houses of Congress. In other words, the grand old party that had come into existence as a protest against human slavery had, after forty years, decided to abandon its great record as the champion of black slaves and become the champion of the trusts and industrial and transportation combinations which were enslaving men. Seeing this change as clearly as I did, there was only one course for me to pursue — I left the party. Still I was a Republican at heart. I never voted but for one Democrat.

After the St. Louis Convention I attended the Democratic Convention at Chicago, and was on the platform when Bryan made the great speech which resulted in his nomination. He was endorsed by the so-called Silver Republican Convention, which was composed of those who bolted the St. Louis Convention of the Republican party and their adherents. In the campaign of 1896 I supported Bryan and made a great many speeches advocating his election. Partly as a result of my activity he carried the State of South Dakota. He was beaten throughout the nation by the industrial combinations which had backed the nomination of McKinley and had adopted the St. Louis platform. These interests put up many millions to purchase and corrupt the voters of the country and to defeat Bryan, so that they could go along with their work of concentrating in the hands of a few the result of the toil of the American people.

Again in 1900 I supported Bryan, who was running on a platform which declared against trusts and combinations in restraint of trade, against the acquisition of colonies to be exploited in the interests of trade; against an enormous army and navy — in fact, which declared against everything that the Republican party in the campaign of 1900 stood for.

After the campaign of 1896 a debate took place in the Senate with regard to free homes on the public domain. In this debate I was contending that the Republican party boasted during the campaign of 1896 that it was the author of the Homestead Law; and that in the convention at St. Louis the party had

150

declared in favor of the Homestead Law. As an advocate of the restoration of the Homestead Law, I told the Republicans that they had put the free homestead plank in their platform at St. Louis and now they were refusing to live up to it. By quoting the plank in the Republican platform and comparing it with the bill that the Republicans were trying to enact, I showed conclusively that they had abandoned it. During this debate, the whole question of party relations and affiliations came to the surface, and above all, the spokesmen of business, who were leading the fight against the bill in the Senate, said plainly and emphatically that they were not there to do the will of the people or to represent them, but that they were rather serving their real masters who paid the party bills.

I quote the Congressional Record:

Mr. PETTIGREW: "That is the measure which the St. Louis Convention specifically and in terms endorsed and said they were in favor of. The Senator from Connecticut (Mr. Piatt) says to me they did not do any such thing. Let us see whether or not they did. This bill was reported to the Senate on the 16th of May, 1896, and on the 18th of June, 1896, the St. Louis platform was adopted. Now, let us see what the platform says:

"'We believe in an immediate return to the free homestead policy of the Republican party and urge the passage by Congress of a satisfactory free-homestead measure, such as has already passed the House and is now pending in the Senate.'"

Mr. PLATT, of Connecticut: "Did they endorse the bill which passed the House?"

Mr. PETTIGREW: "'And is now pending in the Senate.' What bill was pending in the Senate? The bill reported by the Committee on Indian Affairs, the bill I have read here in terms and words."

Mr. PLATT: "What did they endorse? Did they endorse the bill which passed the House or the bill that was pending in the Senate?"

Mr. PETTIGREW: "Both; the bill 'such as has already passed the House and is now pending in the Senate.'"

Mr. PLATT: "Does the Senator think they knew what was pendine: in the Senate?"

Mr. PETTIGREW: "I think they did."

Mr. PLATT: "Or that this bill was any different from the bill pending in the Senate?"

Mr. PETTIGREW: "They knew all about it. There is no question about it. Here is the difference between the two bills. The House bill provided for free homesteaders in Oklahoma, every bit of which had been bought from Indians, and the Senate bill provided that the same provisions should extend to the other states of the West. Now, the Republicans went into the campaign in South Dakota and on every stump they told these people that they should have free homes if the Republican party won and that they could not get them if they did not, and you pointed to the record of the Republican party as being the party in favor of free homesteads, and you showed them that the

Democratic party had voted against it way back in 1860. You gained thousands of votes by that pretense and by that plank in your platform, and now you go back on it.

"It is not the only plank you have gone back on. You have gone back on your whole record as a party. You have left the side of the people of this country. You have abandoned the principles that made your party great and respectable and have become the champions of everything that is corrupt and bad in American politics.

"What is more, we passed this bill as a separate measure at the last session of Congress and it went to the House of Representatives exactly in words and terms as in this bill, being the same measure. Has the House done a thing with it? It is referred to the Calendar — the graveyard of the House. They will not even amend it and pass the provision in regard to Oklahoma; and one of the prominent members of the House stood up the other day and stated that it was made for the purpose of getting votes. One of the most prominent members of the House said that the plank was put in the platform, but the election was over. I wish I had his speech here. I should like to put it in the RECORD along with my statement in regard to it.

Mr. GALLINGER: "If my friend, the Senator from South Dakota, will permit me, we ought to be somewhat exact in these historical matters. Do I understand that that plank was in the platform of the Republican party in 1896?"

Mr. PETTIGREW: "YES."

Mr. GALLINGER: "And the campaign was waged in South Dakota in behalf of that plank by the Republican party?"

Mr. PETTIGREW: "YES."

Mr. GALLINGER: "And the Senator who is speaking fought the Republican party in that campaign."

Mr. PETTIGREW: "I did."

Mr. GALLINGER: "The Republican party had not gone back on that plank at that time. How does it happen that the Senator was with the opposition in that campaign?"

Mr. PETTIGREW: "Oh, Mr. President, that is a long story, but I am willing to answer it. I left the Republican party at the St. Louis Convention, and I am proud of it. There has never been a day from that time to this that I have not been glad of it. I stated in that campaign that if McKinley was elected I never could return to the party, because the forces which would control his administration would make it impossible, but there was a chance to return to the party if he was defeated. Repeatedly on the stump I made that statement. I left the St. Louis Convention, first because it declared for the gold standard, which will ruin every producer in this country and every other country that adopts and adheres to it. I left the Republican party because the trusts had captured your party and had complete control of your convention, and you left out the plank against trusts, which you had heretofore adopted, because the trusts, owning you and your party and in possession of your convention, did not want to abuse each other. Reason enough, reason sufficient to justify my course before the people I represent, and enough, in my opinion, to consign the republican party to eternal oblivion.

"What has been your course since? It is known throughout this country that vast sums of money are collected and that you are in alliance with the accumulated and concentrated wealth of this country, and that you rely upon them not only to carry your campaigns and furnish money to corrupt the elections, but to elect your senators; and after you have done it, after you have elected by corrupt means a man to this body, the great convention of the state where it occurs passes resolutions congratulating themselves upon the infamy and declaring that they are glad of it."

Mr. GALLINGER: "Will the Senator permit me again? He seems to be somewhat specific now, and he says that a man has been corruptly elected to this body and that the party has not only not condemned it, but applauded. I wish to ask the Senator if there is any proof that any man occupying a seat on this floor as a republican was corruptly elected?"

Mr. PETTIGREW: "Oh, yes; and' the proof is with the committee on elections. The proof is before the people of the United States, and they all know it, and it is conclusive and the Senator referred to is Mark Hanna, of Ohio."

Mr. GALLINGER: "That might be said of an accusation against somebody whose case was before a grand jury and where the grand jury had not reported. I do not understand that the committee on elections has made a report to this body giving it as their deliberate conviction, after proper inquiry and investigation, that any accusation against a republican occupying a seat here has been proved; and until that is done I think the Senator ought to be a little more careful about his statements on that point, with all due deference to his rights as a Senator."

Mr. PETTIGREW: "I am willing that the statement I have made shall go to the country. The proof was sufficient to satisfy the Senate of Ohio, and they sent the case here weeks ago. An innocent man would demand that our committee act before we adjourn. Why does the case sleep in the Senate Committee?"

That was my statement to the Senate twenty-five years ago, and during those years, every contact that I have had with the Republican party organization has strengthened my conviction that I understated the case at that time. It did not need the revelations of the 1920 campaign to convince the American people of these facts. Those revelations simply emphasized knowledge that was already common.

But do not let it be supposed for an instant that the Democratic party has been less eager to play handy-man to big business. It has been the opportunity and not the will that was lacking. And even at that, it is a matter of common knowledge that the Wilson Campaign millions in 1912 and again in 1916 were greater than the funds at the disposal of the Republicans, and the bulk of them did not come from either workingmen or farmers. On the contrary, the Democrats, like the republicans got their funds from the only source that yields them in large amounts — the exploiters of the American people.

Bryan was the last of the Democratic leaders to make a stand against the vested interests and while his intentions were of the best, his knowledge of economics was woefully limited. Furthermore, he was far from being the master of Democratic party policy.

The Democratic Convention at Denver (1908), nominated Bryan for the third time. I was a delegate from South Dakota to that convention and was chairman of the sub-committee on the tariff and chairman of the Full Committee on Insular Affairs. In connection with this second committee, I brought in a plan declaring in favor of the independence of the people of the Philippines and against the policy of acquiring colonies peopled by another race for the purposes of commercial exploitation. I brought into the full committee, composed of over fifty members, a tariff plank which resulted in a very active debate. The wheel horses of democracy were all for a high protective tariff and I had introduced a plank which was not sufficiently protective to satisfy their purposes. That debate satisfied me that the difference between the two old political parties was not one of principle. As a result of it, I saw quite clearly that they both were owned by the exploiting interests and that the contest between the two was over which one should hold the offices, dispense the patronage, and collect untold millions for campaign purposes. From that time until now the two have been as like as two peas in a pod. There has never been more than a difference in the wording of their respective platforms, and since 1918, as If to prove that they were one and the same, they have fused in those districts (notably in Wisconsin and in New York) where the Socialist candidates would have been elected in a three cornered fight.

Before the Denver Convention, I was invited by Mr. Bryan to his home near Lincoln, Nebraska, where I spent a week with him. He expected to be nominated, and we put in our time going over a platform for the Denver Convention and discussing and planning the campaign. I had great admiration for Bryan because of his sterling qualities as a man, and because of his ability to state what he had to say in a forceful and eloquent manner, and because I believed that he had the moral courage to stand by his principles.

The week that I spent with him gave me an opportunity to know the man intimately. I had access to his library and conversed with him every day. We walked and drove together and in the course of our conversation we covered many topics. I found that he was fairly well versed in the law; that he had studied Blackstone and Kent and the English precedents, but that he was utterly ignorant of almost everything else except the bible and the evils of intemperance; that his library contained almost no books whatever of value to a man fitting himself to be President of the United States, or even member of a state legislature. I also found that, while his personality was charming, whatever ability nature may have endowed him with had been badly dwarfed and crippled by a narrow education, and that he was not big enough

154

to overcome his training by continuing his investigations of men and affairs after he entered public life.

Bryan asked me to return by way of Lincoln after the Denver Convention and go into greater detail with regard to the campaign. He knew that I was well acquainted with Roger Sullivan, of Chicago, who had become the democratic boss of Illinois and who was reputed to be very rich. He was also aware of the fact that Sullivan for some years had been a resident of South Dakota when a very young man and that I had had his brother, who was a republican, made surveyor-general of the State of South Dakota. He knew, furthermore, that I was well acquainted with Murphy, of New York, the boss of Tammany Hall, as well as with Arthur Brisbane, the editor of the Hearst newspapers. Bryan wished me to see Sullivan, Murphy and Brisbane and authorized me to say to Sullivan and Murphy that he desired their support in the campaign and that they should receive due and proper consideration if he were elected President of the United States; that they would be consulted about affairs in their respective localities and that their political importance would be recognized. I had no trouble with Sullivan and Murphy and easily secured their pledges to stand by the ticket. I then talked with Arthur Brisbane, hoping to receive the support of the Hearst newspapers of which he was the editor.

Brisbane, in my opinion, has more general knowledge of the past and present and of books than any other man in America, and he seems to have the material ready for use. I have always had a high regard for his ability and experience. When I approached him and urged his support of Bryan, he turned to me and said, "Bryan doesn't know enough to be President; he is a provincial fellow, prejudiced by his training. He has none of the knowledge that a man must possess in order to be fit for the position of President of the United States."

I then asked Brisbane how much money he had made the preceding year through his writings. He replied that it was about $70,000. Then I said, "That is nothing. Bryan made $100,000 from the sale of his books and through his lectures, and yet you say Bryan doesn't know enough to be President."

I could make no impression upon Brisbane, however, for he still adhered to his position that Bryan was impossible. So far as I know, he is still of that opinion.

There are other incidents — many of them — that have transpired during the past few years, that I could cite if more proof were necessary to establish my point. But it seems to me that on this score, I have said enough. The able men as a rule, do not go into politics. They stay in business, and with the wealth that they derive through their special privileges and monopolies they support one or both of the old parties — turning their contributions into the channel that will yield the largest net returns.

17. Chauncey M. Depew

The Union and Central Pacific Railroads, from Omaha to San Francisco, had been constructed by a company organized by Ames, of Boston, and his associates. They had succeeded in getting Congress to give a land grant consisting of the odd numbered sections of land — for a strip ten miles wide on each side of the main track from Omaha to San Francisco. Besides that the Government had appropriated money enough to more than build and equip the entire road. In return for this money the Government was given a second mortgage on the property.

The road never paid any interest to the Government, but allowed it to accumulate. They established freight rates that were confiscatory, as far as the public was concerned. For example, on goods shipped from Omaha to Nevada they charged the rate from Omaha to San Francisco and then added the local rate back, from San Francisco to the point in Nevada. The same was true in Utah, except that in Utah the Mormon Church furnished one of the directors of the road and received favorable rates, so that their entire influence was with the railroad and its system of exploitation.

In 1896, the Government's second mortgage was about to mature, and the people controlling the Central and Union Pacific railroads put them in the hands of a receiver and then appointed a re-organization committee. In the meantime a through line had been created by a combination between the Union and Central Pacific from San Francisco to Omaha, the Northwestern Railroad from Omaha to Chicago, and the New York Central Railroad from Chicago to New York. The reorganization committee was appointed for the purpose of swindling the Government out of its entire claim by foreclosing the first mortgage and by separating the Union Pacific from all its branch lines. This reorganization committee included Marvin Hughitt, the President of the Northwestern Railroad and Chauncey Depew, President of the New York Central Railroad. It was, I think, in connection with my efforts to head off this robbery that Chauncey Depew's name first appears in the Congressional Record.

So complete was my exposure of the rascality that the promoters were unable to carry through their scheme. My stand naturally aroused the hostility of the New York Central and the Northwestern Railroad interests.

Nor were these my only offenses against the sacred railroad privileges. I have already related the essential facts concerning my fight on the railway mail pay, during which I showed that the Government paid the railroads for carrying the mail ten times as much per pound as the express companies paid the railroads for carrying express on the same train, in the same car, under almost exactly identical conditions, and that the New York Central Railroad in particular received from the Government, for carrying the mail between New York and Buffalo, a sum sufficient to pay the interest at six per cent upon the total cost of building and equipping a double-tracked railroad from New York to Buffalo. Finally I moved to reduce the railroad mail pay by

20 per cent, and introduced a bill providing for government ownership of the railroads and the fixing of passenger rates at one cent a mile, which I proved would be possible if all passes and other forms of free transportation were eliminated.

It was to guard against such dangerous tendencies that the New York Central Railroad sent Chauncey M. Depew to the Senate in 1898. Depew was not sent to represent the State of New York, or the people of the United States, but to protect and foster the interests of the railroads in general and of the New York Central in particular.

Depew had been in the Senate a little less than sixty days when he found occasion to attack me. I reproduce his entire speech of February 7th, 1900:

Mr. DEPEW: "Mr. President, on the 31st of January, the Senator from South Dakota (Mr. Pettigrew), in the course of his speech on the Philippine question, made the following remarks in reference to the president of the Philippine Commission, President Schurman, of Cornell University. He said:

"'Mr. Schurman, in his Chicago interview (and this is the only authority I will read which is not vouched for by official documents) August 20th, 1899, said:

""General Aguinaldo is believed on the island to be honest, and I think that he is acting honestly in money matters, but whether from moral or political reasons I would not say." (Oriental American, Page 99.)

"'The fact of the matter is that he tried to bribe the insurgents, as near as we can ascertain, and failed; they would not take gold for peace.'

"The speech of the Senator from South Dakota was brought to the attention of the president of Cornell, and I have from him the following letter, which I will read. I do it for the purpose of having the Record corrected by his statement:

"'Cornell University, Office of the President,
Ithaca, N. Y., February 3, 1910.

"'Dear Senator Depew: I see, from page 1362 of the Congressional Record, that Senator Pettigrew, speaking of myself, says:

"' "The fact of the matter is that he tried to bribe the insurgents, as near as we can ascertain, and failed; but they would not take gold for peace."

"'Had this preposterous statement been made anywhere else I should not have paid any attention to it; but as it has been made in the Senate of the United States, I desire to say to you that it is absolutely without foundation.

"Very truly yours,
"'J. G. SCHURMAN.

"'Hon. Chauncey M. Depew,
United States Senate,
Washington, D. C.'

"Now, Mr. President, at the time this speech was being made. President Schurman was in this city upon business connected with his report and the report of his commission on the Philippine matter. He was at that very hour in conference with the President at the White House, and therefore competent to be summoned.

"It seems to me that the alleged facts which have been brought forward by my friend, the Senator from South Dakota, in order to substantiate his contention that the President of the United States is a tyrant and that Aguinaldo is a patriot fail in the important consideration that his alleged facts never turn out to be true.

"He has summoned the two witnesses who were more competent than any others to testify on the question of the original understanding had with Aguinaldo and of the position of the Philippine people, one Admiral Dewey and the other President Schurman, the president of the Philippine Commission.

"Any evidence, any statement, in regard to this matter made by Admiral Dewey would be received at once by the people of the United States without further question and the same can be said of any statement made by the president of Cornell University.

"But instead of presenting his evidence by calling the witnesses themselves, he calls others for the purpose of proving what they have said.

"With Admiral Dewey here in the city, his house well known, himself the most accessible of men, he reads, as proving what Admiral Dewey has said and what his position is, an alleged proclamation of Aguinaldo, translated by an unknown translator and published without any certificate of its authenticity in a New England newspaper; and instead of ascertaining, when President Schurman is in the city, what his views really are and what he really did say and what he really did do, he reads a report of an anonymous and unknown reporter in a Chicago newspaper. Admiral Dewey at once branded the statement affecting him as absolutely and unqualifiedly false, and now President Schurman repudiates the testimony attributed to him.

"I submit, Mr. President, that having, amid the mass of newspaper reports, of anonymous remarks, of testimony of no consideration and no value, subpoenaed the two greatest and most prominent witnesses in the country, he has done it in a way which discredits all the alleged facts which are presented on his side or the contention which Senator Pettigrew and his friends endeavor to make in behalf of Aguinaldo and in discredit of the President and of the Philippine policy of the administration.

'These facts, or alleged facts, cited by the Senator from South Dakota, are like the army of Aguinaldo. Whenever the United States troops appear, there is no army of Aguinaldo. And whenever the truth is let in, as Admiral Dewey and President Schurman let it in, these alleged facts vanish in thin air. The basis of their whole contention has no better foundation than the seat of the Aguinaldo government, which, as far as I can ascertain, is nowhere except in the hat of Aguinaldo."

To this I replied at once and showed by the Record that Mr. Schurman, president of Cornell University, who was the head of the commission that went to the Philippines, sent by the Government to try and pacify the islands, had offered Aguinaldo a Government position with a salary of $5,000 per year if he would cease hostilities. I showed also that the commission had offered to pay a large bounty to any of the Filipinos who would come in and surrender their guns. Furthermore, I showed that Aguinaldo had never talked anything else but absolute independence and that he had talked with Dewey time and again on the point. Finally I charged the following facts as proved by the official records in regard to our conduct of affairs in the Philippine Islands:

I charged the suppression of information, the censorship of the press and tampering with the mails;

I charged that the press was censored, not because there was fear that the enemy would secure important information, but to keep the facts from the American people, and I proved it;

I charged that the President began the war on the Filipinos, and I proved it by Otis' report;

I charged that Aguinaldo, after hostilities had been inaugurated, asked for a truce, with the purpose of endeavoring to settle differences without further bloodshed, and that the administration answered: "War, having commenced, must go on to the grim end;"

I charged that Otis changed the President's proclamation to the Filipinos with the purpose of deceiving those people and concealing our real intention of remaining in the islands;

I charged that the Filipinos were our allies; that we armed them, fought with them, recognized their flag and surrendered Spanish prisoners to them; that despite these facts Dewey finally captured Aguinaldo's ships of war in September or October, 1898; that Otis, on September 8, 1898, threatened to attack the Filipinos, and that we finally did begin the fighting;

I charged that we made a covenant with the Sultan of Sulu, by which the President agreed to sustain slavery and polygamy and pay the Sultan over $700 a month for running Old Glory up over his slave mart every morning and taking it down every night;

Finally, I pointed out that we could not have a republic and an empire under the same flag — that one or the other must go down; that the attempt to govern any people without their consent was a violation of our theory of Government and of the Declaration of Independence; that all governments derived their just powers from the consent of the governed; that satisfying greed of empire by conquest had caused the downfall of every republic and every empire in the past.

To all of this the junior Senator from New York announced, with his incomparable after-dinner, spirited and effervescent logic, that these allegations were all answered and disposed of, because Dewey said that Aguinaldo's statement in relation to him was a tissue of falsehoods and Schurman declared that he did not offer Aguinaldo gold for peace.

That was our first contest. After that, from time to time, as long as I remained in the Senate, Depew went out of his way to attack me. He took the death of Mark Hanna (1904) as a favorable occasion. In the course of a funeral oration, delivered over the remains of Hanna, who had been the factotum of the Republican party and the principal partner of Aldrich as the representative of the corrupt financial interests in the Senate, Depew made the following statement:

"Quite as suddenly as he grew to be supreme in political management Senator Hanna became an orator. He had been accustomed in the boards of directors of many corporations, where the conferences were more in the nature of consultations than arguments, to influence his associates by the lucidity with which from a full mind he could explain situations and suggest policies or remedies. He did not dare, however, except on rare occasions, to trust himself upon his feet. We, his associates, can never forget the day when a mighty passion loosed his tongue and introduced into the debate of this body an original and powerful speaker. It was June, 1900. The presidential campaign for the second nomination and canvass of President McKinley was about to open. Senator Pettigrew, an active and persistent laborer in the ranks of the opposition, was seeking material in every direction which would benefit his side. Without notice he suddenly assailed Senator Hanna in his tenderest point. He attacked his honesty, truthfulness and general character. He accused him of bribery, perjury, and false dealing. Hanna's reply was not a speech but an explosion. It was a gigantic effort, in his almost uncontrollable rage, to keep expression within the limits of senatorial propriety. He shouted in passionate protest:

"'Mr. President, the gentleman will find that he is mistaken in the people of the United States when he attempts, through mud-slinging and accusations, to influence their decision when they are called upon at the polls next November to decide upon the principles that are at issue and not the men. When it comes to personality, I will stand up against him and compare my character to his. I will let him tell what he knows; then I will tell what I know about him.'

"The new-born orator carried his threat into execution by a dramatic and picturesque speaking tour through South Dakota, in which, without mentioning Mr. Pettigrew or referring to him in any way, he took away his constituents by convincing them that the doctrines of their Senator were inimical to their interests and prosperity. The titanic power the Dakota Senator had evoked was his political ruin."

I have given my version of this story in some detail in another chapter (Chapter 21, "A Lost Election"); I need merely say at this point that Mark Hanna's "Explosion" was produced by my calling the attention of the Senate to a report submitted by the Ohio legislature to the Senate Committee on Elections in which careful and detailed data was produced showing that Mark Hanna had been directly implicated in buying his way into the United States Senate.

I read from the majority report of the Committee of the Ohio State Senate, which showed that Mark Hanna purchased the vote of a member of the Ohio legislature for the sum of $20,000; $10,000 to be paid down and $10,000 after he had voted. The testimony disclosed that Mark Hanna had personal knowledge of this purchase and was a party to it and sent the money from Columbus, where the legislature was in session, to Cincinnati to be paid to the purchased member of the Ohio legislature. The testimony also showed that Mark Hanna was negotiating for the purchase of two or three other members of the legislature and through this system of bribery and corruption he succeeded in getting his seat in the Senate of the United States.

I then read the minority report of the Committee on Elections in the Senate which went into the subject fully and disclosed the facts. The Republican members of the Committee on Elections in the Senate — and they were in the majority — simply alluded to the testimony laid before them by the Ohio State Senate and refused to investigate, and gave as a reason that the Ohio State Senate had not sent a man down there to prosecute the case. In other words, Mark Hanna was such a factotum in the Republican party in all its councils that it did not disturb the Republicans at all, as so many of them were used to using money to secure their election. Besides, Mark Hanna at that time was Chairman of the Republican National Committee. Depew says:

"Mark Hanna's reply was not a speech, but an explosion. It was a gigantic effort, in his almost uncontrollable rage, to keep expression within the limits of Senatorial propriety. He shouted in passionate protest:

"'Mr. President, the gentleman will find that he is mistaken in the people of the United States when he attempts, through mud-slinging and accusations, to influence their decision when they are called upon at the polls next November to decide upon the principles that are at issue and not the men. When it comes to personality, I will stand up against him and compare my character to his. I will let him tell what he knows; then I will tell what I know about him.'"

And this is Chauncey Depew's idea of oratory. In other words, the Bowery response, "You're another!" Hanna admitted that he was all that I said he was, but that he could show I was a little worse, which convinced me that Chauncey Depew was a phrase-maker of but little intellect, to balance considerable avoirdupois.

For Depew's part in this whole transaction his name ought to go down in history and he should put a halo on his own statue which he has already erected and presented to his native town in New York. I should suppose it would be appropriate to have a dove come down from Heaven and perch upon his shoulder and say: "I am from the boodle crowd m New York who run the Government of the United States, and this is my beloved son in whom I am well pleased."

18. Bryanism

It is not easy to characterize a complex political situation in a brief and comprehensive manner. If such a thing can be done at all, I believe that it can be done most successfully through the personality of two men who typify the two extremes of American political life. One of these men that I shall select for the purpose is William Jennings Bryan. The other is Joe Cannon of Illinois. The first is a Democrat — the second a Republican.

I have known both of these men for many years. Neither is a statesman in any sense of the word. Both are lawyers and suffer from the disqualifications that go with the study and practice of the law. Bryan has integrity, of a sort; Cannon has a keen mind. Both understand the political game, and both play it according to their lights. Bryan plays prohibition politics; Cannon plays plutocratic politics. Neither has any real grasp of the meaning of the phrase 'the public welfare."

In the previous chapter, I have referred to the support which I gave Mr. Bryan in his fight against the eastern bankers and trust magnates. The fight ended in failure because Mr. Bryan was very weak while the trusts were very strong. Since that fight, Bryan has showed himself for what he is — an American politician, vacillating, uncertain, overlooking the fundamental things, ignorant of the forces that are shaping American public life, incapable of thinking in terms of reality, but making phrases as a substitute for thought.

Mr. Bryan is weak, not corrupt. That is why I wish to describe some of his public activities during the past few years. He is a type of the "good man" that so often fools the American people. By way of illustration, let me refer to two incidents which show Mr. Bryan's attitude toward public questions and his method of judging matters of personal conduct.

When the Spanish Treaty was pending in the Senate of the United States and we believed that we had it defeated beyond a question, Bryan came to Washington from his home in Nebraska and urged a ratification of the treaty. He saw several Senators, before he came to me, and urged them to vote for ratification. Bryan knew the grounds upon which I was opposing the ratification of the treaty and yet he had the temerity to come and ask me to vote for ratification of the treaty. He argued that the treaty would entirely end our troubles with Spain and that, once it was ratified, the nation would have an opportunity to perform a great moral duty — the granting of freedom, under a wise and generous protectorate, to the people of the Philippines. His chief argument was that should the Republicans not give the people of the Philippines their independence, but, instead, should undertake to conquer the islands and annex them to the United States, such a course would and Ought to drive the Republican party from power. The Filipinos had been our allies in the war with Spain, and he held that our repudiation of an alliance by such an act of bad faith as that implied in the conquest of the islands would wreck any administration that attempted it.

Bryan thus made the ratification of the Spanish Treaty an act of political expediency, and did not seem to realize that every person who voted to ratify the treaty at the same time endorsed the doctrine of purchasing a country and its people without their consent — the very doctrine on which he proposed to pillory the Republican administration before the country. Neither did he understand that a Senator holding my views and voting for ratification would be guilty of the most outrageous moral turpitude and depravity.

I called Mr. Bryan's attention to the fact that, if we voted for the treaty, it would be fair for the administration to assume that the Senate sympathized with the spirit of the document which, as I pointed out, besides violating every principle of free government, contravened the Constitution which I had sworn to support. I told him that I would sooner cut off my right arm than cast my vote for the treaty. I was so incensed by his effort to induce me, on the score of expediency, to change front on a matter of principle and stultify myself, that I finally told him emphatically that he had no business in Washington on such an errand; that his stand reflected on his character and reputation as a man, and indicated a lack of knowledge of human affairs which must make his friends feel that he was not a suitable person to be President of the United States.

Despite the vigor of my statement, I doubt if Bryan understood what I was driving at. He was seeking political capital and he was willing to take it where he found it, without paying too much attention to nice questions of principle.

The treaty was ratified by one more vote than was necessary. I do not believe Mr. Bryan's visit changed the result, although several Democrats, who made speeches against it, voted for the treaty. The only effect of his visit was to give an excuse for Democrats, for a cash consideration, to sell out to Aldrich and vote for the treaty.

Andrew Carnegie, in his autobiography, on page 364, refers to this subject as follows:

"Mr. Bryan had it in his power at one time to defeat in the Senate this feature of the Treaty of Peace with Spain. I went to Washington to try to effect this, and remained there until the vote was taken. I was told that when Mr. Bryan was in Washington he had advised his friends that it would be good party policy to allow the treaty to pass. This would discredit the Republican party before the people; that Spaying twenty millions for a revolution' would defeat any party. There were seven staunch Bryan men anxious to vote against Philippines annexation.

"Mr. Bryan had called to see men in New York upon the subject, because my opposition to the purchase had been so pronounced, and I now wired him at Omaha, explaining the situation and begging him to write me that his friends could use their own judgment. His reply was what I have stated — better have the Republicans pass it and let it then go before the people. I thought it unworthy of him to subordinate such an issue, fraught with deplorable consequences, to mere party politics. It required the casting vote of the Speaker to carry the measure. One word from Mr. Bryan would have saved the country from the disaster. I could not be cordial to him for years afterwards. He had seemed to me a man who was willing to sacrifice his country and his personal convictions for party advantage."

This is a significant verification of my conclusions, but it is rather amusing to read Carnegie's comments on the perfidy of Bryan. The facts in his own case do not permit him a great deal of latitude in criticizing others. Carnegie was a very active opponent of the treaty and of the doctrine of imperialism. He was a member of the conference which met at the Plaza Hotel (New York) on the 6th of January, 1900, and he took a prominent part in its discussions (see Chapter 23). The conference was called by the New England Anti-Imperialist League, to organize an Anti-Imperialist political party for the purpose of compelling the old parties to agree to the independence of the Philippines, and for the purpose of opposing the acquisition of tropical countries.

The conference was called ostensibly to discuss the annexation of the Philippines and the Spanish West Indies and Hawaii. Its real purpose was to meet the broader question as to whether we should start on the course of empire. In a vigorous speech Mr. Carnegie urged upon the conference the necessity of a new political party for the purpose of opposing the imperial policy of both the old parties, and said that he would give as much money, dollar for dollar, as all the rest of us could raise toward promoting the campaign. As a pledge of good faith, he subscribed twenty-five thousand dollars on the spot. Afterward, he withdrew completely from the movement because the organizers of the steel trust served notice on him that he must choose between a comfortable berth with them and an Anti-Imperialist party, which threatened the whole success of the steel trust movement; and the organizers of the steel trust told Carnegie that, unless McKinley was elected, they would not attempt to form the trust, as they needed a McKinley tariff in order to justify its great overcapitalization. It was a case of imperialism and a tariff or no trust and Carnegie lined up with the imperialists.

Despite Mr. Carnegie's comments, he and Bryan measure up very much alike. Bryan was willing to sell his convictions for a supposed political advantage; Carnegie sold his for gold. Bryan's act was one of intellectual stupidity. Carnegie's act was prompted by what big business calls enlightened self-interest.

Bryan has the point of view of an ordinary American business man. His ruling passion is "safety first" — not the financial safety of a manufacturer, but the political safety of a visionless manipulation of party machinery. This trait appeared very clearly in his activities during the Baltimore Convention of 1912, where Woodrow Wilson was nominated for President of the United States, with Champ Clark, Speaker of the House, as his chief opponent. The custom in Democratic conventions had always been to disregard the two-thirds rule and give a candidate the nomination when he had secured a majority and held it for several ballots.

At Baltimore, after Clark had for several ballots received the votes of a majority of the delegates, Bryan, who had been instructed at the primaries to vote for Clark and use all honorable means to secure his nomination, arose in the convention and said that he would abandon him and violate the instructions of the Democrats of Nebraska as long as the Democratic delegates in the convention from the state of New York continued to vote for Clark. This occurred after the delegations from New York, Virginia and Illinois had voted in the convention with Bryan to seat the Wilson delegates and oust the Clark delegates from South Dakota, although Clark had carried South Dakota in the primaries by twenty-five hundred majority.

Bryan could vote with Roger Sullivan of Chicago, and Ryan of Virginia, and the Tammany Democrats of New York, to throw Clark delegates out of the convention and seat Wilson delegates, but his pure soul would not permit him to vote for Clark while New York delegates were voting for him. This whole performance branded Bryan as not only a hypocrite, but also as a man lacking in character and in intellect.

Immediately upon Bryan making the announcement, I gave out the following interview which was published in all the leading newspapers of the United States:

"Mr. Bryan's statement that he will support no candidate for President who has the support of New York is the rankest hypocrisy. It is the excuse of the demagogue who believes that such a statement will be popular among the western voters, and has been seized upon by Mr. Bryan as an excuse for doing what he has intended to do ever since he was elected as a delegate to this convention by the Democrats of Nebraska.

"He was not only instructed by the Democrats of Nebraska to vote for Mr. Clark, but instructed by the State Convention to use all honorable means to secure his nomination. After that, he stumped Ohio, Maryland and Florida in Wilson's interest. While claiming that he maintained strict neutrality between Clark and Wilson, during the last week in May, Wilson's managers sent a letter to every Democratic voter in South Dakota saying that Mr. Bryan had endorsed Wilson and made speeches in Ohio and Maryland in support of him.

"This letter was circulated with Mr. Bryan's knowledge and consent. Mr. Bryan was thoroughly familiar with the campaign made in South Dakota. He was familiar with the primary law of that state and knows that there were two Clark tickets in the field and that one of these was put up by Wilson's managers to divide the Clark vote, hoping to give Wilson a plurality.

"He knows that this bogus ticket was not supported by the men who put it into the field, and he is fully aware that Clark carried the state by over twenty-five hundred majority over Wilson. Yet he voted to seat the Wilson delegates in this convention, joining with the ninety votes from New York and the fifty-eight from Illinois and the Virginia delegation, of which Mr. Ryan is a member, to oust the Clark delegates from South Dakota. Yet Mr. Bryan would now have us believe that no honest Democrat can co-operate with New York, Illinois and Virginia in this convention."

The publication of this interview regarding Bryan's hypocrisy and the other facts connected with the Baltimore Convention ended his political career, and yet he still hopes that he will be nominated four years from now, for he honestly believes that he was predestined from his birth to be President of the United States.

This is the William Jennings Bryan, who "led" the Democratic party until he was succeeded by Woodrow Wilson — the Bryan of political expediency and political chicanery. He has traveled around the world, yet he knows little of international affairs. He has been from one end of the United States to another, yet he is ignorant of America.

Furthermore, this is Bryanism — a fluent tongue, a resonant voice, the plausible statement of half-truths, an appeal to the passions and prejudices of the moment, a mediocre mind, and a verbal fealty to "right," "justice," "liberty" and "brotherhood." An ignorant electorate has always followed after such superficial qualities.

Bryan has never told any of the real truths of modern life, because he does not know them. He has never made a fight on an issue of principle because he has no abiding principle. He listens. He watches his audience. He gauges its intelligence and then he makes his point. Mr. Bryan is reputed to be one of the best speakers in the United States. His reputation in this regard has been won not by what he says but by the way in which he says it. Nothing in his public career, with the possible exception of his resignation as Secretary of State, has been based on a hard-fought or hard-won principle. Rather he has yielded to the necessity of the moment, trusting that in the end all would be well, but without foreseeing the end or understanding its import.

Bryanism carries with it no taint of corruption — no suggestion of wilful wrongdoing. It is the politics of an ignorant, unimaginable and of a rather vain mind that is quick in trifles and impotent before major issues. Reform politics in the United States has never existed on any other basis, and therefore reform politics has always proved an easy mark for the machinations of big business.

19. Cannonism

So much for the weak Mr. Bryan. Now for the corrupt Joe Cannon. Bryan never knowingly served the vested interests. He fought them to the extent of his ability and interspersed his political battles by giving lectures on 'Prohibition" and 'Immortality.'" Joe Cannon, on the other hand, was one of the most faithful servants that the vested interests of the United States ever had in either house of Congress. He is a type of those all-too-numerous public men who are the political body-servants of big business.

Joe Cannon is still in Congress. For over forty years he has been a member of the House of Representatives, and, as chairman of the Committee on Appropriations and, as Speaker, has had more to do with shaping legislation than any other man in the House. In fact, he was one of the leaders of the band of plunderers that, in both Houses of Congress, for two generations dominated the public affairs and made the Government of the United States one of the most corrupt in the world.

Under the guidance of this clique of men all legislation was directed to the granting of special privileges to corporations, giving them power to tax and exploit the people of the United States. The tariff became the chief vehicle for the robbery of the public and its beneficiaries were the chief contributors to the great campaign funds collected by the Republican party to demoralize the voters of the nation. Under the regime of Cannonism concessions and privileges of every sort, not only for the public service and industrial corporations, but for the financial institutions of the country, received the chief attention of Congress, and these privileges were so profitable that the halls of the House and Senate swarmed with innumerable lobbyists whose vocation it was to appeal to the ordinary members of both branches with whatever argument was necessary, being assured in advance of the ardent and powerful support of Joe Cannon and the other leaders.

The granting of these concessions and privileges, by which the few planned to plunder the many, is the essence of Cannonism. Elected to office of trust by the franchise of their fellow-citizens, Cannon and his like utilize their position to serve, not the people who elected them, but the great interests which provide the campaign funds and other forms of compensation.

Thus a new profession arose — the profession of public lackeying to the plutocracy. To enter this profession it was necessary, first, to buy or fool the people, and, second, to convince the leaders of the plutocracy of your sincere intention to serve their interests. Thus was perfidy coupled with venality by these "public servants" who had taken an oath to support the Constitution and then busied themselves in robbing the people.

Most of the leaders among the political spoilsmen were content with a reasonably extravagant living, but Cannon in the House and Aldrich in the Senate were not thus easily satisfied. The powerful positions which they held enabled them to become enormously rich.

These men became rich because, through their positions of public trust, they were able to betray the Government and the people into the hands of the exploiters. Let me cite a few illustrations of the way in which this was done.

During the nineties there was much talk about the "land frauds." These frauds were the product of legislation especially secured by Cannon and some of his aids in order that the railroads might secure valuable forest and mineral lands in the West and Northwest without paying anything for them beyond the cost of securing the legislation. I was the author of the law for the regulation and control of the forest reservations of the United States. (See Chapter 2.) It was adopted by the Senate and, as adopted, contained a clause which permitted any homesteader, whose homestead was embraced within a forest reservation, to release his homestead to the Government and be accredited with the time he had lived upon it, and allowed to take land from the Government in some other locality. Mr. Cannon was chairman of the Committee on Appropriations of the House, and chairman of the Conference Committee, and he inserted the words, "or any other claimant," so that, if the lands of a land grant railroad were embraced within a forest reservation, the railroad company could exchange them for any other lands the Government might possess. I did not observe this interlineation in the conference report, which was read rapidly and approved without first being printed. Afterward I found that the Northern Pacific Railroad was receiving scrip for the sections of land of its grant which were on the top of Mount Tacoma in Washington. Lands that were absolutely worthless were exchanged in this way for lands of the greatest value.

I stated these facts in the Senate and suggested an appraisal of those lands that were embraced in the forest reservations on top of snow-capped mountains, and proposed that the exchange be made according to value. If they exchanged a section on top of one of these mountains that wasn't worth over a cent an acre for land worth ten or twenty dollars per acre, they should not get acre for acre, but exact value after appraisal; and I also moved that all operations under the law be suspended pending an investigation by the Interior Department. The Senate passed my amendments, but with a full knowledge of all the facts, showing just what frauds had been practiced and how they were practiced; the House refused to agree to the Senate amendments, and, as is customary, the bill was thrown into conference. Cannon was chairman of the Committee on Conference, and chairman of the Committee on Appropriations in the House, and he insisted upon standing by the railroads and continuing the frauds, and so refused to agree to the Senate amendment, but inserted a provision that thereafter railroads could only exchange for surveyed lands. However, as the law provided that, when three settlers in a township petitioned for the survey of the township the Government was bound to make the survey if the settlers deposited money enough to pay for the work, these railroad thieves would send three men into a township, would have them file three homestead entries, and then make affidavit that they were residing there and wanted the township surveyed; would deposit the money necessary — four or five hundred dollars to get the survey made — and then the railroads would locate their scrip upon these lands all over the township, and when this was done the three men would move on and locate in another township, and so continue the fraud.

Cannon and his henchmen in the House and Senate made the frauds possible, and thus enabled the railroads to secure many millions of dollars' worth of the best land in the West for a small fraction of their true value. Thus the timber and mineral wealth of the public domain was turned over to the great corporations whose handymen were maintained in Congress for just such purposes.

Cannonism is the profession of selling the country to the rich so that they may be enabled to grow still richer by the exploitation of the poor.

Another instance of Cannonism is found in the armor-plate scandals.

For several years the Senate of the United States limited the price to be paid for armor-plate. The armor-plate manufacturers were in a trust. Everybody admitted that. There were only two plants in the United States that could manufacture armor-plate. One was the Carnegie Steel Company; the other the Bethlehem Steel Company. The Carnegie Steel Works and Bethlehem Steel Works were in a combination, and each always bid for just half of what the Government wanted, and always bid the same price.

The Senate passed a bill limiting the price of armor-plate to $300 per ton, and under that provision no armor-plate was purchased because the companies refused to sell at that price. Two years afterwards the Senate passed an amendment to the Navy Appropriation Bill limiting the price of armor-plate to $425 per ton. The Carnegie and Bethlehem companies were asking the United States Government $550 per ton, and were selling the same plate to the Russian Government for $240 per ton. The Senate amendment therefore provided that if the Secretary could not buy armor-plate for $425 per ton, the Government should immediately commence to construct an armor-plate plant and make its own armor-plate. Joe Cannon was chairman of the Committee on Conference in the House, and he absolutely refused to submit to the Senate amendment, but insisted that the armor-plate makers should have their price, although they were in a trust and in collusion. These facts were well known to him and to every member of both Houses.

I could go into the details of the Congressional Record with regard to the duty on white pine. The Senate reduced the duty from $2, the price fixed by the House, to $1 per thousand. Cannon refused to agree to the Senate amendment, but insisted upon $2, which was finally allowed. Under it, the lumber dealers of the whole country formed a combination and plundered the consumers, according to their own statement, of thirty-five millions per year.

These facts were known to Cannon and to both Houses when this duty was put on white pine. It was well known that the duty would not furnish any revenue to the Government or any protection to the building up of an infant industry, but it simply put $2 a thousand into the pockets of the owners of the white pine timber. The statement of Mr. Winchester and other lumbermen that if they could get $2 on lumber it would be worth thirty-five million dollars each year was read in the Senate. And yet Mr. Cannon stood pat on the tariff.

When the tariff was revised, it was revised in the interest of the plutocracy and not in the interest of the people of the United States. Cannon's work in Congress was done in the interest of the scheming jobbery that has cursed and controlled the Republican party for the last thirty years.

I have used Cannon's name, not because I wish to discredit him as an individual, but because his story is so typical of the record of the many who are today holding offices of trust under the Government, and faithfully serving the American plutocracy.

20. Business and Politics

At a number of points in this discussion I have suggested that business men used politicians for the advancement of their interests, and the politicians served the business interests first and the public afterward. My experience showed this to be true in a general way, but there were times when the combination of business and politics rose to the surface of public events and became a gross and scandalous plundering of the public treasury in the interest of some specially favored business group. One such instance, involving the sale of Government bonds to a New York syndicate, is especially deserving of notice.

Grover Cleveland, a New York state lawyer, was closely associated with the big business interests before he became President of the United States. During, his second term as President, the gold reserve in the public treasury fell to a very low point. To meet this emergency, the President, through Carlisle, his Secretary of the Treasury, issued bonds which were to be exchanged for gold and thus keep up the Federal gold reserve.

The Wilson Tariff Bill was passed on August 14, 1894, for the purpose of saving the situation, but the mischief had been done. On November 14, 1894, the Secretary of the Treasury issued a call for $50,000,000 five per cent, ten-year bonds under the Resumption Act

The bonds sold in January, 1894, had been absorbed at home. The Stewart syndicate, which handled these bonds, had been treated fairly by the Government, and there was a disposition on the part of these bankers freely to subscribe for the new issue.

Mr. Stewart and Mr. J. P. Morgan visited Washington in the interest of the syndicate, and it is represented, and generally believed, that Mr. Stewart, at least, had a distinct understanding with the President and with Mr. Carlisle that nothing would be done by the administration in any way whatever to interfere with the marketing of the bonds. These bankers, therefore, went back to New York and forwarded a bid for the whole amount of the bonds at $117.

The total offers for these $50,000,000 of bonds amounted to $58,500,000. The award was made to the Stewart syndicate on the understanding that the gold to be paid for the bonds would not be taken from the treasury. Payment for the bonds was made promptly, $20,000,000 having been turned into the Sub-Treasury by the end of November.

The syndicate immediately arranged to sell the bonds they had bought, and offered a lot of $5,000,000 at 119. It is believed that this amount was sold at the price named, but, before they had an opportunity to dispose of any additional bonds, the President's message and the report of the Secretary of the Treasury recommending changes in the currency law effectually stopped the marketing of Government bonds.

This act, which was very apparently one of bad faith on the part of the administration, resulted in the dissolution of the syndicate and a great depression in the prices of bonds. When it came to subsequent bond issues, the administration turned over the bonds to certain financial groups in New York at a price far below their true value and thus enabled the new syndicate to make millions of dollars without taking any risk, investing any capital or importing any gold.

Senator Peffer, of Kansas, introduced a resolution to investigate the Cleveland bond sales. No sooner had this resolution appeared than David Bennett Hill, of New York, began a fight to prevent its passage. In the course of this struggle he attacked everyone that advocated it, and defended the bond sales with great vigor.

I would not mention Senator Hill in this connection were it not for the fact that his brief career is such a typical illustration of the relation between business and politics.

Hill (a Democrat) came to the Senate with the reputation of being a lawyer of decided ability, and a political manipulator of some cunning and skill, having served as Governor of the state of New York. [1] He remained in the Senate only one term, for, at the end of his six years, Tom Piatt — Boss Piatt, as he was called — took Hill's place.

Among the private jobs which Hill undertook to put through was an amendment to the Indian Appropriation Bill, which practically confiscated the reservation of the Seneca Indians. He made the effort to rob the Indians of their homes under the guise of an old agreement of some sort with the Ogden Land Company, by offering an amendment to the Indian bill, in which it was provided that $300,000 should be paid to the Ogden Land Company out of the sale of the land of the reservation. He was exceedingly persistent, and offered this amendment on the floor of the Senate. The amendment was clearly subject to a point of order and, after a considerable discussion, I stated in the Senate that there was present a lobby of adventurers who were interested in this claim, and that the only result would be that they would divide this money among them; and I finally told Hill that, unless he accepted my amendment which specifically provided that the lands of the Indians of New York should not be sold or any part of them, or any of their property whatever appropriated for the purpose of paying this claim, I would insist upon a point of order and let it go to the House of Representatives for their consideration. He accepted the amendment and it was adopted in conference. Afterwards, the Indians in council passed a resolution thanking me for preventing Hill from plundering them from their property. [2]

After a careful study of the facts and an investigation of the circumstances surrounding the Cleveland bond sales, I made a series of charges against the administration. (May 5, 1896, Cong. Record.)

I charged that the President, through the Treasury officials, sold sixty-two millions of bonds at private sale for $104¾ to his former clients, and that on the day of such sale the market price of these bonds, as quoted in the New York papers, was $117.

I charged that the purchaser and others associated with them, the plutocrats and autocrats of New York, sold these bonds to the public in a short time at a profit of $8,418,000.

I charged that the syndicate was to pay in gold for these bonds sixty-two million dollars, and that one-half of the gold was to be imported and that part of the contract requiring the gold to be imported was not carried out and that less than fifteen millions of gold was imported.

I charged that a secret agreement was made with the syndicate by which they were released from importing the gold and allowed to sell exchange against the gold received for the bonds in England to the great profit and advantage of the syndicate.

I charged that negotiations were completed to sell this same syndicate one hundred millions of bonds at $104¾ and it would have been carried out but for the protests of the public.

I charged that after the public and the Senate had protested against the sale of any more bonds at private sale, the administration delayed action until the syndicate of bankers could get together and corner the gold so that the public could not bid, and then the President offered the bonds at a pretended public sale, and that the bonds were sold at about $111, mostly to the syndicate, while, if there had been an honest effort before the gold had been cornered they would have brought $117 at least.

I charged that about five millions of the bonds were not taken by the bidders and the Secretary of the Treasury could have sold these bonds for $117, but that he gave them to Morgan & Company for $110.68, causing a loss to the Treasury of several hundred thousand dollars.

I had summarized the matter, as I understood it, in the following words (April 29, 1896, Cong. Record, p. 5004):

"Mr. President, the plain statement of the facts connected with the several bond issues by the present administration constitutes an arraignment which no eloquence could make stronger. First, there was the attack upon the credit of the United States by the inspired object lesson from the banks of New York; then the extra session of the Fifty-third Congress; then the passage of the Wilson tariff for a deficit; the further depreciation of the national credit by the demonstration that the revenues were not equal to the necessary expenditures of the Government; then the endless chain — the first bond issue of $50,000,000 of five per cent ten-year bonds at a fixed price of $117,077; the depreciation of the market value of these bonds by the recommendation to Congress that a bill be passed discontinuing the use of them as a basis of bank-note circulation; then the secret contract with the Belmont-Morgan syndicate for the sale of $62,000,000 of thirty-year four per cent bonds at $104¾, which bonds were quoted last December at 121; finally the attempt to give to the Morgan syndicate the last loan of $100,000,000 at the same figure, and the actual award to them at their bid of $110.6877 of about $5,000,000 upon which default was made in payment, for which other parties offered 116, and which were quoted in open market at a higher price.

"Upon this record, Mr. President, the administration and the Democratic party must go before the people next November, and the verdict of the people will be even more emphatic in condemnation than it was in 1894 and in 1895."

Nor was I alone in making a fight to have the facts regarding this infamous transaction brought to light. A number of western senators, backed by Populist constituencies, were as eager as I was to have the facts placed before the country. And in their case, as well as in mine, it was David Bennett Hill that "talked back."

In the debate over the Seneca Indian Reservation I had characterized the claim which Hill was supporting as robbery. This had very much offended Mr. Hill, who waited about three months and, in the meantime, having sent to Dakota for information, he secured some Sioux Falls newspapers containing editorials by J. Tomlinson, Jr., attacking me personally and politically in the most outrageous manner. In the course of a speech on the Cleveland bond sales Hill read these editorials into the record. After reading several of the editorials himself, he asked the clerk to do the reading. As the clerk read. Hill stopped him frequently with such exclamations as "What's that? Read that over." By this trick he had each abusive statement read twice. Throughout the episode he behaved like an endman in a minstrel show.

I had said in my speech in regard to the bond sales that the President and the Secretary of the Treasury were evidently enriching their favorites, for the purchasers of these bonds were all prominent New York people, and they cornered all the gold there was in the country, and were giving for the bonds from ten to fifteen per cent less on the dollar than they would sell for in the open market, and I charged that they had thus made about eighteen millions of dollars, and that it looked like a very disreputable and dishonest job. And so, when Hill had finished his attack upon me by reading these editorials, I simply arose and said that I had charged the administration and the financiers of New -York with acting in collusion to plunder the people of the United States in connection with this bond transaction, and that Mr. Hill seemed to think that the complete answer to charges was to read scurrilous political editorials with regard to myself. I said if he was satisfied with the answer I was entirely satisfied, and that Hill had honored me by this attack in the only way he could honor anybody — he had convinced the Senate and the country that we had nothing in common.

Senator Peffer's resolution to appoint a special committee to investigate the bond sale was finally amended to request the Committee on Finance of the Senate to make the investigation through a sub-committee of four senators, that is, Harris of Tennessee, Walthall of Mississippi, Vest of Missouri and Piatt of Connecticut, all lawyers, three of them Democrats and in sympathy with the administration. This committee made some investigation, but never made a report to the Senate.

Who were the chief actors in this scandalous bond transaction? First, the President of the United States, Grover Cleveland, a Buffalo lawyer; second, John Carlisle, a lawyer from Kentucky, who had been a great advocate of bi-metallism and who sold his convictions in order to get Cleveland to appoint him Secretary of the Treasury; David Bennett Hill, a lawyer from New York, who was the champion on the floor of the Senate; John Sherman, a Republican and a lawyer from Ohio. During the twelve years that I was in the Senate, two-thirds of both Houses of Congress were lawyers and the Presidents were all lawyers — Harrison, Cleveland and McKinley. The consequence was that all legislation was framed in the interests of the exploiters of the people of the United States, whether it dealt with bond sales, armor-plate, railway mail pay, land grants of the public domain, ship bounties — the rights and interests of the people of the United States were never considered. In fact, we have become a government administered by lawyers who were acting as the attorneys and representatives of the great exploiting combinations of banks, railroads and industries.

I have gone into the question of these bond sales because they illustrate one of the methods by which the people of the United States are exploited in the interests of the capitalists. Several millionaires were made as the result of the transaction and the American people footed the bill. It was a comparatively small deal — probably thirty millions were made out of it — but it illustrates very well the operations of the system, and the way the machinery of government is manipulated to accumulate the wealth of the country in the hands of the few.

[1] Some idea of Hill's position in New York State politics may be gained from the following article appearing in a Democratic paper (The Times), February 23rd, 1896:

"Senator Hill is a Democratic statesman of high degree, as statesmen go in that party. His term as senator will close next March and, during his nearly six years in the Senate, he has been responsible for but one bill, and that has not yet become a law. although it has passed the Senate and had been favorably reported from the House Committee on Interstate and Foreign Commerce. And what think you is this great and momentous piece of legislation that is to be the only reminder to posterity — that is, if it becomes a law — that David B. Hill served six years in the Senate? It authorizes the Secretary of the Treasury to detail a revenue cutter to control excursion and other boats which attend yacht races. Now, doesn't that prove the statesmanship of Hill?"

[2] The following is a copy of the Resolution of the New York Indians:

"At a council of the Seneca Nation of New York Indians, assembled at the Council Home at Cold Springs, on the Allegheny Reservation, on the twelfth day of April, in the year one thousand eight hundred and ninety-five, the following resolution was adopted:

"RESOLVED: That we sincerely tender our thanks to the Honorable Richard F. Pettigrew, of Sioux Falls, South Dakota, United States Senator, for his valuable services rendered to our delegates while on their visit to the United States Congress at Washington, D. C, and for the deep interest he has taken in the welfare of his red brethren in opposing the passage of the amendment to the Indian Appropriation Bill relative to the claims of the so-called Ogden Land Company to the lands of the Senecas on the Cataraugus Reservations.

"A true copy.

"William C. Hoag, President, Seneca Nation of Indians.
"Alfred L. Jimson, Clerk, Seneca Nation of Indians.
"Great Seal of the Seneca Nation of New York, 1876."

21. A Lost Election

Before leaving the subject of American political life and its control by big business, I want to refer to one more incident — the election that cost me my place in the United States Senate.

Mark Hanna managed the campaign of 1900 and after McKinley took office Hanna managed the President even more successfully than he had managed the campaign. Through ten strenuous years I had fought Hanna and all that he stood for I had opposed him on the gold standard issue; I had led the opposition to the schemes of the imperialists for annexing Hawaii; I had opposed the acquisition of the Philippines and the other Spanish colonies. I had opposed the trusts, the extortion of the railroads, the armor plate thieves, and had tried to save the public domain for the people. Consequently, when it came to the election of 1900, Mark Hanna spared no pains to insure my elimination from public life.

The incident which inspired Hanna with a particularly strong desire to have me out of the way arose out of a charge concerning a campaign contribution to the Republican party.

In 1895 I went to Europe and stayed several months. I returned on the American Line steamship "St Louis" in company with Cramp, the shipbuilder and owner of the line of ships. During the voyage I became well acquainted with Mr. Cramp and we talked a great deal together.

One day he told me that he had paid $400,000 to Tom Carter, chairman of the Republican National Committee, to re-elect Harrison in 1892. He said that he was assured by Carter that his $400,000 would certainly elect Harrison. Carter told him where he was going to spend the money, and that he "could get it back out of building ships for the Government after Harrison was elected." "Harrison was defeated," said Cramp, "and I lost my money. I have since looked the matter up and have found that Mr. Carter did not spend the money where he said he would spend it, and I feel that I am a victim of misrepresentation."

Mr. Cramp wanted to know of me how he could recover the $400,000, and I told him I knew of no way except to make terms with the next administration and increase his contribution.

In December, when the Senate had convened, I went one day over to Tom Carter's seat and told him what Cramp had said to me. Carter smiled and replied, "Well, we did hit the old man pretty hard."

Some time afterward, in a discussion with regard to the building of an armor-plate factory, I told on the floor of the Senate what Cramp had said to me about the $400,000. Carter, ex-chairman of the Republican National Committee, and Mark Hanna, then chairman of the committee, were both in their seats, but neither of them made any reply or took any notice of my statement. Some time afterwards Senator Bacon, of Georgia, interrupted a speech by Senator Hanna to say:

Mr. BACON: "In this connection I want to call the attention of the Senate to the most remarkable thing I ever heard and the most remarkable thing I ever saw in the Senate. I fancy that the country has never been the witness to what we saw and heard in this chamber a few days ago.

"A senator in his place in this chamber stated as a fact that the manufacturer of ships, a prominent and the most prominent firm engaged in the manufacture of warships for the Government, had stated that in 1892 he was approached by the officers of the Republican party and induced to give $400,000 to the campaign fund of that party upon the assurance that the money would be returned to him or made good to him in the contracts which he should have in the building of warships.

"Now, Mr. President, the remarkable thing that I want to call the attention of the Senate to is this: I heard that statement. I did not doubt that it would then and there be promptly challenged. I did not believe that such a statement could be made in the Senate of the United States in the presence of the leaders of the Republican party and no one deny it or call it in question.

"Now, that was not made in a thin Senate; it was made in a full Senate. It was made when the chairman of the National Committee of the Republican party in the campaign of 1892 was in his seat and heard it, as well as the chairman of the Republican National Committee at the time, Mr. Hannah, and yet no one either challenged it or denied it.

"Mr. President, in the absence of such a challenge and such a denial, the country must believe it is true."

And Mr. Hanna made the following reply:

Mr. HANNA: "Mr. President -

THE PRESIDING OFFICER: "Does the Senator from Georgia yield to the Senator from Ohio?"

Mr. BACON: "I do, with pleasure."

Mr. HANNA: "The Senator alludes to the fact that the chairman of the Republican Committee was in his seat and did not deny the statement made."

Mr. BACON: "If I am incorrect in that, I certainly made it in good faith. I think I saw the Senator present."

Mr. HANNA: "If I undertook to reply to all such statements made upon this floor, I would occupy more time than the Senator from Georgia does in the Senate. I considered it unworthy of notice and declined to dignify it by a reply."

It may well be noticed that Mr. Hanna did not undertake to deny my statement and for this reason: Immediately after I had made the statement in the Senate several of the prominent Republican members of the Senate and a number of newspaper men went to see Cramp, and Cramp told them that what I had said was true; that he did tell me that he made a contribution of over four hundred thousand dollars to Harrison's campaign; that he made it upon the misrepresentations of Tom Carter; that he consulted with me as to how to get the money back; that he had not told it to me in confidence, but for the purpose of securing my assistance in getting the money returned to

176

him. One of the newspaper men reported what Cramp said. Of course, Cramp's statement to these Senators and newspaper men left the Republicans where it was impossible for them to meet my charge except by ignoring it.

After Hanna had said that if he answered such statements he would take more of the Senate's time than was occupied by the Senator from Georgia, and that the source from which the report came was unworthy of notice, I rose and said that perhaps I had something that would be of interest to the great man from Ohio and that did come from a source worthy of his notice. I thereupon stated to the Senate that I had in my hand a petition from the Ohio State Senate, signed by four out of the five members of the Committee on Elections of the Ohio State Senate, asking the United States Senate to investigate the election of Mr. Hanna to that body. I said that this petition charged that Mr. Hanna, to secure his election to the United States Senate, had purchased the votes of two members of the Ohio Legislature from the city of Cincinnati; that the purchasing was done by Hanna agents under Hanna's direction; that the sum of ten thousand dollars had been paid to one of the legislators; and I said that this petition had been referred to the Committee on Elections to the United States Senate. After I called the attention of the Senate and the country to this venal and corrupt practice on the part of Mr. Hanna in purchasing his seat on the Senate, the majority of the Senate Committee on Elections made a report and stated that, as no official person came from the Ohio legislature to present and to prosecute the case against Mr. Hanna before the Committee on Elections, they had concluded not to look into the matter. But the minority of the Committee on Privileges and Elections in the Senate made the following report:

"We cannot concur in the report of the majority of the Committee on Privileges and Elections in the matter of the report of the committee appointed by the Senate of the State of Ohio to investigate the charges of bribery in the election of the Hon. M. A. Hanna to the Senate of the United States.

"The charge is that early in January, 1898, an attempt was made by H. H. Boyce and others to bribe John C. Otis, a member of the House of Representatives of the General Assembly of the State of Ohio to vote for Marcus A. Hanna for the Senate of the United States."

Among other things, the majority of the committee had reported:

"Moreover, it seems clear to this committee that it would not be justified in recommending any action to be taken by the Senate without further testimony to be taken by the committee. The question whether additional evidence should be taken has been the only difficult question which the committee has considered. It is clear that Mr. Otis never had any intention of yielding to bribery. He encouraged Mr. Boyce by the advice of others only in order to entrap him. Then he carefully withdrew and substituted his attorney, Mr. Campbell, to continue the negotiations. Mr. Campbell labored to induce Mr. Boyce to offer money and, finally, as he says, obtained $1,750 from him as part payment on $3,500 to be paid for Mr. Otis' vote for Mr. Hanna, leaving

$6,500 to be paid if Mr. Hanna was elected. At this point, public exposure, through Mr. Otis, Mr. Campbell and their associates, took place, Mr. Boyce disappeared, and the incident was closed.

"That Mr. Boyce, operating in Cincinnati, where Mr. Otis lives, has relations with Mr. Hanna's representatives at Columbus, the state capital, the State Committee undertook to prove by the evidence of various detectives, professional and amateur, who listened at telephone wires and shadowed Mr. Boyce, Mr. Hollenbeck and others. The effort of the committee was carefully and skilfully made. It was not wholly devoid of results; it raises pregnant suspicions that Mr. Hanna's representatives at Columbus knew what Mr. Boyce was doing. But this whole line of inquiry would require verification by testimony to be taken by the Committee on Privileges and Elections before that committee would be willing to found conclusions thereon."

The quotation is from the report of the majority of the committee. Now we will see what the minority further say:

'The attempt on the part of Boyce to buy Otis' vote for Mr. Hanna is clearly proven by Campbell who, from his testimony, seems to have been a lawyer of large practice. One thousand seven hundred and fifty dollars was paid in cash by Boyce to Campbell as attorney for Otis. Boyce agreed to pay $1,750 more when Otis reached Columbus, and a balance of $6,500 if Mr. Hanna was elected...

"We think that the evidence to which we have already referred, standing as it does uncontradicted and unexplained, shows that certain of Mr. Hanna's managers at Columbus not only knew the purposes which Boyce had in view in Cincinnati, but also that they aided, abetted, and advised him in carrying out these purposes, and that this state of affairs existed while Mr. Hanna was present at his headquarters...

"First, That many of the witnesses, whose testimony apparently would have thrown much light upon the subject under inquiry, denied the jurisdiction of the committee and refused to testify under the advice of counsel, who stated that they represented the interests of Majors Rathbone and Dick and Senator Hanna; and,

"Second, That Mr. Hanna and his representatives had subpoenas.

"The report of the majority says they 'do not doubt that if facts appeared from the report of the committee of the State Senate requiring the United States Senate, out of a proper regard for its own reputation, to take further testimony concerning Mr. Hanna's election, it would be the duty of the Senate to proceed without waiting for further prosecution of the case coming from residents of the state of Ohio.'

"We think such facts do appear from the report of the committee of the State Senate, and that this body should direct further inquiry and investigation to be made."

The minority who signed this report was composed of Senators Tubley, Pettus and Caffery.

After reading this and much more of the same kind of evidence to the Senate, I said:

"Mr. President, these things are known to the American people. It will not do for the Senator from Ohio to stand up here and say that charges of this sort — if he answered all that were made he could not do much else — are unworthy of consideration or notice. From the Senate of his own state come these charges; from a minority of the committee of this body come these charges, and yet the Senator from Ohio says they are unworthy of his notice — that they are little things."

This report of the Senate Committee is rather a remarkable document; all who signed the majority report were Republicans and Mark Hanna was chairman of the Republican National Committee, and the general factotum of the whole Republican party. He represented the interests of great business and was a business man. He had collected vast sums of money to corrupt the voters of this country and elect McKinley in 1896. So accustomed had the Republicans of the Senate become to the use of money that it did not disturb them at all that Mr. Hanna had purchased his seat in that body. The facts which I presented did not cause even a ripple of interest, and the Senators did not seem to care if the public knew all about it. During the quarter-century that has elapsed since this episode the purchase of seats in the Senate has become so common that it attracts no public attention. Why should it when even the presidency of the United States is put up at auction in the Republican National Convention and knocked down to the highest bidder?

Mr. Hanna was furious at what I had said about him and he determined that he would have revenge! My term in the Senate would expire in 1901, and Mark Hanna made up his mind to prevent my re-election.

I was not running as a stalwart Republican in the election of 1900, for I had walked out of the St. Louis Republican Convention in 1896. I was running as a Bryanite on the Bryan Free Silver Republican ticket in South Dakota. Mr. Hanna raised a vast sum of money to corrupt the voters of South Dakota, and put in charge of the work Henry Payne, of Milwaukee, one of the well-known hangers-on of every Republican campaign.

Payne came out to South Dakota with $30,000 and in conjunction with the Republican organization of the state and the help of A. B. Kittridge, a Sioux Falls lawyer, afterwards a Republican United States Senator, they polled the state of South Dakota on the probability of my election. This task was not a great one. The total population of the state at that time was only 401,570, with a total vote in 1900 of 96,124. Payne sent out 200 teams and visited every farmer and voter in the state. When they had finished the canvass they found that I had the state by several thousand majority.

This greatly alarmed Mr. Hanna and the Republican campaign managers, for they considered it of great political importance to get rid of me.

Senator Allison, of Iowa, came to Dakota to see how the campaign was going on. He made no speeches, but simply looked over the possibilities of eliminating me from public life. He was being entertained in my home town, when C. C. Bailey, a prominent attorney, asked him about me. Allison replied that I had the greatest power for making trouble of any man he ever knew, and that the interests of the party and the people of this country would be best served by getting me out of the Senate.

Senator Nelson of Minnesota also came to South Dakota and canvassed the State and in his speeches said Mr. Pettigrew should be defeated because he had opposed the great business interests that controlled the Government and the Republican party and therefore, if South Dakota wanted to get anything out of the Government, they should elect a man that would train with the gang.

Theodore Roosevelt also joined in the contest against me as the candidate of the Republicans for vice president on the ticket with McKinley, and sent the following telegram to Senator Piatt in October, 1900:

"Good Lord, I hope we can beat Pettigrew for the Senate. That particular swine seems to me, on the whole, the most obnoxious of the entire drove."

Why was Roosevelt opposed to my election? Because he was the candidate of the predatory interests that own the Government of the United States. Charles Edward Russell answered my question.

Asserting that many public men of value to the country have been cried down by the clamor of subsidized newspapers, Mr. Russell says further:

"I have seen this happen a thousand times. Every observer, particularly if he has been a newspaper man, must be familiar with it. Years ago there was a man in the United States Senate that certain newspapers did not like, because he had attacked the interests that owned these newspapers. The newspapers covered that man with ridicule by misrepresenting everything he did or said. They convinced a large part of the country that he was a wild, erratic, absurd, visionary; when, as a matter of fact, he had one of the coolest, clearest and steadiest minds I have ever known in a long acquaintance with public men and affairs. Yet the news columns drove him out of public life, to the great interest of the public interests. I have no objection to mentioning his name. It was R. F. Pettigrew.

"He was ahead of the times, for his vision was clearer than most men now occupying positions of public trust, and he realized then that the interests were weaving the web of autocratic control about the several departments of the Government.

"Possessing the courage of his convictions, he stood almost alone as a target for the shafts of mendacious newspapers, many of them instigated by the sullen command of great wealth. They were merciless and the people believed them rather than the man who had interceded in their behalf."

After Henry Payne's canvassers had reported the result of their poll of the people of the state of Dakota, Hanna went out among the railroad interests, the trust interests and the financial interests of this country, and raised a special fund of $500,000 to be expended in the purchase of Dakota votes. I did not believe that it could be done because I had great confidence in the farmers of Dakota and I had underestimated the resources of the business interests, overestimated the possibilities of ordinary human nature. Hanna himself came to South Dakota and stumped the state with Senator Fry, of Maine. The railroads furnished a special train. The State Committee had been lavish with its publicity and great crowds met the Hanna special at every station.

At Midson, where there is a normal school, Hanna began his speech by taking off his hat and saying, "You see, I have no horns."

The next day I addressed the same crowd — largely composed of farmers — and said, "Of course Mark Hanna has no horns, I dehorned him in the Senate." And then I told the story of how he had bought his seat in that body. A day or two after my speech at Midson, Hanna came to Sioux Falls and addressed a large outdoor meeting and someone in the crowd yelled to Hanna to take off his hat and show the crowd where Pettigrew dehorned him.

I was very badly beaten in the election. After it was over I made an investigation to determine how the work had been done. The Republicans had visited every banker in every country town in the State; had deposited a sum of money with him, and had given him minute instructions as to the part that he was to play in the campaign.

The local representatives of the Republican party would then take a list of the farmers, and watch for each man. When he came into town they would take him over the bank and the banker would hand him ten dollars in cash.

"That is yours," the representative of the Republican party would state, "and if Pettigrew loses this township (or county) in the election there is ten dollars more for you at the bank that you can get by coming in and asking for it after election."

In some cases, in several cases of which I know personally, the sum was twenty dollars before election and twenty dollars after election.

Hanna boasted, after the election, that my name was never mentioned in any of his campaign speeches by either himself or Senator Fry. But his statement is false in this respect, for a Roberts County paper published the following just after Mark Hanna's visit:

"Mark Hanna at Sisseton Indian Agency, South Dakota, in an address to Two Stars, chief of the Sissetons, chaperoned by Mr. Sapackman, chairman of the Roberts County Republican Committee:

"I understand that half of you Indians are going to vote for Bryan and Pettigrew. I understand that your annuities from the Government, due in about six weeks, are $22 per capita. That is enough for Indians who vote against the Great Father. If all the Sisseton Indians will vote the Republican ticket, I will have the Government increase their annuities $75 per head. This will give to the Sisseton Indians $75 apiece instead of $22 apiece. Do you tumble?

"They tumbled and God did not forbid that citizen Mark Hanna should attempt to divert the will of the sovereign people or tamper with the sanctity of their ballots."

I have since talked with many of these Indians who heard Mark Hanna's statement to them, and who corroborate this story from the local newspaper.

They also told me that Mark Hanna never made any effort to secure for them seventy-five dollars per capita which he had promised them if they would vote against me.

I also learned that, during the campaign, the Republican Committee of South Dakota had trunkfuls of blank passes from every railroad in the country. Upon these passes they could send a man and his family to any point in the United States or the adjacent countries and return, free of cost and at the expense of the railroad. I know of several prominent Democrats who made long excursions after the election, one of them taking his family to the Hawaiian Islands.

Mark Hanna had secured these passes by appealing to the railroads when they made their effort to swindle the Government out of the money which had been advanced to build the roads. He had also cited my bills for the Government ownership of all the roads in the United States, as well as my exposures of the swindles in connection with the Railway Mail Pay. Consequently the railroads not only furnished transportation, but a considerable amount of the money used against me. James J. Hill, president of the Great Northern Road, told me afterwards that Mark Hanna had assessed him fifty thousand dollars, and he told Hanna that he not only would not give a single dollar towards trying to defeat me in South Dakota, but he would not give the Republican National Committee any money whatever if they were going to undertake the purchase of the voters of South Dakota.

After the election, I was in the Auditorium Hotel, in Chicago, getting lunch one day, when a young man came in and asked, 'Is this ex-Senator Pettigrew?'

"Yes," I said, "it is."

"Well," said the young man, "I want to tell you of an incident that might be of interest to you. I was Mark Hanna's private secretary in 1900, and on election day Hanna left Chicago and went back to Cleveland to vote, leaving me in charge of the Republican headquarters. About ten o'clock election night, Hanna called me up over the phone and wanted to know about the election. I told him that McKinley was undoubtedly elected, and Hanna replied, 'Oh, I know that; but how about Pettigrew?' I thereupon replied, 'Pettigrew is undoubtedly beaten,' and Hanna said, 'If you are sure of that I can go home and go to bed and to sleep. I wanted to accomplish two things in this election — to elect McKinley and to beat Pettigrew, and I did not know which I wanted the worst.'"

I think that was the most striking compliment that was ever paid to my work in the Senate. I had kept up my attacks upon the plutocracy until their spokesman was as anxious to defeat me as he was to elect a president. I sent thousands of copies of the following letter to the voters of South Dakota in my campaign for re-election to the United States Senate in 1900:

"Dear Sir:

"I enclose herewith a copy of the platform adopted at Kansas City. It is a new Declaration of Independence. It is the platform upon which I am running for re-election to the United States Senate. I have been twice elected to the Senate from South Dakota, receiving the united support of the Republicans of the state, and in both instances also of very many of the Democrats and Populists.

"I am now a candidate for re-election upon the platform which I enclose, because I think it embraces the best settlement of the great principles involved in the coming political contest that I have seen. I am not therefore a candidate for re-election as a Republican, for the reason that I believe this contest is not one between political parties, but is a contest between those who wish to preserve Republican institutions in this country and prevent the Republic from becoming an aristocracy. It is a battle between the Man and the Dollar; between concentrated wealth in the hands of a few people and the great mass of the people who have produced the wealth, but who are unable, owing to a pernicious system of transportation and combination of capital, to enjoy that which they produce.

"The Republican party has been captured by the evil elements, by the great transportation companies, the great money trusts, and the great combinations of capital which have gained control of our manufacturing industries. It is therefore for the interest of the Republican party to perpetuate that legislation which has produced the condition in regard to the distribution of wealth in this country, against which I protest.

"I have not changed my views upon these great issues since I ceased to act with the Republican party politically. My votes in the Senate on all these questions have been the same during the past four years as they were during the previous seven years. If I had changed my position on these questions my enemies would have ample proof of the fact in the Record of the Senate; but the votes which I have recorded show that my position has not been changed, but the position of the Republican party has changed completely — so much so that, when I offered an amendment to the last Republican Tariff Bill, refusing protection to articles controlled by the trusts unless they dissolved the trusts, and allowed free competition within our own country, every Republican Senator voted against it and defeated the measure.

"When the War Revenue Bill, to pay the expenses of carrying on the war with Spain, was under consideration, I offered an amendment to tax the products of the trusts as a means of raising revenue, or compelling the dissolution of the trusts, and every Republican Senator voted against my amendment.

"We offered an amendment to levy a tax upon incomes to support our armies in the contest with Spain, and all the Republican members of the Senate voted against it, and the bill was so framed as to lay the entire burden of taxation upon the individual — upon consumption — so that the poor man would pay just as much as the man of enormous wealth.

"Against this unequal and unfair distribution of the burdens of taxation I protested, on the ground that it tended to the unequal distribution of wealth; and that where the wealth of a country was once gathered into the hands of a few men the manhood of the masses was destroyed and the institutions of our country endangered. But the Republican party, controlled by evil influences and headed by Mark Hanna, persisted in their policy, which has made it impossible for me to act with them politically.

"I left the Republican party in 1896 for the reason that I felt that the party had left the side of the people in its abandonment of bimetallism; but, above all, because of the fact that it omitted from its platform at St. Louis all allusion whatever to the trusts. Since that time, its course has been more and more in the direction of plutocracy, more and more in the direction of the government of the few to the disregard of the many, and their interests; and it has culminated in an effort to conquer people living in the tropics, and to annex to this country territory that will never be organized into states, and in the establishment of a colonial policy in violation of the Constitution of the United States and of the Declaration of Independence, and of every theory of Government we have advocated as a people.'"

"I believe that colonial possessions mean a standing army of great proportions, and a vast horde of officeholders serving a long distance from home, governing an unwilling people, which must result in constant conflict, and end in the curtailment of the right to vote among our own people, and a suppression of all protest by the armed forces assembled and equipped in the first instance for the purpose of conquering these distant possessions.

"Under these circumstances, no matter what may be the consequences to me personally, I feel it my duty to do everything in my power to overthrow at the polls the dominion and control of the Republican party, and thus restore this country in letter and in spirit back to the principles and doctrines of its founders, so that it may continue to be an example to all people who believe in the doctrine of self-government, and that governments derive their just powers from the consent of the governed.

"I thus write you this long letter, hoping to make my own position clear, and stimulate you to greater activity and effort in the coming campaign. I should like very much to hear from you on this subject.

"Yours truly,
"R. F. PETTIGREW."

22. Hawaii — A Revolution to Order

During the years of my acquaintance with American public life, I have seen the center of power move from Washington to Wall Street. When I first entered the Senate they talked of the "invisible empire of business." During the nineties that empire ceased to be invisible — it came out in the open, and through its representatives and attorneys on the floor of the Senate and the House it fought its battles for privilege and plunder — fought them and won them.

The plutocracy established its right to plunder the people of the United States. Through the banks, the railroads and the trusts, it robbed them openly and shamelessly, and those few of us who fought on the side of the people and against these masters of privilege, were driven out of public life for our pains. Laws aimed to promote the general welfare were not so much as considered in Washington. The work of Congress was, first and last, to protect and safeguard the interests of big business.

I saw this thing and faced it. I fought it in the Senate during twelve years with all the strength and ability at my command, and when those twelve years of struggle were ended, the business power was immeasurably stronger than it was when they began.

The real strength of big business came over the issue of imperialism. The right to plunder at home had been pretty firmly established by the time the Sherman Law was passed in 1890. The right to plunder abroad had never come up for serious consideration.

From 1870 to 1890 the business interests of the United States were busy building railroads, opening mines and establishing factories. Even as late as the nineties there were only a few of the business groups that were looking outside the country for a chance to exploit and rob. Among these few were the sugar men.

The United States has never provided its own sugar supply. The sugar business is a profitable one, however, and the American business men made up their minds that if profits were to be made in sugar they might as well have them.

The fight turned on Hawaii.

The Hawaiian Islands have a climate well adapted to sugar-growing and the soil, a deep volcanic ash overlying boulders, is the best sugar-cane soil in the world. In Hawaii they raise eight tons of sugar to the acre.

Hawaii was owned by foreign capitalists among whom the Americans were the largest single holders.

I had an investigation made when I was in Hawaii of the books of the interior department, for their law required that every sugar corporation should file a report giving the names of the stockholders. All of the corporations did not comply with the law, but several did comply. I had their reports studied and from them it appeared that the holdings in sugar corporations, arranged by nationality, were: American, $3,225,750; British, $1,642,350; Hawaiian, $792,000; German, $458,700; and Portuguese, $1,200, making a total of $6,120,000. In short, more than half of the sugar plantation values were American owned.

The estimates of taxable property in the Islands showed that the Hawaiians, who numbered together 39,504 individuals, owned taxable property to the amount of $8,101,701, while the Americans, British and Germans, 6,768 in number, owned taxable property to the amount of $26,701,908. The "foreigners," while numbering only one-seventh of the taxpayers, owned more than three-quarters of the taxable wealth in the Islands.

Foreign economic interests on the Islands were paramount, and it was these interests that fostered the Revolution of 1893. I need not go into this matter in detail, as I have elaborated on it elsewhere (The Course of Empire,

Chapter 5). Let it suffice to say that the United States Minister, resident at Honolulu, entered into a conspiracy with a few business men and their representatives for the purpose of overthrowing the native government, and deposing the reigning queen. As a part of this conspiracy, the United States Minister used American marines to protect the conspirators while they organized a government, which was immediately recognized by the United States Minister. A treaty, based on this disgraceful incident, was sent to the Senate of the United States for ratification on the recommendation of President Harrison, and was reported favorably by the Committee on Foreign Relations.

The report of the Committee on Foreign Relations did not tell the facts regarding the overthrowing of the Hawaiian Government; neither did the message to the President transmitting the treaty give the essential facts, and it was with great difficulty that the facts were obtained. But the infamy of the whole transaction was finally disclosed and, after a great many months of controversy, the treaty failed to command the two-thirds vote necessary for its ratification.

I was the leader of the fight in the Senate against the treaty and its ratification. The question excited widespread attention. Most of the great newspapers were outspokenly in favor of ratifying the annexation treaty. They filled their columns with false headlines on the subject, and even resorted to the practice of making up press dispatches purported to come from the Islands. Despite all their efforts, however, the treaty could not pass.

There is no longer any dispute over the material facts of the Hawaiian Revolution.

What were the essential facts behind the revolution that led the United States to make its first annexation of non-continental territory. There is no longer any serious dispute concerning them.

George W. Merrill, who was our Minister to Hawaii, wrote Mr. Secretary Blaine, September 7, 1889, as follows:

"It is also noticeable that among the American residents here there are several who, from personal motives, contemplate with satisfaction periodical disquietude in this kingdom, hoping that frequent revolutionary epochs will force the United States Government to make this group a part of its territory and to absorb into its body politic this heterogeneous population of 80,000, consisting of Chinese, Japanese, Portuguese, native Hawaiians, half-castes, and only about 5,000 of those who may be properly denominated the white race.

"In order to keep affairs in as much turmoil as possible, baseless rumors are constantly put in circulation, many of which find publication in other countries."

This was from our minister who was superseded shortly afterward by Mr. Stevens. Mr. Stevens was appointed minister in October, 1889. Harrison had been elected President. One of the issues of the campaign was free sugar. The McKinley Act became a law August 27, 1890. On August 20, 1891, Mr. Stevens wrote to Mr. Blaine as follows:

"The probabilities strongly favor the presumption that a United States warship will not be pressingly necessary in the two or three immediate months. But as early as the first of December, without fail, the month preceding the election, and for some time thereafter, there should be a United States vessel here to render things secure...There are increasing indications that the annexation sentiment is growing among the business men. The present political situation is feverish, and I see no prospect of its being permanently otherwise until these islands become a part of the American Union or a possession of Great Britain."

Here, then, is our minister, accredited to a friendly government, contemplating the destruction of that government and the annexation of its territory. Further on, in his next dispatch, he asked the State Department to keep secret his statement in regard to the overthrow of that government; and he says in the dispatch that it would be uncomfortable for him if the facts were known in Hawaii.

On November 20, 1892, Stevens again writes:

"I think it understating the truth to express the opinion that the loss to the owners of the sugar plantations and mills, etc., and the consequent depreciation of other property by the passage of the McKinley Bill, has not been less than $12,000,000, a large portion of this loss falling on Americans residing here and in California.

"Unless some positive measures of relief be granted, the depreciation of sugar property will go on...

"One of two courses seems to me absolutely necessary to be followed, either bold and vigorous measures for annexation, or a "customs' union," and ocean cable from the Californian coast to Honolulu, Pearl Harbor perpetually ceded to the United States, with an implied, but not necessarily stipulated, American protectorate over the islands. I believe the former to be the better, that which will prove much the more advantageous to the islands, and the cheapest and least embarrassing in the end for the United States."

Here, in 1892, two months before the final revolution, our minister outlines the reason for it and advises annexation as a remedy for the situation. This statement of Minister Stevens is supplied by ample evidence published in the official investigation which President Cleveland caused to be made of the whole situation.

The American Minister had been converted into an advocate of the overthrow of the friendly government to which he was sent; and what was done by these conspirators, few in number, having vast wealth — fortunes made absolutely out of the people of the United States in the profit upon sugar? The American Minister having been secured, the next step was to find an excuse for overthrowing the existing government.

On the 14th of January, 1893, being Saturday, the Queen took steps to promulgate a new constitution. Petitions had been received by her signed by two-thirds of all of the voters of the island, protesting against the Constitution of 1887 and asking that a new one be promulgated. The Constitution of

1887 deprived a large per cent of her people of the right to vote for members of the Senate or any voice in the government. The Constitution left the control of the country in the hands of the foreign business men and the people resented it.

Immediately on the proposition being made to adopt a new Constitution, nine business men had a meeting in Smith's office. Smith was a lawyer in Honolulu. Later, he became an attorney-general of the so-called republic. There they began to plan and plot for the overthrow of the Queen. But, finding that there was opposition to her movement, the Queen abandoned the idea of issuing a new Constitution and, on Monday, January 16, 1893, she issued a statement to that effect.

On Saturday, the 14th, a committee of safety composed of thirteen members had been organized at W. V. Smith's office. At this meeting the feeling was expressed that this was a good time to get rid of the old regime and provide for annexation to the United States. There was no fear of disorder, no thought that life and property were in danger.

Mr. Smith stated that the committee at his office debated whether they would ask the United States to establish a protectorate. They concluded that as the Queen had an armed force it was best to appoint a committee to see the United States Minister, and ascertain what he would do.

After the meeting, Smith went to see the American Minister and arranged with him as to what should be done if Smith and his conspirators were arrested. He secured the required assurances and the call for troops was issued.

These conspirators then held a public meeting and Thurston made some lurid remarks — talked about freedom, etc., and about liberty and tyrannical government — and after his fiery speech they passed the tamest sort of resolutions embodying their protest against the new Constitution, but said not a word about overthrowing the government or establishing a new government.

At every step in the proceeding great care was taken to consult the American Minister and to know just what he should do in case the conspirators were arrested. There was a great sense of fear and apprehension of danger on the part of these thirteen men only. All honest citizens felt safe and secure in life and property.

Troops were landed from the United States gunboat in the harbor, and distributed, not for the purpose of protecting Americans or American property, but to guard the government building and show the Queen that they were assisting the revolutionists. This was Monday evening. On Tuesday morning the Committee of Thirteen met again and signed the proclamation declaring the establishment of a new government, and about two o'clock started, in two parties on different streets, to go to the government buildings, now guarded by United States troops, to read the proclamation, according to a previously arranged plan with our minister.

Without a single armed man they proceeded to the government building and, in front of it, within seventy-five yards of the 150 marines landed from the United States vessel, they proceeded to read the proclamation declaring that they were the government. They, however» took the precaution to go in two parties, one party going up one street and the other party another street, so as not to attract attention. They took the precaution to send one of their number up to see if there were any armed men likely to interfere.

The proclamation having been read at the government building, guarded by United States troops, the United States Minister proceeded at once to recognize the new government. They had not an armed man — they had proceeded to the government building where there were clerks and officers of the Hawaiian Government, with not even a policeman present. They stood up in front of that building within seventy-five yards of the Gatling guns of the marines from an American battleship, and read a paper declaring that they were the government. Three-quarters of a mile away the Queen had five hundred men under arms and, without waiting, the moment they read the proclamation our minister recognized these thirteen men as the government of Hawaii — without any armed forces whatever, knowing that he had violated international law and violated the precedents followed by all civilized nations, and he undertook to falsify the facts.

He claimed that he recognized the government after the Queen had surrendered — after the old government had given up — after she had abdicated and said that she would submit her case to Washington. An investigation of the facts proved that this statement is false.

After the recognition of this so-called government, before the surrender of the Queen or the armed forces which she had, a delegation was sent to her and she surrendered to the armed forces of the United States, saying:

"I yield to the superior force of the United States of America, whose minister plenipotentiary, His Excellency John L. Stevens, has caused the United States troops to be landed at Honolulu and declared that he would support the said provisional government."

To avoid collision and bloodshed, she submitted the question to the Government at Washington, surrendering to the armed forces of the United States; surrendering after Stevens had recognized the so-called government; surrendering because she was told that the Government of the United States, whose people she had always been taught to reverence and respect, would do justice and restore her to the throne, and they cited a precedent in Hawaiian history as a justification for this claim:

"On the 10th of February, 1843, the British frigate Carrysfort, commanded by Lord George Paulet, arrived at Honolulu and showed displeasure by withholding the usual salutes.

"He proceeded at once to take the King prisoner and make such demands upon him that he surrendered his crown on condition that the question would be submitted to the British Government. The "History of the Hawaiian People" says:

"Under the circumstances the King resolved to bear it no longer. 'I will not die piecemeal,' said he; 'they may cut off my head at once. Let them take what they please; I will give no more.'

"Dr. Judd (he was an American) advised him to forestall the intended seizure of the islands by a temporary cession to Lord Paulet, pending an appeal to the British Government. The event proved the wisdom of this advice.

"On the next day the subject was discussed by the King and his council, and preliminaries were arranged with Lord Paulet for the cession. On the morning of the 25th the King and premier signed a provisional cession of the islands to Lord George Paulet, 'subject to the decision of the British Government after the receipt of full information from both parties.'

"At 3 o'clock p. m., February 25th, the King, standing on the ramparts of the fort, read a brief and eloquent address to his people."

Then they submitted the question to Great Britain, and the English Government promptly restored the King to his throne, refusing to accept an usurpation of that sort. So, in this case, the Queen, having in mind this historic incident, said:

"I, Liliuokalani, by the grace of God and under the Constitution of the Hawaiian Kingdom, Queen, do hereby solemnly protest against any and all acts done against myself and constitutional Government of the Hawaiian Kingdom by certain persons claiming to have established a provisional government of and for this kingdom.

"That I yield to the superior force of the United States of America, whose minister plenipotentiary, His Excellency John L. Stevens, has caused United States troops to be landed at Honolulu and declared that he would support the said provisional government.

"Now, to avoid collision of armed forces and perhaps the loss of life, I do, under this protest, and impelled by said force, yield my authority until such time as the Government of the United States shall, upon the facts being presented to it, undo the actions of its representatives and reinstate me in the authority which I claim as the constitutional sovereign of the Hawaiian Islands."

When Kamehameha, in 1843, surrendered and ceded the islands to the British admiral, because he could not resist the force of an armed ship of war, the English Government promptly repudiated the act and restored him to the throne; and when Queen Liliuokalani, deprived of her authority by the armed forces of the United States, proposed to submit the question to this Government, she had good reason to suppose that the great republic would preserve its honor and dignity among the nations of the world and restore her to the throne. Yet, in the face of these facts, the treaty made with this revolutionary government of business men was passed by the Congress of the United States and this country took title to Hawaii against the will of the majority of the people in that country.

On January 31st, thirteen days after the revolution, President Dole wrote Mr. Stevens that his government could not maintain itself, and asked for the protection of the United States troops. Stevens complied, and our flag was put up, over the public buildings, and remained up until April 1, 1893, when Mr. Blount ordered it taken down. If there was a government that had been able to create and establish itself and to maintain itself with an armed force, why was it that thirteen days afterwards they begged of Mr. Stevens, admitting their impotency to maintain their government, to again land the troops of the United States and put the United States flag upon the buildings? This was done on the 31st of January, and the flag remained there sixty days. The flag went up in dishonor. When it was raised under such circumstances it was a disgrace to the Republic.

During the sixty days while our flag remained upon this building, the provisional government brought in foreign mercenaries from San Francisco, collected an armed force, gathered up every gun upon the islands, passed the strictest penal laws against the importation of guns, and made it a criminal and penal offense to have a gun. The so-called republic was surrounded by armed men. Back and forth in front of the public offices marched men with Winchester rifles.

The new government proceeded rapidly to enact laws. It consisted, not of a legislative body, but of nineteen men, self-constituted, supported by our armed forces. They provided that no one should be eligible to be a senator, a representative or a juror until he should have subscribed to the following oath or affirmation:

"I do solemnly swear (or affirm), in the presence of Almighty God, that I will support the constitution, laws and government of the Republic of Hawaii; and will not, either directly or indirectly, encourage or assist in the restoration or establishment of a monarchial form of government in the Hawaiian Islands."

On the 31st an act concerning seditious offenses was published. This law made it an offense to speak, write or print anything which might bring hatred or contem.pt against the government. On the same day was published a law prohibiting the importation of firearms and ammunition without first obtaining the permission of the government. On the same day an act relating to contempts became law: "Any person who shall publish any false report of the proceedings of said council, or insulting comment upon the same," etc., was liable to imprisonment for thirty days.

What did this revolutionary government do? It set up a republic! For nearly a year after the government was created they had no constitution. But after a year the nineteen concluded to organize the Republic of Hawaii. Such a republic was never known to history before. An election was called for a constitutional convention. The call provided that the people who would take an oath to support their government might elect eighteen delegates to the constitutional convention. The revolutionists, nineteen of them, constituted themselves members of the convention without any election, making the election of delegates absolutely a farce. What kind of a constitution did they adopt? Their constitution provided for an oligarchy. It provided that the government should consist of Mr. Dole as president — he was named in the constitution — who was to hold office until the year 1900, a senate of fifteen members and a house of representatives of fifteen members, and the senate and house sitting together were to elect Mr. Dole's successor president after the year 1900, but no successor was to be elected unless he received a majority of the senate; and, if no successor was elected, Dole continued to hold the office.

Under this constitution no person could vote for a senator unless he was worth $3,000 in personal property or $1,500 in real estate, according to the last assessment for taxation, or unless he had an income of $600 a year.

These provisions shut out everybody in the Hawaiian Islands from the right of suffrage except the sugar planters and their fellow business and professional men. Such a qualification would have disfranchised ninety per cent of the voters of the United States.

The constitution created a council of state, five of whom were to be selected by the president, five by the senate and five by the house of representatives; and this very constitution provided that a majority of the council could do business. Then it provided that they could make laws and appropriations when the legislature was not in session, and that their laws and their acts and their appropriations should hold good until the last day of the session of the legislature.

They put into the constitution a provision for a union, commercial or political, with the United States. Did that come from the people? They had no voice in it. The constitution was not endorsed by the people or submitted to the people. After this self-constituted convention had adopted its constitution, it declared the document the constitution of the Republic of Hawaii, and never submitted it to a vote at all. And yet it was from this gang of sugar-raising conspirators that we took the islands.

The annexation of Hawaii was the first big victory won by the business interests in their campaign to plunder outside of the United States. It was the precedent that they needed — the precedent that made easy the annexation of Porto Rico, the Piatt Amendment to the Cuban Treaty, the conquest of the Philippines and the other imperialistic infamies that have sullied the good name of the United States during the past twenty years.

When I entered this fight against the annexation of Hawaii, I had a vague impression of the power that could be exerted by big business. The fight lasted five years, and when it was ended, I had a clear, full knowledge of the methods and the strength of the American plutocracy. I entered the fight, knowing that it would be a hard one. I left it, wondering that we had been able to hold off the interests for as many as five years.

23. Anti-Imperialism

The Senate debates over the annexation of Hawaii had roused millions of Americans to the imperial menace that was threatening the life of the Republic. Between 1893, when the revolution occurred in Hawaii, and 1898, when the annexation of the islands was finally approved under the stress of the war frenzy that possessed the country, I carried on almost a continual fight against the policy of those who were advocating annexation. The friends of the treaty were not able, during those five years, to secure anything like the necessary two-thirds of the Senate, and the fight against annexation might have been won but for the Spanish-American War with its tidal wave of patriotic frenzy.

It was on July 7, 1898, after the war had been in progress for more than two months, and after the public attention had been turned from the problems of imperialism to the celebration of victory, that Hawaii was annexed, and even then the imperialists still lacked their two-thirds of the Senators, so that it was necessary to provide for annexation by a joint resolution which required only a majority of both Houses of Congress.

With the end of the war there was a swing back toward sanity and a vigorous protest rose from all parts of the country.

Millions of the plain people were eager to stem the tide of imperialism that was running so strongly in favor of the big business interests and their policies.

As one means of checking imperialism an Anti-Imperialist League was formed about 1899. The league had a large popular membership — about half a million, I believe — held mass meetings and conferences in all parts of the country — adopted a platform that denounced the imperialism of the McKinley administration, and pledged itself to enter politics and fight the issue through to a finish in every voting precinct in the United States.

Pursuant to this program, a conference was called at the Plaza Hotel in New York, for the 6th of January, 1900. The national elections were due in November of the same year; it seemed certain that McKinley would seek a second presidential term on his record as an advocate of annexation and conquest; there was, therefore, an excellent chance to make a clear issue and to organize a large enough sentiment within the ranks of both old parties to administer a severe rebuke to the business interests that were behind the Republican party and its imperial policies.

The meeting of January 6th turned out to be an eventful one. Andrew Carnegie was present, as well as Carl Schurz, ex-Senator Henderson, Brisbane Walker, Gamaliel Bradford, Edward Burrett Smith, Prof. Franklin H. Giddings, and about ten others. All were prominent men, and all were radically opposed to any movement that looked towards the holding of colonies against the will of the inhabitants and in violation of the principles enunciated in the Constitution and the Declaration of Independence. I was the only Senator or member of the House present at this meeting.

We had our meals brought to us, and talked all day. Finally we decided that we would organize a third political party.

It was agreed by Carnegie and Schurz and Henderson and by Prof. Giddings that the two old political parties — Democratic and Republican — were just alike; that as parties they were simply the servants of the great combinations and corporations who were the real rulers of the country; that it was foolish to depend upon either of them to oppose a policy which was being pushed by their financial backers and, therefore, it was decided to start a third party and to organize it in every county in the United States.

Mr. Carnegie, in a vigorous speech, urged the necessity of a new political party for the purpose of opposing the imperial policy of both of the old parties, and said that he would give as much money, dollar for dollar, as all the rest of us could raise toward promoting the campaign. As a pledge of good faith, he subscribed twenty-five thousand dollars on the spot.

The others present subscribed a like amount, elected Edward Burrett Smith, of Chicago, chairman of the political organization which they were forming, and authorized him, in consultation with the committee which had been appointed, to take charge of the campaign, to secure an organization in every county in the United States, and to have national committeemen from every state.

Carnegie paid in $15,000 of the $25,000 he had subscribed. The others paid in the whole of their subscription ($25,000) and active work was begun within a month. Shortly after the New York meeting Carnegie came to my house in Washington, talked about the whole matter with me, and expressed great earnestness and anxiety about the success of the movement. I had every reason to believe that Carnegie meant to stand by the movement, and I felt convinced that his financial position and influence would enable us to raise a sufficient amount of money to carry on an effective campaign against McKinley and his imperialist backers.

I had known Andrew Carnegie very well for many years. I first became intimately acquainted with him during the contest in the Senate over the annexation of the Hawaiian Islands. I led the opposition to the annexation of those islands chiefly because the annexation would mean that we were starting upon a colonial system, acquiring a territory inhabited by a people not suited to our form of government, and that such a move would be the first step in the course of empire. Carnegie was of the same view, and, during the contest, often came to my house in Washington and discussed the question with me.

At the same time, I was investigating the question of the distribution of wealth in the United States, and I discussed the matter with him and, finally, made a speech in the Senate on that question. Carnegie agreed with me that the concentration of wealth in a few hands and the move for imperialism were both serious menaces to the American people and their liberties. Carnegie was not then so enormously rich as he afterwards became.

194

Carnegie was a rich man even in 1900, but he had liberal views. I had known him for years, and had known during all of that time that he was vigorously opposed to imperialism. His support of the anti-imperialist movement, therefore, seemed to represent a very substantial part of the foundation upon which the movement was built.

The story of our plans was soon noised abroad, and it became known that an effort was being made to organize a third political party with the backing of Andrew Carnegie. About the middle of February I received a letter from Mr. Smith urging me to come to New York. I went at once, and was told by Mr. Smith that Carnegie had refused to pay in any more money after his first fifteen thousand dollars, and that he had refused to have anything to do with the members of the committee, although they had made repeated efforts to see him and to get into communication with him. In view of my acquaintance with Carnegie, Mr. Smith thought that I was the best person to see him and ascertain why he had abandoned the project about which he had been so enthusiastic only a month before.

I called upon Mr. Carnegie, but he refused to see me. I then went down to Wall Street to see some friends and acquaintances who were interested in the business side of national affairs, and to inquire why Carnegie had abandoned his effort to organize a third party, and had gone back on the whole anti-imperialist position of which he was an acknowledged advocate. I was not long in discovering the real difficulty.

The steel trust had been talked about and planned by the great capitalistic combinations of this country, and Carnegie was one of the parties to the negotiations. The matter had gone so far that the following propositions were agreed upon: First, they were to organize a corporation with one billion dollars of stock, none of which was to be paid for; second, they were to issue four hundred million dollars of bonds to pay for the properties and furnish working capital. Carnegie was to receive one hundred and sixty millions of this four hundred millions of bonds and, in addition, a like amount of the stock, and he was, of course, very anxious to consummate this deal which was of enormous financial advantage to him.

No sooner was it noised abroad that Carnegie was actively engaged in organizing a third political party, which would oppose McKinley and his imperialist policy, than he was waited on by a committee, with the ultimatum that they would go no further with the organization of the steel trust unless he abandoned his third party activities and stopped his contributions towards the movement. The members of the committee told him that it was absolutely necessary that they should have a protective tariff in order to justify the organization of the steel trust; that in order to have a tariff satisfactory to them, McKinley must be elected; that the organization of a third party would jeopardize his election, and, consequently, the tariff, and as they were going to capitalize the tariff by the issue of stock for which they paid nothing, they would have nothing further to do with the steel trust if Carnegie insisted upon pursuing the political course he had outlined.

The issue was a very clear one — political principles on one side and immense financial profits on the other. After weighing the matter, Carnegie abandoned the whole third party movement and went in for the election of McKinley.

Subsequently, the steel trust organization was completed and Carnegie received his quota of the bonds and stock of the combination. He then retired from active business and began to build monuments to himself all over the world.

The anti-imperialist movement, which had depended so largely upon Carnegie's support, worked on for a time, hampered by a shortage of funds and a lack of effective interest in influential quarters. Its efforts were virtually nullified by Carnegie's withdrawal and the lukewarm support from other sources. The Republicans won the election. The steel trust secured the tariff it needed. The combination was perfected. The imperial policy of the preceding four years was confirmed by the election, and the hopes of those who had worked so loyally against the change of national policy were destroyed.

Undoubtedly we made a mistake to pin so much faith on the actions of one man — particularly in view of his business connections. On the other hand, his friendship, his determination and his apparent sincerity gave us every reason to believe that he could be relied upon to see the movement through.

We had made the issue — in Congress and out. We had set the Declaration of Independence against the conquest of the Philippines and the Constitution against the Hawaiian Treaty. We had placed the rights of man against the interests of the plutocracy. We had done everything that human ingenuity and energy and foresight could do to make our fight effective, and we had lost out. McKinley, the steel trust, big business and imperialism had won.

24. Criminal Aggression in the Philippines

The annexation of Hawaii and the Spanish Treaty, which provided for the acquisition by the United States of Porto Rico, Guam and the Philippines, started this country definitely on the course of empire. From that point — the years 1898 and 1899 — we were committed to an imperial policy.

"Imperial policy" is a phrase with a pleasant sound and a dismal echo — dismal for the rights of man and women. The moment we adopted an imperial policy we committed ourselves to certain lines of national conduct that are as far from the principles of the Declaration of Independence as the east is from the west. In our new possessions it was necessary:

First, to beat into submission any of the native population which displays a spirit of independence;

Second, to extend the imperial boundaries in order to have more opportunity for exploitation;

Third, to establish measures that will insure the effective exploitation of the native population.

Our first imperial duty — that of beating the native population into submission — was presented only in the Philippines. The Cubans were nominally self-governing; the inhabitants of Porto Rico had welcomed the Americans as saviors.

The Filipinos had followed the same course at first, but, when they found that they were not to be free, they turned about and fought as stubbornly for their independence of American rule as they had fought during the preceding century for their independence of Spanish rule. It was the strength of the American army, not the justice of the American cause, that reduced the Filipinos to submission.

Perhaps nowhere in American history is there a record so black as that which describes our dealings with the Filipinos. Before the seizure of the islands by Admiral Dewey, McKinley had taken a high moral stand on the subject of forcible annexation. In his message to Congress (April 11, 1898) he had said: "I speak not of forcible annexation, for that cannot be thought of. That, by our code of morals, would be criminal aggression." So it would, but we practiced it toward the Filipinos with the same zest that the British have displayed in India or the Japanese in Korea.

When we decided to attack Spain, when Dewey was ordered to sail from Hong Kong and to destroy the Spanish fleet, a rebellion was going on in the Philippine Islands. The inhabitants of those islands were trying to throw off the Spanish yoke. Knowing that at Singapore there was a man, the most capable among the Filipinos, who had led a former revolt, our officers in the East induced this man to go back to Manila and organize the insurgent forces. Aguinaldo arrived on the 17th day of May, 1898. He immediately organized the insurgent forces. He purchased arms in Hong Kong. Admiral Dewey furnished him with arms taken from the Spanish forces, and he attacked the Spanish garrisons all over the province of Cavite and secured arms from his prisoners. He pursued this course during the summer of 1898, until he had captured the entire island of Luzon except two Spanish garrisons — very small ones — and before winter he captured those. Dewey, in his report, says his progress was wonderful. He took 9,000 prisoners. After having captured the entire island, he set up a government, which was a peaceful government, a government suitable to those people, a government which protected life and property throughout the entire area of that country. He also captured the Southern Islands, the Island of Panay, of Cebu, and Negros, and organized governments there.

He assembled an army of 30,000 men and surrounded Manila. His army was intrenched. He invested the city on the land side while our navy blockaded the port on the ocean side. We acted in absolute concert with each other, consulted together, and, when Manila was finally taken, our troops landed, asking the insurgents to give up about a quarter of a mile of their trenches. They marched out and allowed our troops to occupy a portion of their works. They believed that they were to act in concert with us in the attack upon Manila. When the attack was ordered their troops marched into the city

197

along with ours. They took the principal suburb of Manila. We took and occupied the walled city. When they came to the walled city, which contained less than one-fifth of the population of the city of Manila, they found our bayonets turned against them. They were told that they could not enter. They had lost thousands of lives in their contest with Spain; they were in possession of that entire country, and yet, although in the assault upon the city they had lost more men than we did, they were denied admittance to the city, and they yielded and occupied the suburbs for some time.

Finally, we requested that they retire from the suburbs and they retired. Aguinaldo asked that he might be permitted to retire slowly, as it was difficult to govern his people and convince them that it was right that they should surrender possession of territory which they had conquered and for which many of their comrades had laid down their lives. He also asked that, in case we made a treaty with Spain, the territory which he had conquered should be restored to him; and this we refused. So we did not conquer the islands from Spain, for Spain had been conquered and driven out by the government of Aguinaldo. We had simply helped to take the city of Manila. Therefore, we took no title by conquest from Spain, for, at the time of making the treaty with Spain, we had not conquered any territory from her.

We did not acquire title by purchase, because title by purchase required delivery of possession and, as Spain was not in possession, she could not and did not deliver the islands to us. By what right are we there? By no right in morals of law; by no right that can be defended before God or man. We are there as conquerors; we are there as armed banditti that would enter your premises in daytime, and we have no more right to be there than the bandit has to enter and despoil your home.

If our title is by conquest, then it is as yet incomplete. If our title is by conquest, we did not acquire it from Spain, and it is nearly two years since the war with Spain has ceased, and yet the conquest is in progress.

In October Aguinaldo was again asked to give up more territory. He was again asked to retire his troops beyond not only the city of Manila, but the adjoining towns. Then he called the attention of General Otis to the fact that the towns which Otis desired him to surrender were not a part of Manila — you will find it on pages 20 and 21 of General Otis' report. General Otis said, "You are right; the territory which I now demand I cannot find as embraced in the city of Manila or its suburbs, but," he said, "that makes no difference; I insist on the possession of the territory anyway." So our lines were pushed out constantly, creating irritation and bad feeling.

Finally Dewey seized the ships of the Filipinos in the harbor. Was not that an act of war? Why talk longer about who commenced the war in the Philippines, when in October we seized the vessels of our allies — and they were vessels of war — dismissed the men who manned them, took down the Filipino flag, and removed it from the sea?

On the 24th of November, Otis again wrote to Aguinaldo, saying that he must retire beyond the village of Santa Mesa, and that if he did not he would attack him. On the 21st of December the President sent a proclamation to be published in the Philippines, telling the inhabitants that the United States has assumed sovereignty over the islands — a proclamation which was a clear declaration of war — a declaration that we would extend our military control, then existing in the city of Manila, throughout the entire area of the group.

This proclamation was published in the Philippines on the 4th of January, 1899. We seized their ships in October; we drove them beyond the territorial limits of the city of Manila — the only country we had occupied or had any right to occupy under the protocol with Spain; we, on the 4th day of February, attacked their forces and fired the first and second shots, and killed three of their people. After that, on the 5th day of February, the day after hostilities were inaugurated, Aguinaldo asked to have hostilities cease, and said that he had no notion of making an attack on our people and had not done so. The reply was that fighting having once commenced, it should go on to the grim end.

Under these circumstances, we are precluded from taking any other position than that we betrayed and attacked an ally; that we conquered and reduced to subjection an unwilling people; that because we are mighty and because our army is strong enough to destroy the independence of an ally, we have deliberately taken possession of territory that was desired by our big business men for their enrichment.

By our "code of morals" our very presence in the Philippines, after the natives had established their own government, was an offense. By the same code, our greatest crime in the Philippines was the denial by the Washington administration, backed by the army and navy, of the right of self-government. The Filipinos not only desired self-government, but they actually established it before the American army began the conquest of the islands.

One of Lincoln's most famous remarks is as follows:

'Those who deny freedom to others deserve it not for themselves; and under the rule of a just God cannot long retain it."

I believe that is true. I believe the reflex action upon our own people of the conquest of other peoples and their government, against their will, has undermined the free institutions of this country, and has already resulted in the destruction of the republic.

President McKinley urged the conquest of the Philippines because he said they were not fit for self-government. I believe that there are no people fit for any other form of government. Governments are instituted, not bestowed, and therefore derive their just powers from the consent of the governed.

Any nation of people is capable of maintaining as good a government as they are entitled to have. When people can maintain a better government they will evolve it. It is impossible to give them a better government than they can maintain for themselves. A form of government will be as good as the average of the individuals composing the community are willing to have. The American Indians maintained a government and, for them, a better one than we have been able to bestow upon them. The Esquimeaux in the arctic region maintain a government of their own suited to their condition and their circumstances, and it is a better government than anybody else can give them. Would their condition be improved by sending them foreign governors and a foreign council to enact laws and direct their course and method in life and to guide them in their civic and civil affairs? So it is with every other people the world around. There is nothing in the history of the colonies of the so-called Christian nations of the world to encourage the idea that we can give to this people a better government than they can maintain by themselves.

The old doctrine of the divine right of kings, of the hereditary right to rule, is a doctrine that we Americans disputed and controverted when we established our government, and when we announced the doctrine of the Declaration of Independence. So proud have we been of that discovery that each year we have celebrated the birth into the world of a new theory, a new doctrine with regard to governments; and four hundred constitutions have been framed after ours. So powerful has been our example throughout the world that nation after nation, struggling to be free, has adopted our form of government.

No nation, no people, in all time and in all history ever impressed such a powerful influence upon the human race as this republic, and for this reason alone. Empires have been established; since history began a trail of blood has been drawn across the world, and a vast aggregation of people has been brought under the rule of an emperor or monarch, but no people in the history of the world has ever produced such a powerful effect for good upon the human race as this great republic, and simply because of the doctrine laid down by our forefathers in the Declaration of Independence.

Is it an old doctrine that all governments derive their just powers from the consent of the governed? Some have said that it was a nursery rhyme sung around the cradle of the republic. The doctrine is new. It was announced little more than a century ago, a day in the birth and life of nations, and yet this great republic deliberately abandoned it for the old doctrine and the old theory and the old idea of selfishness.

Lincoln, in his speech at Springfield on June 26, 1857, thus defined his notions of the Declaration of Independence:

"In those days our Declaration of Independence was held sacred by all and thought to include all; but now, to aid in making the bondage of the negro universal and eternal, it is assailed and sneered at, and construed, and hawked at, and torn, till, if its framers could rise from their graves, they could not at all recognize it. All the powers of earth seem rapidly combining against him, mammon is after him, ambition follows, philosophy follows, and the theology is fast joining the cry...

"I think the authors of that notable instrument intended to include all men; they did not mean to say all were equal in color, size, intellect, moral development or social capacity. They defined with tolerable distinctness in what

200

respects they did consider all men created equal — equal with "certain inalienable rights, among which are life, liberty and the pursuit of happiness." This they said, and this they meant. They did not mean to assert the obvious untruth that all were actually then enjoying that equality, not yet that they were about to confer it immediately upon them. In fact, they had no power to confer such a boon. They meant simply to declare the right, so that the enforcement of it might follow as fast as circumstances should permit.

"They meant to set up a standard maxim for free society, which should be familiar to all, and revered by all, constantly looked to, constantly labored for, and, even though never perfectly attained, constantly approximated, and thereby constantly spreading and deepening its influence and augmenting the happiness and value of life to all people of all colors everywhere. The assertion that "all men are created equal" was of no practical use in effecting our separation from Great Britain, and it was placed in the Declaration not for that, but for future use. Its authors meant it to be as, thank God, it now is proving itself, a stumbling block to all those who, in after tim.es, might seek to turn a free people back into the hateful paths of despotism. They knew the proneness of prosperity to breed tyrants, and they meant that when such should reappear in this fair land and commence their vocation they should find left for them at least one hard nut to crack."

It seems to me that Lincoln, with his prophetic vision, must have foreseen this day when prosperity, breeding tyrants, should undertake to declare that the Declaration of Independence no longer applies to anybody but the people whom we decide are capable of self-government.

The holding of tropical countries, the conquest of unwilling people, their retention in subjugation by a standing army, means of necessity not a republic where all the people must be consulted, but a despotism where the will of one man can march armies, declare war and act with great rapidity. A republic is naturally slow in action, because the people must be considered and must be consulted.

We took on many of the semblances of monarchy and of imperialism during the McKinley administration — concealment of facts from the people, denial of news and information, no knowledge of what is going on, no announcement of policy and purpose; and the excuse for it all was that if we should allow the people to know the facts there was danger of creating disapproval of the course of our monarch, and if the enemy should secure these facts it would be of some assistance to them. This is necessary in a monarchy. Press censorship too is a necessary adjunct of imperialism — one of the things our forefathers would not have tolerated for a day. And yet our people are becoming so numb that they are willing to accept it, and even criticize men who protest.

We annexed the Philippines forcibly. That, according to the principles laid down in the Declaration of Independence, is criminal aggression. We departed from the foundation principles of this country; violated its most sacred obligations to the world, and pursued the same brutal, unjustified policy that

Great Britain has pursued wherever her conquering armies have mowed down naked savages with machine guns.

25. Imperialism at Work

The story of our criminal aggression in the Philippines makes bad reading for the liberty-loving American, but it is not the only shameful page in American imperial history — far from it. The United States has been following the course of empire for many a year. Since the days when the white man first came into contact with the American Indians, the English-speaking people of North America, after the example of their cousins across the water, have been robbing weaker nations of their property and calling it civilization.

Our first aggressive war after the Revolution, which made us a nation, was the war in 1846 with Mexico. We invaded Mexico without any provocation and stole from Mexico half her territory and annexed it to the United States. General Grant, in his Memoirs, writes:

'The occupation and annexation of Texas were, from the inception of the movement to its final culmination, to acquire territory out of which slave states might be formed for the American slave-holders. Even if the annexation of Texas could be justified, the manner in which the subsequent war was forced upon Mexico could not." (Vol. 1, p. 33.)

At another point Grant holds that "the war was one of conquest in the interest of an institution." (Vol. 1, p. 115.) Again he states: "It was an instance of a republic following the bad example of European monarchies in not considering justice in their desire to acquire additional territory." (Vol. 1, p. 32.) These are the sentiments of a man who was an officer in the American army that conquered Mexico and who later distinguished himself in the Civil War.

Abraham Lincoln, in the House of Representatives, voted against and denounced the war with Mexico as a great wrong. (See his speech in the House of Representatives, January 12, 1848.) Later in the same year, in a letter to J. M. Peck, Washington, May 21, 1848

(Complete Works, N. Y. Century Company, 1894, Vol. 1, pp. 120-122), he writes:

"It is a fact that the United States army, in marching to the Rio Grande, marched into a peaceful Mexican settlement, and frightened the inhabitants away from their homes and their growing crops. It is a fact that Fort Brown, opposite Matamoras, was built by that army within a Mexican cotton field...It is a fact that when the Mexicans captured Captain Thornton and his command they captured them within another Mexican cotton field."

We went into Mexico because we had taken a fancy to some of Mexico's territory. After a war that lasted two years we helped ourselves to nearly nine hundred thousand square miles of land. That was the first great military triumph of the American imperialists.

Our next performance was the annexation of the Hawaiian Islands, and this was closely followed by the conquest of the Philippines. This robbery did not inure to the benefit of the laboring people of the United States, but exclusively to the advantage of the exploiting speculators and plunderers.

The Mexican War occurred more than seventy years ago. Between that time and the Spanish War exactly fifty years elapsed without a single act of aggression or a single war of conquest waged by the United States. Those were the years during which the slave oligarchy of the South was replaced by the power of an exploiting plutocracy of the North — the years that saw the rise to power of a new ruling class in the United States. The new rulers were busy with their internal affairs at first. By the time of the Spanish-American War, however, they had found their stride and they have been lengthening it ever since.

We had scarcely reduced the Philippines to subjection when the Roosevelt administration became involved in the taking of Panama, one of the most infamous episodes that ever disgraced American history.

The Republic of Colombia is situated on the north coast of South America and embraced the whole of the Isthmus of Panama. It has a government modeled after that of the United States, and is composed of several independent states having governors and legislative bodies of their own. The Isthmus of Panama was the State of Panama, one of the states composing this Republic of Colombia.

In 1903, while Roosevelt was President, he negotiated with the French company that held the franchise for the purchase of the then uncompleted canal across the Isthmus and approached the Republic of Colombia with an offer of ten million dollars if they would cede to the United States a strip ten miles wide across the Isthmus. The cession was to grant sovereign rights and thus give the United States exclusive control over the Canal. At the same time this cession would cut the State of Panama in two. Colombia was afraid to deal with us for fear that we, having obtained a foothold at Panama, might take the whole country. She therefore declined to sell the Canal Zone.

Roosevelt thereupon sent out navy and our marines to Colon, which is the port on the Gulf side of the Isthmus of Panama, and secretly notified the government of the State of Panama that, if they would set up a republic and revolt against the Republic of Colombia, he would give them the ten millions of dollars for the canal strip, and would also see that Colombia did not send any troops to suppress their rebellion. The Governor of Panama agreed to this arrangement, and, at the proper time, started a rebellion to set up an independent government.

The Republic of Colombia sent sufficient troops to overthrow and suppress the rebellion, but Roosevelt had instructed the officers in control of the American marines not to allow Colombia to land any troops in Panama or to interfere with what went on there. Pursuant to their instructions, our officers refused to allow the Colombian troops to proceed to the scene of rebellion, but, instead, turned them back and compelled them to return to Colombia.

On November 2, 1903, the Department of State at Washington telegraphed the naval authorities at the Isthmus as follows:

"(a) Keep the transit free and uninterrupted. Should there be a threat of interruption by armed force, occupy the railroad line; prevent the landing of any armed force having hostile intentions, whether the government or insurgent, at Colon, Portobelo, or any other point. Prevent landing if in your judgment it might precipitate a conflict.

"(b) In case of doubt regarding the intentions of any armed force, occupy Ancon Hill and fortify it with artillery."

About 3:40 P. M. on November 3, 1903, Loomis, Acting Secretary of State, sent the following telegram to the person in charge of the United States consulate at Panama:

"We are informed that there has been an uprising on the Isthmus; keep this department informed of everything without delay." The Consul of the United States answered on the same day: "The uprising has not occurred yet; it is announced that it will take place this evening. The situation is critical." [1]

Later on the same day (November 3) at about nine o'clock, Loomis sent the following telegram to the United States consulate at Panama: "Troops which landed from Cartagena must not continue to Panama."

At 10:30 the same day, another telegram was sent to the same official: "If the cablegram to the Nashville (one of the war vessels then at Panama) has not been delivered, inform her captain immediately that he must prevent the government troops from continuing on to Panama or from assuming an attitude which might result in bloodshed."

On the same day, November 3, the following telegram was sent to the Secretary of the Navy by the commander of one of the war vessels stationed at Colon:

"I acknowledge receipt of your telegram of November 2 (above referred to). Before receiving it, there were landed here this morning by the Colombian government about four hundred from Cartagena. There is no revolution on the Isthmus, nor any disturbance. It is possible that the movement to proclaim independence may take place in Panama this evening."

At about 10 o'clock P. M. of the same day, the Department of State at Washington received from the Vice-Consul of the United States in Panama the following telegram: 'The revolt took place this evening at six; there has been no bloodshed. The government will be organized this evening and will be composed of three consuls and a cabinet. It is believed that a similar movement will take place in Colon."

On the same day General Tovar arrived at Colon with a battalion of sharpshooters from the Colombian army, a force more than adequate to handle the uprising on the Isthmus.

On the following day, November 4, Hubbard, commander of one of our war vessels at Colon, sent the Secretary of the Navy the following dispatch: "Government troops (Colombian) now at Colon. I have prohibited the movement of troops in either direction. There has been no interruption of transit yet. I shall make every effort to preserve peace and order."

On November 6, the Secretary of State at Washington, telegraphed to the Vice-Consul in Panama in the following terms: "The people of Panama by an apparently unanimous movement have severed their political bonds with the Republic of Colombia and have assumed their independence. As soon as you are convinced that a de facto government, republican in form and without substantial opposition on the part of its own people, has been established on the Isthmus of Panama, you will enter into relations with it as the responsible government of the territory."

Here, then, was a rebellion by one state against a sister republic — a rebellion which we helped to organize, a rebellion which was assisted by our troops and navy, which were sent in advance to help make the rebellion a success. Is there any more glaring chapter of infamous conduct in the treatment of one nation by another than this proceeding on the part of the United States? I know of nothing that parallels it in its infamy except the annexation of Texas, the acquisition of Hawaii and of the Philippines.

Let me cite one more illustration of the imperialistic methods employed by the United States in its recent dealings with Latin-America. Central America is a country about four times as large as the state of Ohio, and has a population of a little over five million people. The country is divided into five republics — Guatemala, Honduras, Salvador, Nicaragua and Costa Rica. During Taft's administration the United States intervened during a difficulty between some of the Central American states, in which Nicaragua was involved. The United States thereupon said: "Let us have a conference," and the result was that all of the states of Central America except Nicaragua sent delegates to Costa Rica to attend the conference, the object of which was to make perpetual peace in Central America.

The president of Nicaragua refused to send a delegate because the conference had been called by the United States, and he would not recognize the right of the United States to interfere in Central American affairs. Thereupon the United States sent down troops and drove him out of office and put a puppet in his place. Afterwards a meeting was held in Washington of the Central American states, and Nicaragua participated.

At that meeting a League of Nations was formed of the Central American republics, and it was agreed to arbitrate all their differences and thus to end war forever. There was to be an international court to decide the international problems of Central America. Carnegie hailed the proposition with delight, and furnished one hundred thousand dollars to build a marble peace building in Costa Rica.

Meanwhile, the puppet we had set up in the place of the duly elected president of Nicaragua began looting the treasury of Nicaragua, and was finally forced to borrow money. The United States Government thereupon notified their puppet that the New York bankers would let him have all the money he wanted.

In 1912 the people of Nicaragua revolted against the government set up by us, and in order to support our man in authority we landed marines in the capital of Nicaragua, and we have kept them there, and our creatures have been ruling there ever since. Nicaragua contracted further debts, until at last they could not meet their interest payments.

In 1916 Nicaragua was very hard up, and we said to her: "Your case is practically hopeless. You cannot pay interest on your debt. The United States may some time want to build a canal up the San Juan River and through Lake Nicaragua to the Pacific Ocean. Give us the San Juan River and the lake, with the privilege of building the canal when we get ready to do it, and give us that splendid bay of Fonesca, and a little island for a naval base, and we will loan you the money to pay your interest and put things on a new basis." The result was that Nicaragua, having a president of our choice, maintained by our blue jackets, said: "Very good. We will give you the right of way and we will sell you the island, and will take the funds to pay the interest on the money we owe you."

Costa Rica claimed a partial right in the San Juan River, which is the boundary between the two nations. We were therefore proposing to purchase from Nicaragua a part of the territory belonging to Costa Rica. There was a long debate over the subject, and it was finally appealed to the United States during the administration of Grover Cleveland. Cleveland was the judge and gave a clear-cut decision that was just and equitable and satisfactory to all parties.

Another nation now came into the case — San Salvador. The Gulf of Fonesca abuts Nicaragua and it abuts San Salvador. An island in that bay commands the shores of San Salvador, and San Salvodar said: "We object to giving away any naval base in Fonesca Bay, even to the United States, because it threatens our coast." So the case came before the court at Costa Rica — before the League of Nations — and was thoroughly considered and a decision rendered, which was against Nicaragua and the United States and in favor of San Salvador and Costa Rica. Yet, Nicaragua, backed by the United States, refused to recognize the decision of the court. The League of Nations, formed to secure perpetual peace, vanished into thin air.

In 1917 the president of Costa Rica was overthrown, and another president took his place. The matter was referred to President Wilson, and he refused to recognize the rebellion which had occurred over the question of an election during which it appears that Timco, the new president, represented the majority of the people. At any rate, the matter was purely a local one. But Wilson said, "I will not recognize him." Thereupon, the Costa Rica Congress met and recognized the administration of the new president; but Wilson still refused, although the new president had been recognized by every Latin-American country except Panama, Nicaragua and Cuba — all three dominated by the President of the United States.

Recently we have purchased the Danish West Indies, which lie on the ocean side of the Caribbean Sea, without asking the consent of the people living there. We have taken over Santo Domingo; we collect the customs of the country; the finest building in the republic is our customs house, built with Dominican money by Americans and officered by Americans. Haiti, the other half of the island, without any declaration of war by the United States Congress, was seized by President Wilson and is now being administered in every detail by the United States. The excuse given for this action by the Wilson administration was that the Republic of Haiti owed money to the National City Bank of New York. On their account the United States invaded the island, placed it under martial law, suppressed the newspapers, dispersed the legislative assembly, dominated the elections and murdered several thousands of the people. [2]

The Declaration of Independence holds that "All men are created equal; that they are endowed by their Creator with certain inalienable rights; that among them are life, liberty and the pursuit of happiness. That to secure these rights, governments are instituted among men, deriving their just powers from the consent of the governed." I should like to call Jefferson as a witness and have him tell us what he thinks of these disgusting perversions of American foreign policy.

Again and again the United States has fastened its eyes on a desirable piece of territory and then sent its armies to fulfill its territorial ambitions. Again and again the American flag has floated over battlefields where the victors were invaders from the United States, while the men, fighting desperately in defense of their homes, their children and their liberties, were the inhabitants of small, weak, defenseless countries that could not stand before the organized might at the disposal of the great northern empire.

The essence of imperialism is the extension, by armed force, of the rule of one people over another — as we extend our rule over the southwest; over the Philippines; over Haiti and over Nicaragua. Such armed conquest is recorded among the acts of imperialists in every age. During the past two generations our American imperialists have greatly extended the list.

One annexation leads to another annexation. One act of aggression is followed by a second. The principle of expansion established by Jefferson, and which he considered to be "beyond the Constitution," is acclaimed by Roosevelt with enthusiasm. Meanwhile, Roosevelt, who boasted of the taking of Panama from Colombia, scores "the feeble diplomacy of Jefferson's administration" (Winning of the West, Vol. VI, p. 261) and refers to Jefferson and Madison as "peaceful men, quite unfitted to grapple with an enemy who expressed himself through deeds rather than words," and as "two timid, well-meaning statesmen." (Ibid. p. 271.) In 1803 the Constitution was still virile and respected. Even a President of the United States hesitated to transgress it. Exactly a century later a President could act as Roosevelt acted in Panama; could consider himself an exemplary American, and could taunt those who had tried to observe the Constitution during an earlier generation with being "peaceful," "timid," and "well-meaning."

Between Jefferson's hesitancy over the purchase of Louisiana in 1803 (a contiguous territory) and Roosevelt's eager seizure of Panama in 1903, there stretched a century that witnessed a slow, but steady shifting from the principles of Jefferson and the Declaration of Independence to the principles of Caesar, Napoleon, McKinley, Roosevelt, Wilson, the Piatt Amendment and the Peace Treaty of Versailles.

Since the annexation of Hawaii in 1898 the United States has been speeding away from her old policies; abandoning her old positions and devoting herself to a venture in imperialism that drags her down to the level of the British Empire, the Japanese Empire, the Roman Empire, the great empire of Alexander, or of any other conquering people, past or present.

[1] This correspondence will be found in House Document 8, 58th Congress, 1st Session, which contains the official correspondence connected with the Panama Revolution of 1903.
[2] General Barnett placed the number killed by the American forces at 3,250.

26. Benevolent Assimilation

During the five eventful years that intervened between the Hawaiian Revolution and the passage of the treaty of annexation, I did all that a man could do to prevent the American people from taking this fatal step. As a reward for my efforts I was denounced, vilified and condemned. The lawyers in the Senate, representing the business interests that were seeking the ratification of the treaty, put everything possible in the way of my work. Still I succeeded in blocking the ratification of the treaty for five years. Then came the break with Spain. When the Spanish War fever swept the country I knew that the fight on the Hawaiian Treaty was lost. Since that day in July, 1898, when the Hawaiian Treaty was ratified, for twenty-two years I have watched the progress of the United States along the path of empire. Through these years, likewise, I have done what I could to bring the real facts of the situation to the attention of the American people. It may be too late to save them from the fate that hangs over them, but at least I want them to know where they are going, and why.

I want the American people to know what to say when they are told that United States business men and United States soldiers are in the Philippines, Porto Rico, Santo Domingo and Panama to bless the inhabitants of these countries. I want them to know that it is an oft-repeated story — the plea of "helping the backward nations."

The cry that we have entered upon our imperial course in order to benefit the native populations in the lands that we have conquered or annexed is an old one. Dickens personified it splendidly in his character, the Reverend Mr. Chadband. Dickens' description of the encounter between the reverend gentleman and a street waif is as follows:

"Stretching forth his flabby paw, Mr. Chadband lays the same on Jo's arm and considers where to station him. Jo, very doubtful of his reverend friend's intentions and not at all clear but that something practical and painful is going to be done to him, mutters, 'You let me alone. I never said nothing to you. You let me alone.'

"'No. my young friend,' says Chadband, smoothly, 'I will not let you alone. And why? Because I am a harvest laborer, because I am a toiler and a moiler, because you are delivered over unto me and are become as a precious instrument in my hands. My friends, may I so employ this instrument as to use it to your advantage, to your profit, to your gain, to your welfare, to your enrichment. My young friend, sit upon this stool.'

"Jo, apparently possessed by an impression that the reverend gentleman wants to cut his hair, shields his head with both arms."

How well Dickens knew human nature! How characteristically he describes the crafty gentry who use fair words to cover up foul deeds. Had he lived today and watched the practice of American imperialism, he would have been satisfied to let Mr. Chadband give way before his betters.

I have before me McKinley's proclamation to the Filipinos, and I have placed it side by side with a proclamation of the King of Assyria, written eighteen hundred years before Christ. A man would think that McKinley had plagiarized the idea from Asshurbanipal.

Ragozin, in his History of Assyria, gives a literal translation of a proclamation issued by Asshurbanipal to the people of Elam. The Elamites had gone to war. Rather, their country had been invaded by Asshurbanipal's forces, which had overrun the land, cut down the trees, filled up the wells and killed the inhabitants. Asshurbanipal captured the capital city of the Elamites, killed their king, took 208,000 of their people into captivity as slaves, drove off most of the cattle belonging to those that were left, and then sent them this affectionate greeting:

"The will of the king to the men of the coast, the sea,

the sons of my servants.

"My peace to your hearts; may you be well.

"I am. watching over you, and from the sin of your king, Nabubelzikri, I separated you. Now I send you my servant Belibni to be my deputy over you; I have joined with you, keeping your good and your benefit in my sight."

McKinley writes to the Filipinos:

"Finally, it should be the earnest and paramount aim of the administration to win the confidence, respect and affection of the inhabitants of the Philippines by insuring to them in every possible way the full measure of individual rights and liberties which is the heritage of a free people, and by proving to them that the mission of the United States is one of benevolent assimilation, which will substitute the mild sway of justice and right for arbitrary rule. In the fulfillment of this high mission, while upholding the temporary administration of affairs for the greatest good of the governed, there will be sedulously maintained the strong arm of authority to repress disturbance and to overcome all obstacles to the bestowal of good and stable government upon the people of the Philippine Islands."

This reads very much like King George III of Great Britain, who said, with reference to the rebellious American colonists:

"I am desirous of restoring to them the blessings of law and liberty equally enjoyed by every British subject, which they have fatally and desperately exchanged for the calamities of war and the arbitrary tyranny of their chiefs."

Every conqueror, every tyrant, every oppressor, utters just such pious phrases to justify his course of action. The English-speaking people are particularly adept at this form of hypocrisy. Each act of aggression, each new expedition of conquest is prefaced by a pronouncement containing a moral justification and an assurance to the victims of the imperial aggression that all is being done for their benefit.

What are we about in the United States? Why this rush to control the Philippines, Haiti, Costa Rica? The answer can be given in one word — exploitation! It is the search for markets; the search for trade; the search for foreign investment opportunities that is leading us to the South and to the East. The plutocracy is after more profits — that is the cause behind American imperialism.

The imperialists' aim is to assimilate, not the people of these possessions, but their lands and their wealth. If the people will work, the American plutocrats will exploit their labor as well as the resources of their respective countries. If the people refuse to work, they will be brushed aside, and men and women who will be more amenable to discipline will be imported from some other country to take their places. Who was responsible for the Hawaiian revolution and for the subsequent annexation to the United States? The American and other capitalists who had gained possession of the best land on the islands. What interests led the State Department to interfere in Haiti and in Nicaragua? The same business forces. Imperialism is imperialism the world over. Occasionally it is sufficiently enlightened to have some regard for the welfare of the exploited populations. At other times it is as blind and ignorant and ferocious as the policy of the British imperialists in China.

I spent a portion of the year 1898 in China and Japan, traveling extensively over both empires. At first hand, and from the best authority, I learned the policy that the British Government had pursued with regard to the traffic in opium, and I submit it as an excellent example of the way in which the empire builders act where they have an opportunity to make profits out of the wretchedness and suffering of a weaker people.

In Peking, I had several conferences with Li Hung Chang, who was then an old man, having been the virtual ruler of China for very many years under the Empress Dowager. In one of the conferences I asked Li Hung Chang why he did not stamp out opium smoking in China. He replied that he could not because the English Government refused to allow the Chinese to interfere with the trade. He then told me that in some of the provinces of China (for China is divided into a number of States) the Governors were raising poppies and making opium, in order to beat the English out of the trade in China. He said that he had tried to secure an agreement with the English under which he was to stop the raising of poppies in China provided the English would stop importing opium. This he had been unable to do, as the trade in opium was an English monopoly conducted by the Government itself.

According to his statement, the English had set apart a million acres of the best land in India for the purpose of raising poppies, and had compelled the people of India to raise the poppies and sell the product exclusively to the English Government. The English had built a factory to manufacture the opium, and every package that left the factory was decorated with the coat of arms of Queen Victoria. Opium was little used in China until the English introduced it early in the nineteenth century. The Emperor had protested against the opium trade, but the English Government insisted upon its right to sell opium to the Chinese. Finally, the Emperor of China sent his men aboard some English ships that were lying, loaded with opium, in the harbor of Canton and threw the poison into the sea. Seventy years earlier the American colonists had set the precedent for this Canton opium party by going aboard the British ships in Boston Harbor and throwing the tea overboard. Today the anniversary of the "Boston Tea Party" is one of the fete days of the people of New England. The British liked the exploit as little as the other, however, and they began a war with China (1840). This war, sometimes called the First Opium War, went against China, and she was compelled to cede Hong Kong to the British, to open four other ports to British trade, and to pay an indemnity of 5,525,000 pounds sterling into the British Treasury. The matter came in for a good deal of comment in Parliament, but eventually it was dropped. [1] In 1857 a new controversy arose, and the Emperor again undertook to exclude English opium, giving as the reason that it was destroying his people; that the drug was a deadly drug and was causing great injury, and he enacted laws making it a criminal offense for the people of China to smoke opium, or for anyone to import the drug. In connection with this campaign he confiscated the opium that the English had already imported and imprisoned the people who handled it.

England thereupon declared another war upon China which was called the Second Opium War (1858-1862). Again China was defeated. Canton was bombarded; Peking was threatened; and, after a disastrous struggle, the Chinese made a treaty under which several new ports were opened to British trade; a British Ambassador was received at Peking, and China paid an indemnity of 4,000,000 pounds sterling to the British. After each war, the British were able to bring opium into a few more Chinese ports.

Li Hung Chang spoke with great bitterness of this conduct on the part of a so-called Christian nation, and went quite largely into the question of the injurious use of opium. He also presented me with a copy of the treaty made between China and Japan after the China-Japanese War, which had occurred only a few years before I visited Peking. This treaty was written in English and Chinese, and the book handed me contained Li Hung Chang's picture and autograph, and the entire record of the conversations held at Shimonoseki between the ruler of China and Count Ito, the representative of Japan.

The terms of the treaty compelled China to cede to Japan the Island of Formosa, which had an area of 13,000 square miles, and was inhabited by four million Chinamen. In the conversation which preceded this treaty, Count Ito asked Li Hung Chang why he did not stamp out the opium traffic in China, as he had promised to do at Tientsin ten years before. Li Hung Chang answered that he could not do it because the English Government would not allow it. "Furthermore," said he to Count Ito, "if you take the island of Formosa and stop opium smoking, it will result in a war with England." To this Ito replied: "That may be true, but we will stamp out opium smoking even if it does result in war."

When I heard that story, told impressively by a member of the race that had suffered such wrong at the hands of British imperialism, I could not help comparing it in my mind with the participation of America in the slave trade, and wondering what new infamies the imperialist policy in which we were then, and still are engaged, would lead us to in the course of the present century.

The British had nothing against the Chinese. They sold them opium because there was money in it. If there had been no profits in the trade there would have been no opium war. Our imperial ventures, like those of the British, are financial. We are in the imperialist business because it pays the plutocrats to be there.

I never realized this so completely as in the winter of 1900, when a delegation from Porto Rico visited the city of Washington for the purpose of having the products of Porto Rico admitted free of duty to the United States. The delegation came before the Committee on Insular Affairs, of which I was then chairman, and asked for a hearing. I therefore called the members of the committee together so that they might hear the Porto Rican delegation present its case.

There were five members in the delegation— two Englishmen, two Spaniards and a Frenchman. I had one of the Englishmen take the stand first and asked him what it was he desired the Congress of the United States to do. He answered that the delegation desired to have the products of Porto Rico — sugar, tobacco and tropical fruits— admitted to the United States free of duty.

I then asked him. "Are you a citizen of the United States?"

"No," was his reply. "I am a citizen of England, but a resident of the United States."

"Are you going to become a citizen of the United States?" I asked. He replied that he was not.

I then asked what interest he had in Porto Rico. He answered that he owned 200,000 acres of land.

"You are working your land at the present time?" I asked.

"Not to any great extent," he replied. He then explained that the land could raise great crops of sugar that might very nearly supply the United States if the industry were encouraged by having the sugar admitted free of duty.

In answer to a question about the people that were occupying his lands in Porto Rico, the Englishman explained that they were "natives."

"Are they your tenants?" I said to him. "Do they rent the land from you?"

"Yes," he answered. "They live in single-room houses as a rule, elevated from the ground on posts, one post at each corner. As a rule the houses are from six to eight feet from the ground." He then told us how the natives built a floor on top of these posts and then made a palm-leaf hut in which they resided. For support they planted yams and dry-land bananas and raised chickens and pigs. They paid their rent for the use of the land by a certain number of days' work on the Englishman's plantation.

To my question as to the character of the people, he replied that they were "good people." When I asked him whether they could read or write, he said they could not, since there were no provisions on the island for their education.

I then put the other Englishman on the stand. He told the same story. After that I questioned the two Spaniards and the Frenchman. They all owned several hundred thousand acres of land, which were being used more or less in the way already described. All spoke of the native inhabitants as "good people," as mostly white people, and as entirely illiterate.

I asked if there were any of the natives who owned their own land. All agreed that there were very few such.

After I had taken their testimony in full, and had showed up the enormities of the economic system then existing in Porto Rico, I told them that the hearing was closed; that as long as I remained chairman of the Committee on Insular Affairs they would get no legislation enacted admitting their product free of duty; that if I could have my way about it I would cancel their title to every acre of the lands of Porto Rico and make the title out to the people of the United States. That I would then give an inalienable title to every person in Porto Rico for all the land that he could actually use, and levy taxes upon them for the compulsory education of their children.

"What!" they exclaimed. "Take our property without paying us for it?"

"It is not your property," I answered. "The land of Porto Rico belongs to the people who inhabit it and who work it. I would not pay you a dollar for your pretended title or allow you to remain there for one day to exploit the inhabitants of that island or to hold a single acre of that land in excess of the amount actually occupied and cultivated by you in person."

Of course, when my term of office expired in 1901 these foreign highwaymen, waiting to prey upon the people of Porto Rico, returned to Washington and secured the legislation they desired. They also secured control of the Government of Porto Rico, and made arrangements for a large armed police force to preserve law and order. They also appealed to Congress to put a duty on Cuban sugar in order to prevent it from competing with Porto Rican sugar. They then returned to the islands and began their work of "economic development."

About the first thing they did was to cancel the leases of the inhabitants who occupied the land. Then they compelled them to work for wages, raising sugar and tobacco, and they refused them the use of any land to raise yams, bananas, pigs and chickens, and they fixed the wages at 50 cents a day in silver. Little provision was made for the education of the people, and the wages were so low that, with their large families, the laborers found it impossible to buy adequate food and clothing. Consequently, their children grew up without clothes — ran naked in the fields and even in the towns — and were put to work as soon as they grew old enough to be of use.

Shortly after this beautiful plan of "economic development" was put in effect, the owners of Porto Rico began to boast of the great things they had done for the people. They told how they had furnished employment; had put up the mills and factories and brought in the machinery to make the sugar out of the raw cane, and to manufacture the tobacco, so that Porto Rico exported §150,000,000 worth of the product per annum to the United States. With it all, the miserable peons of Porto Rico went naked and starving in one of the richest spots of the whole world.

After the first few crops had been harvested, the laborers of Porto Rico went on strike, leaving the cane to sour in the field. Thereupon these foreign pirates, the English, the Spanish, the French and the American planters, called in the police force and the armed men of the United States and shot up the strikers and arrested them and put them back to work in the fields — those they had not wounded or murdered. Thus, economic development pursued its imperial course in Porto Rico, where conditions are as bad today as they were when we took possession of the island twenty-two years ago, and always will remain as bad until the system of exploitation at home and abroad is abandoned and labor is given its just reward.

Lest anyone should think that I am exaggerating, I should like to call attention to a report recently published by the United States Department of Labor, giving a full description of the working and living conditions in Porto Rico. (Labor Conditions in Porto Rico, by Joseph Marcus, Washington, 1919.) The special investigator who wrote the report for the Labor Department, as a result of a careful study of conditions, states that:

The American flag has been flying over the island of Porto Rico for twenty years, yet the percentage of illiteracy is still abnormally high. During the years 1917 and 1918 "only 142,846 children out of a total of 427,666 of school age actually enrolled in the public schools." "The difficulty," says Mr. Marcus, "lies in the bad economic condition" in which the worker finds himself. "Porto Rico is an island of wealthy land proprietors and of landless workers. There is a law in Porto Rico prohibiting any single individual from owning more than 500 acres of land. * * * With the American occupation the price of cane land rose very high — from thirty to three hundred dollars per acre — and this induced many a small holder to sell his land and join the ranks of the laborers." Under the circumstances, the law limiting land holdings was not enforced, and at the present time "of the best land of Porto Rico, 537,193 acres are owned and 229,203 acres are leased by 477 individuals, partnerships, or corporations from the United States, Spain, France and other countries." The total wealth of the island is in the hands of fifteen per cent, of the population. Fourteen per cent of the wealth is in the hands of native Porto Ricans. Sixty-seven per cent is owned by Americans. Four-fifths of the people of Porto Rico live in the rural districts. They build their little shacks on land that does not belong to them; they work when work is to be had on the nearest plantation; the men dress in a pair of trousers, a shirt and a straw hat. "Throughout the island thousands of children of the ages from one to seven years go naked, in the towns as well as in the rural districts."

When the laborer is at work he and his family share the following diet:

Breakfast — Black coffee, without milk, and quite often without sugar.

Lunch — Rice and beans, or rice and codfish, or codfish and plantains.

Supper — The same as lunch.

This diet holds good while the laborer has steady work, but, during a large part of the year — five or six months — there is no work. "How he pulls through the slow season is a mystery to many who are interested in the welfare of the laborer."

The Porto Rican laborer is a sick man. "Hookworm disease, anemia, etc., are very widespread."

The low energy value of the diet, together with the prevalence of sickness, has so undermined the endurance of the Porto Rican laborer that a number of experiments in scientific diet, carried on by the employers themselves, resulted in increasing the working capacity of the men from 50 to 100 per cent. Mr. Marcus finds that, with an increase in wages which would enable the laborer to purchase some meat and dairy products, the charge of laziness and inefficiency, which is frequently lodged against the workers, might well be withdrawn.

The investigation upon which Mr. Marcus bases his report was made during the year 1919. At that time machinists in the sugar mills received about one dollar per day. Laborers in the busy season were paid ninety cents per day; in the slow season seventy cents. The working day is from ten to twelve hours. On the tobacco plantations men's wages during the busy season are from sixty to eighty cents a day and, during the dull season, from forty to sixty cents a day. Women receive from thirty-five to forty-five cents a day in the busy season and from twenty-five to thirty-five a day in the dull season. On the coffee plantations wages are lower. Men receive from fifty to sixty cents per day in the busy season and from thirty-five to forty-five cents per day in the dull season.

Mr. Marcus reports that the needle industry is making considerable headway in Porto Rico. Men's and children's suits are manufactured by women operators who earn from three dollars and fifty cents to five dollars per week. Embroidery manufacturing, lace-making and drawing work pay from one dollar and twenty-five cents to four dollars per week. The work is done exclusively by women.

Detailed descriptions are given of living and working conditions in these and other industries. Enough has been said here to indicate very clearly that the American people, having assumed the responsibility for directing the lives of 1,118,012 Porto Ricans, are far behind the standard of "health and decency" which civilization prescribes as the minimum below which human beings cannot be expected to live and to work.

Here are two examples of the work of modern empires. Great Britain fought two wars in order to force the drug habit on China. The United States took Porto Rico away from its "Spanish oppressors" and then turned the island over to absentee landlords, whose sole interest in the island was to make out of it all the money they could. This is imperialism at its worst — hard, grasping, western imperialism. With it I should like to contrast an instance of imperialism among the "heathen" of the Orient.

Japan took the Island of Formosa from China about 1897. Formosa is a very fertile island lying off the coast of China in the Pacific Ocean. Its population is almost exclusively Chinese, and it has been a part of the Chinese Empire for over four thousand years. The inhabitants nearly all smoked opium which had been forced upon them by England as a result of the two "Opium wars." When Japan compelled China to relinquish her right to the Island of Formosa (she had already occupied the island during the war) she sent eight hundred surveyors to the island and surveyed all of the land in Formosa. When the survey was completed she made maps showing who occupied each tract and describing the title by which it was held.

The Japanese found that the land in Formosa was owned in great tracts by Chinese mandarins, most of whom lived over in the cities on the main coast of China, many of them in Amboy. The holdings of these absentee landlords were from 200,000 to 500,000 acres. On the island itself practically all of the 4,000,000 inhabitants were landless and were paying rent to owners who lived abroad. No provision whatever was made for the education of the Formosan children.

Japan at the same time registered every opium smoker in Formosa and ascertained the amount of opium he smoked each day. She also destroyed every poppy field in Formosa and built an opium factory and purchased the raw opium from the Indian (English) Government to supply the registered opium smokers each day with the amount they smoked. She then passed a statute making the raising of poppies a crime and making it a criminal offense for any person except a registered opium smoker to have any opium in his possession. Consequently, when all the registered opium smokers died off, opium smoking was wiped out all over the island.

Having surveyed the land and ascertained just who owned it, Japan passed a law taking the title of the Island of Formosa from the landlords and conveying it to the Empire of Japan. As compensation to the landlords, Japan issued 4,000,000 yen of Formosan trust bonds and divided these bonds arbitrarily among those who had owned the island. Then she gave to each farmer who tilled the soil in Formosa the land he occupied and used, as well as the improvements which he already owned, and accompanied this gift with a provision that the farmer might dispose of his improvements to any other person who actually used and occupied the same, or that his improvements might descend to his children. In the case of the land, however, he was denied the right to alienate any portion of it. The Japanese also established schools all over Formosa for the compulsory education of the people.

I cite these facts because they present a picture of imperialism at its best — as it was practiced by Japan — in contrast with imperialism at its worst, as it is practiced by Great Britain and the United States. At bottom, however, imperialism is imperialism and is the same in principle, wherever it is found.

After all, why talk nonsense? Why lie to others? Why seek to deceive ourselves? An imperial policy has as its object the enrichment of the imperial class. The plain man — the farmer, the miner, the factory worker — is not the gainer through imperialism. Rather the monopolist, the land owner, the manufacturer, the trader, the banker — who have stolen what there is to steal at home, devote their energies to the pursuit of empire because the pursuit of empire gives them an opportunity to exploit and rob abroad.

We annexed Hawaii, not to help the Hawaiians, but because it was a good business proposition for the sugar interests. We took the Philippine Islands because the far-seeing among the plutocrats believed that there was a future economic advantage in the East. For the same reason we are in Haiti, Costa Rica and Panama. Each step along the imperial path is taken for the economic advantage of the business men of the United States and at the expense of the liberty and the lives of the natives over whom we secure dominion.

[1] "Ashley even brought forward a resolution for the suppression of the opium trade, but withdrew it after a debate turning on the inability of the Indian Government to part with a revenue of 1,000,000 pounds sterling or more." — The History of England. Sydney Law and L. C. Sanders. Longmans. 1913, Vol. 12, p. 41.

27. The U. S. and the Course of Empire

The United States has entered upon the course of empire. There is no limit to imperial policy; if we can justify the taking of the Philippines and governing them against their will — if we can justify conquering countries where our Constitution cannot go — our armies will soon be marching across Mexico, down the Isthmus to South America, leaving death and desolation in their track, rearing upon the ruins of those free governments a tyrannical, despotic power.

Let a free people once set out on an imperial course and the institutions that are dear to every lover of liberty disappear like April snow.

Imperial power cannot possibly be maintained without an immense navy and a standing army. Do not the very existence of such an army and such a navy constitute a denial of all that the old America stood for?

Armies and navies are fighting machines. If they are to be successfully operated there must be one man to whom is given supreme control. If there is to be an empire, there must be a dictator, so that he can move with rapidity; so that decisions can be made in a day and armies marched and ships moved where danger is seen. Is despotism what the people of America desire? If so, they will have it — indeed, they now have it under the imperial realities that are cloaked under the guise of republican names and republican traditions. Is it freedom that the American people seek? Then they must abandon the course of empire.

It is impossible for a republican form of government to function as an empire. Republican institutions invariably are corrupted when imperialism is established. Creasy, in his Fifteen Decisive Battles of the World, puts the matter tersely in these words:

"There has never been a republic yet in history that acquired dominion over another nation that did not rule it selfishly and oppressively. There is no single exception to this rule, either in ancient or modern times. Carthage, Rome, Venice, Genoa, Florence, Pisa, Holland and Republican France, all tyrannized over every province and subject-state where they gained authority."

Imperialism is tyranny and in the process of destroying liberty abroad you crush it effectively at home. Senator Hoar saw the peril. When the question of imperialism was up for discussion in the Senate he said (January 9, 1899):

"We have now to meet a greater danger than we have encountered since the Pilgrims landed at Plymouth — the danger that we are to be transformed from a republic, founded on the Declaration of Independence, guided by the counsels of Washington, into a vulgar, commonplace empire, founded upon physical force."

Read history! The record is unmistakable.

Among the plutocracies and the monarchies of the past, whenever property and power have been gathered into the hands of the few and discontent has appeared among the masses, it has been the policy to acquire foreign possessions, to enlarge the army and the navy, so as to keep discontent occupied and thus distract its attention. A foreign war has cut many a domestic tangle. The recent record of the United States in its acquisition of foreign territory, coming as it does with an increase of the army and the navy, tells the sinister story of the decision which the ruling classes of America have made to pursue an imperial policy.

The growth of the army and navy of the United States during the past twenty years has been phenomenal. When I entered the Senate, the authorized strength of the army was 28,417 men and the annual army appropriation was $44,582,838. Today the authorized strength of the army is 175,000 and the appropriation requested by the War Department is $935,000,000. The navy, which received an appropriation of $22,006,206 in 1890, is asking this year for $695,000,000. A generation has seen the army and navy of the United States increased from defensive organizations to the powerful, imperial fighting machines — the dogs of war, larger, stronger and better fed than those belonging to any other nation in the world.

Rome was organized as a republic. For the first six hundred years of her history she had the best government then existing on the globe. To be a Roman citizen was a greater honor than to be a king in another country.

Rome consolidated her power until she ruled all Italy. Then she began to spread out along the northern coast of the Mediterranean to reach into Asia Minor and Africa. But, when the policy of acquiring and ruling peoples who could have no part in her republican form of government began, Rome ceased to exist as a Republic and became an Empire. From that point the historian dates the ruin of her government, and the misery of her population. When Rome had acquired Egypt and Asia Minor with their populations of low consuming power and great tenacity of life, the Roman citizen found that he could not compete against them in the growing of crops or in other industrial enterprises.

The Roman of those days was like the Anglo-Saxon of today — a man of great vitality, requiring excellent nurture, the best food and plenty of it. When he came into competition with the Asiatic races, people of low vitality and with a great tenacity of life — human machines who could subsist upon the least food and perform the most work — the Roman farmer was destroyed, the foundation of power was shattered and the Roman Empire passed away.

When the Roman Republic was established m.ost of its people were farmers. Their farms did not average more than twelve acres in area, indicating a dense rural population. No foreign foe could march through that stockade of individual farm owners to the walls of Rome. They were successful farmers and prosperous, and they made mighty soldiers. Cincinnatus left the plow to lead his victorious legions. This was the situation during the early days of the Roman state.

During the first century of the Christian era centralization of wealth power revolutionized this simple life of the small farm. The lands were absorbed by the wealthy; the mines of silver and gold in Spain and Greece had been worked out; the old republic disappeared and in its place was erected the structure of an empire.

James Bryce says of this period of Roman history:

"The ostentation of humility which the subtle policy of Augustus had conceived, and the jealous hypocrisy of Tiberius maintained, was gradually dropped by their successors until despotism became at last recognized in principle as the government of the Roman Empire. With an aristocracy decayed, a populace degraded, an army no longer recruited from Italy, the semblance of liberty that yet survived might be swept away with impunity. Republican forms had never been known in the provinces at all and the aspect which the imperial administration had originally assumed there soon reacted on its position in the capital... This increased concentration of power was mainly required by the necessities of frontier defense, for within there was more decay than disaffection."

Great Britain rules over the mightiest of modern empires, but the British people have not been enriched by her conquests. Study the facts with regard to her laboring population. Compare the English factory worker of today with the English yeoman of four or five hundred years ago — compare them in health, in vigor, in quickness of eye and hand, in love of life — in anything you will, and the result will be to the disadvantage of the present-day Britisher.

Where are the people of Europe best off at the present time? Is it in Great Britain — mistress of the sea and ruler of territory scattered over six continents? Not at all! It is in little Switzerland, Holland, Norway. Where is there the best distribution of wealth, the best opportunity for the individual man? Where is there the least poverty, misery and distress? It is in Switzerland and Norway. It is not in England. Her conquests have bestowed no blessings upon her people. Two-thirds of them own nothing, while about a quarter of a million own all the property of the British Islands.

What blessings has England conferred upon her colonies that would justify the adoption of her policy by the United States? Her course in Ireland has been one of the blackest pages in the history of the world — a record of starvation and plunder.

If England will govern Ireland as she has done, what right has she to claim that she can govern any country? What is there in England's example that can justify us in undertaking the same work?

England began with Ireland. She followed with India. How has that country fared? In India, the English have made practically no converts to Christianity. Neither have the natives learned the English language. A great army, paid for by the native governments themselves, has been maintained to hold the Indian peoples in subjection and to prevent them from securing modern arms and modern implements of destruction. Indian raw materials cannot be manufactured at home because of the taxes imposed by the British authorities. Instead, they are shipped, in English ships, to Great Britain; manufactured and underrated by British manufacturers and merchants, and then transported back to India and sold to the Indian people. As trader, manufacturer, merchant, insurance agent and banker, Great Britain has profited, and India has paid.

What blessing has England conferred upon India? No blessings! On the contrary, she has taken away the food supply of the native population and left millions to die of starvation.

At the time of annexing the Philippines President McKinley said that moral reasons compelled us to stay in the Philippines, and that we, under God's direction, owed a duty to mankind, and more of similar cant. Here is what John Morley, the English statesman and writer and biographer of Gladstone says with regard to England's policy in this same connection:

"First, you push on into territories where you have no business to be and where you promised not to go; secondly, your intrusion provokes resentment and, in these wild countries, resentment means resistance; thirdly, you instantly cry out that the people are rebellious and that their act is rebellion (this in spite of your own assurance that you have no intention of setting up a permanent sovereignty over them); fourthly, you send a force to stamp out the rebellion; and, fifthly, having spread bloodshed, confusion and anarchy, you declare, with eyes uplifted to the heavens, that moral reasons force you to stay, for if you were to leave, this territory would be left in a condition which no civilized power could contemplate with equanimity or composure. These are the five stages in the Forward Rake's progress."

There is not a word in that passage that does not accord with the excuses given by those American imperialists who are in favor of conquering and ruling unwilling peoples.

Does the United States wish to follow the British example? From it no money will come into the Treasury for the benefit of the people of the United States. The laborers of this land, from whom we raise our taxes in the same way that England raises hers — by a per capita levy on consumption — are invited to contribute this taxation to support an army of occupation and subsidize ships to carry the trade, in order that the people in the outlying territory may be exploited by the trusts of the United States.

There is another reason behind the imperialist program that is being followed by the United States. It is well when people become restless and dissatisfied with the conditions which exist; when the workers of a land learn to believe that they are not receiving their just share of the products of their toil, to give them amusement — to distract their attention by distant problems — to supply them with bread and circuses, as in Rome, or to do as England has done — begin the killing of men in some far-off land and then appeal to the patriotism of the folks at home. By such means are the minds of the people diverted from the pressing economic and social problems, the right solution of which is essential to the happiness of the toilers of the nation.

There is no justification in history for the imperial course upon which we have entered. Rather, every page in history is a warning to us — that we desist before it is too late. And why should we not desist? What reason can be given for our imperial policy save the desire of the ruling class to plunder and invest?

The area of this country is great enough, if we would maintain free institutions under a republican form of government, for in a republic, founded upon the principles of equality and universal suffrage, it is essential that the individual voter shall have a knowledge of, and be familiar with, the methods of government; and if the country is so great and the problems of government are so complicated that it is impossible for the individual voter to acquire this familiar knowledge, how is it possible for him to vote intelligently? How is it possible for him to know that by his vote he is maintaining free institutions? In the past, republics have been of quite limited area — a single city perhaps — with a comparatively small population. The founders of this government, recognizing the difficulty of maintaining as a unit a republic of extensive proportions, inaugurated the Federal system, a union of sovereign states, hoping thereby to extend self-government over vast areas and to maintain at the same time the purity of republican principles by making each sovereign state a free republic.

For the purpose of unifying a vast area within the bounds of a republic it was enacted that the central government, the Government of the United States, should be a government of limited powers, a government possessing only such powers as were conferred upon it by the Constitution. All other sovereign rights — all other powers common to a sovereign — were retained by the States themselves, or by the people themselves as inhabitants of the States. If we follow our present policy of acquiring tropical countries, where republics cannot live, and where free, self-governing people have never lived since the world had a history, we overturn the theory upon which this government was established.

The whole theory of our government precludes centralization of power; the whole theory of our government sustains the idea that the United States as a government shall only do those things which cannot be done with equal effectiveness by the states or by the individual citizens.

But our Federal system has not accomplished the purpose for which it was created; it has not fulfilled the expectation of its authors.

Before we acquire more territory; before we start on a policy of imperialism and of conquest, it is our duty to inquire whether our area and population are not already too great. Centralization went on rapidly after the War of the Rebellion. It was hastened by the Spanish War. It received an immense impetus during the World War. As a result, our people are looking to the Government of the United States as the source of all power and the channel through which all relief must come. The American people have ceased to rely on the states. They are forgetting how to rely upon themselves.

This concentration of power in the hands of the Federal Government has been followed by encroachments by the Federal courts upon the sovereignty of the states and upon the legislative and executive branches of the government itself, until a point has been reached in our public life where the courts are almost supreme.

Within the past fifty years the wealth of the United states, which was once fairly distributed, has been accumulated in the hands of a few, so that five per cent of the people own three-quarters of the nation's wealth, while two-thirds of the citizens — the workers are practically without property. Recent events point unmistakably to the fact that the few men who own nearly all the wealth have gained control of the machinery of public life. They have usurped the functions of government and established a plutocracy.

Those who favor an imperial policy for the United States, who favor a departure from those customs and practices that have created the proudest pages in our history, say it is manifest destiny. Throughout all recorded time manifest destiny has been the murderer of men.

Manifest destiny has caused the strong to rob the weak and has reduced the weak to slavery. Manifest destiny built the feudal castle and supplied the feudal lord with his serfs. Manifest destiny compelled republics to go forth and conquer weaker races and to subject the conquered people to slavery; to impose taxation against their will, and to inflict upon them forms of government which they considered odious. Manifest destiny is the cry of the strong in justification of their plunder of the weak. This cry sent forth the nations of Europe to divide among them the weaker nations of Africa and Asia.

If we pursue the course to which "manifest destiny" is alluring us; if we annex weaker nations to which we cannot apply our system of government; if we acquire territory in the Tropics where men cannot live who are capable of self-government, then republican forms cannot exist in those distant possessions. The vigorous blood, the best blood, the young men of our land, will be drawn away to mix with distant races and to hold them in subjection. Gradually the reflex of the conquest and of this tyrannical government will work its effect upon our own people, and free institutions will disappear from this land, as well as from the land we conquer and undertake to hold in subjection.

Whenever England concludes to go upon an expedition and plunder some of the weaker nations of the world, she makes her first appeal to patriotism. Then, step by step, she goes on until she has committed the wrong, has transgressed the rights of the natives; has aroused their resistance, and then she declares that the flag has been fired on, and that no Englishman must question the right or wrong of what is being done until the enemy is defeated and the country annexed.

Contemplate the course of every republic in the past; watch its surrender to the lust of power and the greed for wealth; then turn to our own shores, examine our present conduct and see our flag go down in misery and in shame. The glory of this republic has been that we have offered an asylum to the oppressed and a hope to mankind which has been followed wherever freedom has flowered throughout the world. Shall we stain that record? Shall we abandon history? Shall we become one of the robber nations of the world?

The United States is on the wrong course — the course that leads to national disgrace and finally to national destruction. The wealth lords who desire imperialism are not the American people. The jingoes and exploiters who are out for conquest and for annexation are not the American people. They are merely the representatives of a ruling class that would use the American people to fill their own money bags.

We have a task— clear and well defined.

Our duty is to educate and elevate the population we already have, and thus perpetuate our institutions. In the past every republic has sown the seeds of its final destruction by gratifying the desire for conquest and for glory. Let us profit by their example and pursue a course that will make the masses happy and prosperous rather than dazzle and allay the mutterings of misery and discontent by the march of armies and the glory of conquest.

28. The Profiteers

The test of a man or of a social system is the way he acts in a crisis. The great war was the crisis that tested American capitalism and that showed it up for what it was — a brutal game of profit-making at the expense of the people who work and pay.

When the war broke out in Europe, I knew that the American business men would take advantage of the emergency in which Europe found herself to charge the highest possible price for the worst possible product and when, three years later, the United States decided to enter the war I was equally convinced that the American business men would rob their own country of every farthing on which they could lay their hands.

Not for a moment was I deceived by the glib talk of "patriotism" that sounded from every Chamber of Commerce and every business office and banking institution. I had dealt with the armor-plate contracts in the United States Senate twenty years before; I had investigated the sickening details of the beef contracts made by the packers with the government during the Spanish war. Besides these details and beyond them, I knew the whole business system for what it was — a device for enabling the strong to rob the weak; for permitting the capitalist to coin every private or public need into profits.

A reference to the situation which was unearthed in the Senate away back in 1897 will give the justification of the conclusions I have reached with regard to the capitalist system, as such.

In the closing days of the 54th Congress a question arose regarding the cost of armor-plate. After an exhaustive discussion, in which great quantities of evidence were submitted, the question was put to a vote of the Senate in this form: — Shall the Senate vote for armor-plate at $300 or $400 per ton? Only twelve Senators favored the $400 limit. They were Aldrich, Allison, Brice, Cullom, Gibson, Gorman, Hale, Hawley, McMillan, Murphy, Squire and Wetmore. There were 36 votes cast on the other side, of which mine was one.

The evidence seemed perfectly clear. We had summoned experts and ascertained that the cost of labor and materials entering into a ton of armor-plate was about $160. This figure included a charge for "keeping plant ready for use," a charge for "shop expenses," a charge for "office expenses and contingencies," and a charge for "administration, superintendence and engineering, beside the charges for "materials in ingots," "materials consumed in manufacture" and for "labor." Ten per cent was allowed for re-pipings and 10 per cent for rejected plates, making a total of about $200 per ton. The company claimed a return on the "investment," but it was proved that profit on the first armor-plate contract secured by these companies had been equal to the entire cost of the plant. An allowance of 5 to 10 per cent was made, however, for repairs and maintenance, and the total cost of a ton of armor-plate was brought up to $225.

At that figure, the profit to the companies on the 8,000 tons of armor would be about $600,000 on a $300 figure. Under the circumstances the Senate voted 36 to 12 for the $300 figure.

After Congress had adjourned the Secretary of the Navy endeavored to get bids at $300. None was forthcoming. Instead, representatives of the companies waited on him and advised him that they could not make the plate for less than $425 — a figure which allowed for a profit of about $1,600,000 on the contract.

An amendment was therefore made to the deficiency appropriation bill (July 13, 1897, p. 2,553) allowing for armor-plate at that price.

"Last winter we appropriated money for the purpose of buying armor-plate and limited the price to $300 a ton. The evidence taken before the Committee on Naval Affairs showed conclusively that the plate could be made for $250 a ton. The two armor-plate factories, being in collusion and having been in collusion as to every bid they have had heretofore, as was shown by the evidence before the Committee on Naval Affairs, refused to make the plate for $300, but insisted that they should have $425.

"Instead of bringing in a proposition to build a factory and make the plate ourselves and thus protect the interests of the government, the Committee on Appropriations propose to accede to the demands of these men, who are in a trust to plunder the Treasury, and they bring in an amendment to pay them $425, thus cowardly surrendering to this admitted combination. It seems to me too disgraceful to be tolerated."

(It was shown that the two plants could be duplicated at one or one and a half millions each.)

These facts and many others that had come to my attention during the years of my public life led me to look behind the patriotic professions of the business leaders — their talk about Belgium and the Lusitania, and "Humanity" and "Democracy" — to see what were the real reasons that were leading the United States into the war. I did not have to look far before discovering the answer. American banks, like the Morgans, and American manufacturers, like the Bethlehem Steel Company, had granted large extensions of credit to the Allies and, if the Allies lost, they were bankrupt. Furthermore, they saw an unequaled opportunity to strengthen their hold in the United States and to run a pipeline into the public treasury. The entrance of the United States into the war would validate their European speculations at the same time that it gave them tens of billions in American war contracts.

By the time these facts were clear in my mind, the United States had entered the war. I opposed the step with all of the energy that I had, and, after it was taken, I said very frankly what I thought about it in the following newspaper interview that appeared in the Sioux Falls "Argus Leader" of October 6, 1917:

"There is no excuse for this war."

"We should back right out of it."

"We never should have gone into a war to help the Schwabs make $40,000,000 per year."

"This man McAdoo said here that we are in the war from principle to protect our right to trade on the open sea. Not an American was killed except on ammunition boats, and they had no right to be there."

"Sympathy is being extended to Belgium. She deserves none. For fifty years Belgium robbed the Congo. This made Belgium wealthy, but three-fourths of her people did not share in this wealth. If she is now indemnified it will go to the men who robbed the negroes of the Congo."

"One hundred years ago we fought out the alien and sedition law. The party back of it failed at the next election. The same struggle is on again."

"People desire to know if they are living in the United States or in Russia."

Since the day that I had refused to take sides with Mr. Wilson in his 1912 campaign he had disliked me. This statement gave him his chance and within ten days of the date on which it appeared I was indicted by the Federal Grand Jury at Sioux Falls, S. D.

The indictment is a curious document. One day, with the many others that were issued during the same period, it will be historic:

"The District Court of the United States of America for the Southern Division of the District of South Dakota in the Eighth Judicial Circuit.

"At a stated term of the District Court of the United States of America for the Southern Division of the District of South Dakota begun and held at the City of Sioux Falls, within and for the district and circuit aforesaid, on the third Tuesday of October, in the year of our Lord one thousand nine hundred and seventeen: "The Grand jurors of the United States of America, good and lawful men, summoned from the body of the district aforesaid, then and there being duly empaneled, sworn and charged by the court aforesaid, to diligently inquire and true presentment make for said district of South Dakota, in the name and by the authority of the United States of America, upon their oaths, do present:

"That Richard Franklin Pettigrew, late of Minnehaha County, State of South Dakota, in said district heretofore, to wit: on or about the sixth day of October, in the year of our Lord one thousand nine hundred and seventeen, at and in the County of Minnehaha, State of South Dakota, and in the division and district aforesaid, and within the exclusive jurisdiction of this court, and while and when the United States was at war with the Imperial German Government, pursuant to a joint resolution of the Congress of the United States, approved by the President of the United States on April 6, A. D. 1917, did then and there knowingly, feloniously and wilfully make, say and utter certain false statements, with intent to promote the success of the enemy of the United States, that is to say, the Imperial German Government, to-wit: that he, the said Pettigrew did then and there wilfully and feloniously publicly state and say to one P. F. Leavins, and to other persons to the Grand Jurors unknown, and did then and there direct and cause to be published, printed and circulated through and by means of the 'Daily Argus Leader,' a daily newspaper, published in the City of Sioux Falls, State of South Dakota, in words and substance, as follows, that is to say:

"'There is no excuse for this war.'

"'We should back right out of it.' "'We never should have gone into a war to help the Schwabs make $40,000,000 per year.' "This man McAdoo said here that we are in the war from principle to protect our right to trade on the open sea. Not an American was killed except on ammunition boats, and they had no right to be there.'

"Sympathy is being extended to Belgium. She deserves none. Fifty years ago Belgium robbed the Congo. This made Belgium wealthy, but three-fourths of her people did not share in this wealth. If she is now indemnified it will go to the men who robbed the negroes of the Congo.'

"'One hundred years ago we fought out the alien and sedition law. The party back of it failed at the next election. The same struggle is on again.'

"'People desire to know if they are living in the United States or in Russia.'
against the peace and dignity of the United States of America and contrary to the form, force and effect of the statute of the United States in such case made and provided.

"Count Two.

"And the Grand Jurors aforesaid, upon their oaths aforesaid, do further present and say:

"That Richard Franklin Pettigrew, late of Minnehaha County, State of South Dakota, in the said district heretofore, to-wit: On the sixth day of October, in the year of our Lord one thousand nine hundred and seventeen, with force and arms, at and in the County of Minnehaha, State of South Dakota, and in the division and district aforesaid, and within the exclusive jurisdiction of this court, and while and when the United States was at war with the Imperial German Government, pursuant to a joint resolution of the Congress of the United States, approved by the President of the United States on April 6, A. D. 1917, did then and there, knowingly, feloniously and wilfully obstruct the recruiting and enlistment service of the United States, to the injury of the United States, in that he, the said Richard Franklin Pettigrew, did then and there feloniously publicly state, say and utter to one P. F. Leavins, and to other persons to the Grand Jurors unknown, and did then and there direct and cause to be published, printed and circulated through and by means of the 'Daily Argus Leader,' a daily newspaper, published and circulated in the City of Sioux Falls, State of South Dakota, in words and substance, as follows, that is to say:

"There is no excuse for this war,

"'We should back right out of it.'

"'We never should have gone into a war to help the Schwabs make $40,000,000 per year.'

"'This man McAdoo said here that we are in the war from principle to protect our right to trade on the open sea. Not an American was killed except on ammunition boats, and they had no right to be there.'

"'Sympathy is being extended to Belgium. She deserves none. Fifty years ago Belgium robbed the Congo. This made Belgium wealthy, but three-fourths of her people did not share in this wealth. If she is now indemnified it will go to the men who robbed the negroes of the Congo.'

"'One hundred years ago we fought out the alien and sedition law. The party back of it failed at the next election; the same struggle is on again.'

"'People desire to know if they are living in the United States or in Russia.'"
against the peace and dignity of the United States of America, and contrary to the form, force and effect of the statute of the United States in such case made and provided.

"Count Three.

"And the Grand Jurors aforesaid, upon their oaths aforesaid, do further present and say:

"That Richard Franklin Pettigrew, late of Minnehaha County, State of South Dakota, in said district heretofore, to-wit: on the sixth day of October, in the year of our Lord one thousand nine hundred and seventeen, at and in the County of Minnehaha, State of South Dakota, and in the division and district aforesaid, and within the exclusive jurisdiction of this court, and while and when the United States was at war with the Imperial German Government, pursuant to a joint resolution of the Congress of the United States, approved by the President of the United States on April 6, A. D. 1917, did then and there feloniously and wilfully cause and attempt to cause disloyalty, insubordination, mutiny and refusal of duty in the military forces of the United States, to the injury of the United States, in that he, the said Richard Franklin Pettigrew, did then and there feloniously publicly state, say and utter to one P. F. Leavins, and to other persons to the Grand Jurors unknown, and did then and there direct and cause to be published, printed and circulated through and by means of the 'Daily Argus Leader,' a daily newspaper, published and circulated in the City of Sioux Falls, State of South Dakota, in words and substance, as follows, that is to say:

"'There is no excuse for this war.'

"'We should back right out of it.'"

"'We never should have gone into a war to help the Schwabs make $40,000,000 per year.'"

"'This man McAdoo said here that we are in the war from principle, to protect our right to trade on the open sea. Not an American was killed except on ammunition boats, and they had no right to be there.'

"'Sympathy is being extended to Belgium. She deserves none. Fifty years ago Belgium robbed the Congo. This made Belgium wealthy, but three-fourths of her people did not share in this wealth. If she is now indemnified it will go to the men who robbed the negroes of the Congo.'

"'One hundred years ago we fought out the alien and sedition law. The party back of it failed at the next election. The same struggle is on again.'

"'People desire to know if they are living in the United States or in Russia.' against the peace and dignity of the United States of America, and contrary to the form, force and effect of the statute of the United States in such case made and provided.

"R. P. STEWART,

United States Attorney in and for the State and District of South Dakota.

"JAMES ELLIOTT, Judge.

"Names of witnesses sworn and examined before the Grand Jurors: P. F. Leavins."

Was I indicted because I had told a lie or because I had told the truth? Was I right in my charges or was I wrong? Was it a war for democracy or was it a profiteers' war?

I did not have to wait long for the answer to these questions. In fact, the answer came with a rapidity and with a completeness that was overwhelming. First there was the statement from the Chairman of the Federal Reserve (Bank) Board, Mr. Harding; then came the revelations with regard to Hog Island and to the airplane contracts; later Mr. Wilson, in his St. Louis speech, blurted out the frank admission — "Of course this was a commercial war," and finally there appeared the figures showing the profits made by the leading industries during the war years.

For example, there was Bethlehem Steel, Schwab's own plant. The profits of this company for 1911, 1912 and 1913 averaged $3,075,108 per year. In 1915, the profits had jumped to $17,762,813; in 1916 to $43,593,968. For 1918, the corporation made a profit of $57,188,769. Improvements and extensions of the plant ate up $24,329,245, while depreciation took $31,510,366. See my indictment. Schwab exceeded forty million a year.

Again, there was du Pont Powder which reports its war profits in the following words, which are taken from its financial report for 1918. "The stock of the E. I. du Pont de Nemours Powder Company, the predecessor of the E. I. du Pont de Nemours Company, sold during the early months of the war at $125 per share. The share of debenture stock and two shares of common stock of E. I. du Pont de Nemours Company, which were exchanged for the former security, are worth in today's market (Dec. 31, 1918) $593, or an increase in value of 374 per cent. In the meantime (1915-18) the total dividends on the common stock of the E. I. du Pont de Nemours Powder Company and on the exchanged securities of E. I. du Pont de Nemours Company have amounted to 458 per cent on the par value of the original stock. It is difficult to imagine a more satisfactory financial result."

It is difficult. But it is very easy to picture the misery and suffering of war and the great price in excessive taxation that the purchasers of the du Pont product have saddled on the working people in their respective countries.

Then there were the producers of copper. The Anaconda Copper Mining Company paid $65,275,000 in cash dividends during the years 1915 to 1918.

It also paid off a funded debt of $15,000,000 in the same period, and invested, besides, $54,466,703 in betterments. After this outlay, it had, on January 1, 1919, a net quick surplus of $39,926,000 as compared with $4,688,204 in 1914. The twenty-nine leading copper producing companies paid $540,846,855 in cash dividends during 1915, 1916, 1917 and 1918; expended $354,704,290 in betterments and improvements during 1915, 1916 and 1917, and in 1918 their surplus was $330,798,593 as compared with a surplus of $96,711,392 on the same day of 1914.

The United States Steel Corporation, with a capital stock of about $750,000,000, made a profit, in 1916 and 1917, of $888,931,511. These are figures published by the company itself. When the steel Trust was formed this capital stock represented little besides water, but during two war years the corporation made over 100 per cent on it.

These are individual cases. In Senate Document 259, 65th Congress, Second Session, are published the figures showing the profits made by American business men during the year 1917. This document contains 388 pages, and in it are listed, by number, the amount and per cent of profits made in 1917 by American business men. The results are almost unbelievable. Among the industries engaged in manufacturing and selling the principal necessaries of life there is not a single trade in which at least one concern did not make 100 per cent or more on the capital stock.

The profits for 122 meat-packing concerns are reported as follows: 31 concerns made profits for the year of less than 25 per cent; 45 made profits of from 25 per cent to 50 per cent: 46 made profits of over 50 per cent; and 22 of over 100 per cent. In this industry, half of the concerns made a profit of more than 50 per cent and a sixth of over 100 per cent.

These sound like large returns, but they are outdistanced by the figure for the 340 bituminous coal producers in the Appalachian field. Among these concerns there were only 23 that reported profits of less than 25 per cent; 68 reported profits of 25 but less than 50 per cent; 79 reported profits of from 50 to 100 per cent; 135 reported profits of 100 to 500 per cent; 21 reported profits of from 100 to 1000 per cent, and 14 reported profits of over 1000 per cent. Half of the concerns in this industry showed profits of more than 100 per cent, and one in each ten reported profits of more than 500 per cent.

The whole report is filled with just such figures. Profits of under 25 per cent are unusual. Profits of 50 per cent; 100 per cent, and 500 per cent in a single year are quite common.

How moderate I had been! I had talked about our entrance into the war enabling Schwab and his associates to make forty millions a year. What they had actually done was to make billions. I had only half stated the case for the profiteers. True to the principles of their ferocious system, they had taken advantage of a national emergency to become fabulously rich.

In July, 1920, I wrote the Pittsburgh Dispatch the following letter which they published at once.

"Sioux Falls, S. Dak., July 24, 1920.

"The Pittsburgh Dispatch, Pittsburgh, Pa.

"You asked me to answer this question: 'Was the object of the war gained?'

"I suppose my answer must be confined to the United States' participation in that contest. So far as the United States is concerned, the very object and only object for which we entered the war has been fully gained. We went into the war because the great financial and industrial interests centered in New York, who are the real government of the United States, conceived it to be for their gain or profit to put the United States into the European conflict. They had sold billions of dollars' worth of material to England, Russia, France and Italy, at enormous prices, reaping a marvelous profit. But as the war progressed and the demands on the part of those nations for credit increased, the financiers and controllers of American industry who were furnishing war material, became alarmed, and feared they would not be able to collect their claims against these European nations who were approaching bankruptcy, and they therefore determined to put the United States into that controversy, and have the United States loan money to the European nations, to pay off the obligations which they held against them.

"They, therefore, started an agitation in the United States to work up the people of this country in favor of going into the war. They bought up, or already owned, all the great daily newspapers. They ordered and paid for preparedness parades in every town of consequence in the United States. *They lied to and deceived the American people with exaggerated stories of the German atrocities,* until they created a war frenzy in this country.

"They had been at work on the President for months. They had a committee, a secret committee, paid by them, planning every phase of the war before we went into it.

"E. P. C. Harding, of the Federal Reserve, President of the Bank Board of the United States, on March 22, 1917, published the following statement:

"'*As banker and creditor, the United States would have a place at the peace conference table, and be in a much better position to resist any proposed repudiation of debts, FOR IT MIGHT AS WELL BE REMEMBERED THAT WE WILL BE FORCED TO TAKE UP THE CUDGELS FOR ANY OF OUR CITIZENS OWNING BONDS THAT MIGHT BE REPUDIATED.'*"

"The above was issued before we entered the war, and immediately on our entering the war, these corporations rushed through a loan to the European countries, not one dollar of which ever went to Europe except in the form of war material.

"*As a result of the war the United States is a debtor and these corporations and their representatives, are creditors of the United States instead of the European nations. Their profits run into the tens of billions. The very object for which we went to war has, therefore, been fully gained.*

"Conclusive proof in the fact we have 16,500 more millionaires than we had before we went into the war.   — R. F. Pettigrew."

This letter states the whole issue.

The country was in peril. Men were dying. The energies of the nation were being directed to the winning of a victory. The ignorant, unthinking millions were being mobilized to make the world safe for democracy, and the profiteers were piling up their wealth.

There was no misunderstanding about this matter. It was not an accident.

The profiteers did not and could not stop profiteering because the system to which they belong is a profiteering system. The profiteer is a product of a system of society that provides the largest rewards for the man who is most successful in robbing his fellows of the results of their labor. There was profiteering before the war — on a small scale. But during the war — in a critical period — the system was tested and it proved to be what many of us had thought it — a legalized system of robbery; a method of enabling the rich to live off the toil of the poor, and to fatten out of their privations.

The World War showed capitalism at its best and at its worst. In every one of the great capitalist countries engaged in the war, the same kind of profiteering went on. The American profiteers made more than their European competitors because there was more to make. Everywhere they got what they could. Capitalism produced the war. Capitalism profited by the war. The utter incompetence; the crass brutality of the system caused it to break in Russia, in Germany and Austria. Today it is in full swing, stronger than ever in England, France and the United States. Will the people who do the work and produce the wealth ever realize that capital is stolen labor and its only function is to steal more labor?

29. The Russian Revolution

The war was an affirmation of capitalism. The Russian Revolution was the answer of the workers. The war wrecked most of the capitalist nations of Europe — wrecked them financially and economically — and those that survived the period of hostilities were caught in the maelstrom of high prices that followed the signing of the Armistice. During more than four years the producers of Europe turned from making useful things and devoted themselves to making the means of destruction. The result was fatal. European capitalism had written its own death sentence.

The old system broke down first in Russia. The revolution began there, and no sooner did it show itself than the other capitalist nations — the former Allies of Russia, — turned against her and fought her with armies, with a blockade, and with every other device that military and diplomatic experts could devise.

The demands of the Russian people were very simple, They asked for work, bread and peace — three things that the capitalist system in Russia was unable to provide. Hence the Revolution.

There have been scores of revolutions during the past two centuries, and after each one of them that proved successful, the people have written a Constitution modeled on the Constitution of the United States — a constitution that permitted the economic masters to carry on their work of exploitation with impunity. The Russians abandoned this precedent.

Instead of writing a political constitution, they did a very new and a very wonderful thing — they wrote an economic constitution, based on the proposition that the exploitation of one man by another must cease.

The Bill of Rights was added to the Constitution of the United States as an afterthought. It is not in the body of the Constitution at all, but takes the form of "amendments." The Russian Constitution begins with a Bill of Rights.

The rights enumerated in our Constitution are civil rights, free speech, free press, religious freedom, rights of accused persons, rights in the case of civil trials. The right to be admitted to bail, etc. The Russian Bill of Rights begins with a statement of economic principles. Chapter 1 of the Bill of Rights declares the existence of a Soviet Republic in Russia. Chapter 2 begins with these words, — "Bearing in mind, as its fundamental problem, the abolition of exploitation of men by men, the entire abolition of the division of the people in classes, the suppression of exploiters; the establishment of a Socialist society, and the victory of Socialism in all lands, the Third All-Russian Congress of Soviets of Workers', Soldiers' and Peasants' Deputies further resolves:

"*a.* for the purpose of realizing the socialization of land, all private property in land is abolished, and the entire land is declared to be national property and is to be apportioned among husbandmen without any compensation to the former owners, in the measures of each one's ability to till it.

"*b.* all forests, treasures of the earth, and waters of general public utility, all implements, whether animate or inanimate, model farms and agricultural enterprises, are declared to be national property.

"*c.* as a first step towards the complete transfer of ownership to the Soviet Republic of all factories, mills, mines, railways, and other means of production and transportation, the Soviet law for the control by workmen and the establishment of the Supreme Soviet of National Economy is hereby confirmed, so as to assure the power of the workers over the exploiters.

"*d.* with reference to international banking and finance, the third Congress of Soviets is discussing the Soviet decree regarding the annulment of loans made by the Government of the Czar, by landowners and the bourgeoisie, and it trusts that the Soviet Government will firmly follow this course until the final victory of the international workers' revolt against the oppression of capital.

"*e.* the transfer of all banks into the ownership of the Workers' and Peasants' Government, as one of the conditions of the liberation of the toiling masses from the yoke of capital, is confirmed.

"*f.* universal obligation to work is introduced for the purpose of eliminating the parasitic strata of society and organizing the economic life of the country."

All wealth and all the comforts of civilization are the products of labor applied to the earth. Man is a land animal and his right to the soil is inherent and fundamental. The chance to reach the land and the right to reach it are as great as the right to use the air and the water of the earth.

The Soviet Constitution allows every person over eighteen years of age to vote if they are engaged in some useful employment.

Thus disfranchising the lawyers and the preachers.

A lawyer spends the first half of his life over the past and the last half trying to apply the past to the present and lets the future go to hell.

A preacher spends the first half of his life over the past and the last half over the future and lets the present go to hell. I am sure neither are engaged in a useful occupation.

Then follows a provision regarding the right to bear arms. After it there comes the forceful and splendid declaration against capitalist imperialism and in favor of a self-governing and self-determining world. Sections 4 and 5 of Chapter 3 provide:

"Expressing its absolute resolve to liberate mankind from the grip of capital and imperialism, which flooded the earth with blood in this present most criminal of all wars, the third Congress of Soviets fully agrees with the Soviet Government in its policy of breaking secret treaties, of organizing on a wide scale the fraternization of the workers and peasants of the belligerent armies, and of making all efforts to conclude a general democratic peace without annexations or indemnities, upon the basis of the free determination of the peoples.

"It is also to this end that the third Congress of Soviets insists upon putting an end to the barbarous policy of the bourgeois civilization which enables the exploiters of a few chosen nations to enslave hundreds of millions of the toiling population of Asia, of the colonies, and of small countries generally."

Following this protest there is a section (8) setting forth the attitude of the Soviet Government toward those portions of the former Russian Empire which were not yet incorporated into the Soviet Republic:

"In its effort to create a league — free and voluntary, and for that reason all the more complete and secure — of the working classes of all the peoples of Russia, the third Congress of Soviets merely establishes the fundamental principles of the federation of Russian Soviet Republics, leaving to the workers and peasants of every people to decide the following question at their plenary sessions of their Soviets: *whether or not they desire to participate, and on what basis, in the federal government and other federal Soviet institutions.*"

Conservative thinkers and publicists deride these provisions on the ground that the Soviet Government has not yet been able to put them fully into practice. They jest. Have we been able to enforce the Prohibition Amendment?, to enfranchise the Negroes in accordance with the provisions of amendment 14?, to guarantee the right of free speech in accordance with amendment 1?, or to protect American citizens against unreasonable search and seizure in accordance with amendment 4? To ask these questions, is to answer them.

A Bill of Rights presents the aspirations and the political ideals of a people — nothing more. The ideals of our forefathers were of a political nature, as is clearly indicated in the Bill of Rights which they drew up. In the same way, the ideals of the Russian workers are of an economic nature, as is clearly indicated by the Bill of Rights which they have drawn up.

The times have changed since the Constitutional Convention met in 1787. Then men were striving for political freedom. Now they are seeking economic emancipation. It is all part of the same struggle — for liberty, but the new times have called forth new ideals. The Russian Bill of Rights is a new step and a long step in the direction of freedom.

There were nearly 170 millions of people in Russia when the war began in 1914. After three years of bloody struggle they demanded work, bread and peace, and they proceeded to get these things in the only way that the workers will ever get them from the masters — by taking them. The beneficiaries of privilege will not yield unless they are compelled to by force of circumstances that are too strong for them to control. The embodiment of that force is the organized will of the people who do the worlds' work.

The Russian Revolution is the greatest event of our times. It marks the beginning of the epoch when the working people will assume the task of directing and controlling industry. It blazes a path into this unknown country, where the workers of the world are destined to take from their exploiters the right to control and direct the economic affairs of the community.

30. The League to Perpetuate War

The war has just begun. I said that when the Armistice terms were published and when I read the Treaty and the League Covenant I felt more than ever convinced of the justice of my conclusion. The Treaty of Versailles is merely an armistice — a suspension of hostilities, while the combatants get their wind. There is a war in every chapter of the Treaty and in every section of the League Covenant; war all over the world; war without end so long as the conditions endure which produce these documents. The League of Nations is a League to perpetuate war. I do not charge that its sponsors intended this, though I have sufficient respect for the intellectual ability of men like Balfour and Lloyd George, Makino and Orlando to believe that they knew quite well what they were about. But whether by intention or accident, the "Big Five" presented the world with two documents, the attempted enforcement of which is destined to bathe the earth in blood and wipe out what remains of "western civilization."

The advocates of the League of Nations claim for it that it will end war. "If we do not adopt it," says Mr. Wilson, "we will break the heart of the world." If we do adopt it, we shall help to bleed the western world white in the series of frightful international struggles that will follow upon any attempt to enforce the Treaty and the League Covenant as they are written.

Let me state, briefly, my reasons for believing that the League of Nations is a War League rather than a Peace League.

1. The League of Nations is not a league of all nations. On the contrary, three kinds of nations are deliberately excluded from it, — the Socialist nations like Russia; the enemy nations, like Germany; and the "undeveloped

nations," like Mexico. The "Big Five" who wrote the Armistice Terms, the Peace Treaty and the League Covenant were Great Britain, France, Italy, Japan and the United States. These are the five great capitalist empires of the world. They are also the five leaders among the allied nations. The League is therefore a Holy Alliance of capitalist empires against socialist states; a League of the Allies against the Central Powers; a League of the five great exploiting nations of the world against those whom they propose to rob. This situation creates a series of alignments any one of which may lead to an outbreak at almost any moment.

2. On the one hand, there is the alignment against Russia. Ever since the Revolution of 1917, the Allies have done everything in their power to destroy the government of Russia. They have sent their armies against her at Vladivostock and at Archangel; they have attacked her with their fleets on the Black Sea and in the Baltic; they have financed and equipped 'those like Yudenich, Kolchak, Denikine and Wrangel who were in rebellion against the established government of Russia; they have financed and equipped the Ukranians, the Finns and the Poles, on condition that they should make war on Russia; they have established a "sanitary cordon" of border states in an effort to cut Russia off from the rest of Europe; they have maintained a blockade which has resulted in the death, by starvation and by disease, of Russian men, women and children. During three long years, the Allies have carried on these activities without succeeding in forcing a declaration of war from Russia.

The Russian people are very patient. They had need of patience under the Czars, but there is a limit to everything. There are a hundred and fifty million of Russians. These people feel bitter against the capitalist governments that have attacked and blockaded them. They have an army — the largest now in Europe, if report speaks true. Some day that army will come into action against the armies of the Allies — come with the fervor and ardor of revolution, and when it comes, Europe will witness another terrible massacre and another fearful destruction of wealth.

3. Then, there are the enemy countries — defeated in the great war, stripped of their navies and of their merchant ships; of their colonies; of their investments in foreign countries; of their coal and iron; dismembered, saddled with heavy indemnities in addition to their onerous taxes. These enemy countries are suffering under the smart of a terrible military defeat. But more than that, after revolting and driving out their despotic rulers they have been subjected to an economic punishment more frightful than any that has ever been administered in modern times. The governing classes feel this; the people feel it, and they are all ready, at the first opportunity, to rush to arms in vindication of their international position and of their national rights, which they believe were grossly violated by the Treaty of Versailles. No opportunity was lost; no effort was spared to humiliate the defeated and to visit upon them a drastic economic punishment. The vanquished and humiliated are preparing to come back, and the Allied Nations know it.

4. There are the exploited countries; the "undeveloped" portions of the earth; the promising investment field; the good markets — Mexico, India, Korea, Egypt, Persia, China and the others. Africa has been under the heel of Western business men for generations. The same thing is true of India and other portions of Western and Southern Asia. These peoples, numbering hundreds of millions, have been kept in ignorance and held in bondage, while the British, German, French, Belgian and other traders and investors made free with their property and their lives. In the Belgian Congo, the black men were treated with indescribable cruelty; the people of India, after a century and a half of British rule, are almost wholly illiterate, while their industries have been deliberately curtailed in order that the Indian market might be open for British manufacturers. Mexico has been victimized again and again by the United States. Hayti, Santo Domingo and Nicaragua have felt the weight of America's imperial fist. Under the Treaty, with its "Mandates" and its guarantees of territorial integrity, these peoples, comprising the bulk of the world's populations, are to be continued in "tutelage" while' Allied Capitalists plunder and allied governments tax and kill.

The Baku Conference of the Eastern People (September, 1920) is the beginning of an organized protest that challenges the right of the west to continue its exploitation of the East. India is aflame with revolt, and the smaller eastern countries are awaiting the signal to begin a holy war, a religious crusade, against the domination of Western Civilization. Whether the proposed expulsion of the Sultan from Europe will start the conflagration, or whether some other spark will set it off remains to be seen. But the spirit of liberation is abroad in the earth, and any group of nations that seeks, with or without a covenant, to continue a system of virtual slavery, is heading for bitter and terrible conflicts.

5. Finally, there is an item of immense significance. The "Big Five" are five capitalist empires, each one of which is struggling for markets and for investment opportunities. Britain and Germany fought the recent war because Germany challenged Britain's economic supremacy. Today each of the Big Five is busy with just such an economic battle as that which preceded the war of 1914. British and American oil interests are in open conflict; Japan is seeking to exclude western bankers from the Chinese field; France and Italy are bitter rivals for the control of the Mediterranean; Britain and France are contending for the resources of Central Europe and of the near East. Besides that, it must not be forgotten that naval and military appropriations are larger among the Big Five than they were before the world war.

Any one of these issues may lead to war — between the Allies and Russia; between the Allies and the Central Powers; between the Allies and the victims of their exploitation; between the Allies themselves. One or more of them is sure to result in war within a decade, if the Treaty and the League Covenant are enforced. The League of Nations is a League of War; its present form, its very existence spells war.

I have another reason for insisting that the League will make for war rather than for peace — a reason growing out of the League's own record. During its brief existence, the League has witnessed more than a score of wars in Europe, Africa, and in Asia. These wars have been participated in by Great Britain, France, Italy and Japan— the leading exponents of the League. France has sent men and money to back Poland and to uphold General Wrangel's insurrection against the Russian Government, while her armies are busy conquering and subjugating Syria. Great Britain is fighting in Ireland and in Mesopotamia. Spain, France and Italy all are fighting in North Africa, and Thrace is being ravaged by contending armies.

Since the League came into being, Europe has blazed with war. The League is not a war preventer, but a war maker.

So much for the character and history of the League. Now as to its purposes. These are three in number:

1. To crush out Socialism.
2. To safeguard the British Empire.
3. To unite the exploiters against the exploited.

The relation of the League and of its principal members toward Soviet Russia is a sufficient guarantee of the first point. The position of the British Empire, combined with the working of Article X of the League Covenant establishes the second.

British statesmen insisted that they desired nothing as a result of the war. As things turned out, however, they received over two million square miles, including important possessions in East Africa, Mesopotamia, the lands bordering the Red Sea and the Persian Gulf, Persia, Thibet, and the German possessions in the South Pacific. This gives the British Empire control over something like a third of the earth, including a continuous stretch of territory from the Cape of Good Hope to Cairo and from Cairo to Bengal. These things are guaranteed under the Treaty, and Article X of the Covenant provides that: "The members of the League undertake to respect and preserve against external aggression, the territorial integrity and existing political independence of all members of the League." This clause commits all members of the League to back the British Empire in its efforts to hold hundreds of millions of human beings in subjection.

The original Holy Alliance organized in 1815 between Austria, Russia, Prussia and France, carried a mutual guarantee to protect from internal disturbances like the French Revolution, the members of the Alliance. This new Alliance guarantees its members against the possible loss of their colonies and possessions by any form of external oppression. They bind each other to help hold what they have stolen in this and previous wars. According to the original plan, the United States was to furnish the men and the money necessary to carry this Covenant into effect.

The League is intended to organize and unite the exploiter nations. Under Covenant provisions, the exploited nations have no rights that the exploiters are bound to respect. Japanese troops will remain in Korea; British rule stays

238

in India and American Marines hold their ground in Hayti. The robbers will unite and plunder their victims in severalty.

Thus, the League is intended, not to secure freedom and self-determination, but to perpetuate autocracy and the rule of force of which the leading members of the league are the chief exponents.

The Treaty and the League Covenant intensify every cause that led up to the world war. International Capitalism, with its economic rivalries and commercial struggles is perpetuated and consecrated; the exploitation of the weak by the rich and the strong is provided for; out of such a situation there can come nothing less than revolution and a struggle for independence on the one hand and the bitterest conflicts between the members of the League on the other. The League will perpetuate, will compel war. It makes peace unthinkable; impossible. It condemns the world to generations of blood-letting and destruction. The League is a logical product of the forces that made the last war and will prove an instrument of immense value in bringing about the next one.

31. The 1920 Election

The World War gave the business interests the opportunity for which they had been waiting. At the same time that they made millions they were able to come out in the open as the controlling force in American public life. Their answer to the Russian Revolution revealed their international stand. The events surrounding the election of 1920 showed how far they were ready to go in dominating the lives of the American people.

I spent the winter of 1919-1920 in Washington and New York, where I paid close attention to the business situation. I was particularly interested in the question as to whether a panic was going to be ordered by the New York bankers.

The masters of business life discussed the high cost of living, in other words, the cost of food and raw material, and how to reduce prices. They knew that the inflation of the currency was what had increased the price of all articles not controlled by the trusts, and they discussed the question of contracting the volume of money, for we have in circulation in the United States today nearly fifty-nine dollars per capita as against seventeen dollars in 1880. But the issue of money under the present system is very profitable to the bankers. They had made more than a billion out of the issue of money since the United States went into the war, and had inflated the currency, since the present bank act went into effect, by several billions of dollars. The bankers disliked to contract the currency because the issue of money is so profitable, and they finally hit upon another method and said, "We will con-tract the credit."

There were two fields in which it was possible to contract credit. One was the field of big business. The other was the field of agriculture. A contraction of credit to big business would have hit manufacturers and merchants (themselves). A contraction of agricultural credits, on the other hand, would hit only the farmers who are unorganized and in no position to strike back. A decision was therefore made to curtail credit by compelling all the banks to restrict their loans in the farm-producing area of the United States.

After the whole matter had been argued through, an order was sent out from New York to all of the reserve banks throughout the United States to restrict their loans and to refuse credit on all the products of human toil not controlled by the combinations. The result has been, of course, the reduction in the price of everything that is produced on the farm. Meat, corn, cotton, oats and hay are all far below their spring selling prices, not because crops were unusually large, but because the farmers were compelled to sell all of their crops in the market at the same time. They were compelled to sell because they could not borrow. They would not borrow, not because money was scarce — there is more money in the country than at any time in its history — but because the banks refused it to the farmers. During this same time loans were made to Norway, Belgium, France. There was plenty of money for that, but food prices must come down, and the way to bring them down was to compel the farmers to sell by withdrawing all credits and calling all existing loans.

While American farmers were being refused credit, the Bankers' Club, which is the government of the United States, entered into a "consortium" with the bankers of England, France and Japan to loan money to China for railroad concessions and concessions of minerals and coal. Vanderlip and Lamont were in China all through April getting these concessions. This contract between the United States, England, France and Japan is a written contract and the Secretary of State is a party to it; and yet the people of the United States are refused access to it.

This same club in New York, composed of the bankers and the great industries, discussed the question of the cost of labor. They said, "Labor is clamoring for more pay because of the high cost of living. We can reduce the cost of living by withdrawing credit and robbing the farmers, but we must also reduce wages," and they discussed for weeks the question of importing Chinese and Japanese laborers from the Orient. Their newspapers began to agitate the question, feeling out the public, but the opposition was so strong against taking down the bars and importing coolie labor that they turned their attention to Europe and made arrangements for the importation of laborers from the starving centers of Europe at wages that would send an American laborer to the poorhouse. These Europeans are now coming in at the rate of 100,000 a month. It is contract labor, in violation of the laws of the United States.

Unless American wages were reduced, it would be impossible for American manufacturers to compete in foreign markets, and unless food prices came down, wages could not be reduced without lowering efficiency. Therefore, the food prices came down and the farmers stood the loss, and this was done on the eve of an election. In years gone by the business interests would not have dared to operate so openly. That they do it now is the proof of their power, and of the contempt in which they hold the American people.

So much for the events which preceded the election. It was a period of open-handed assumption of power by the business interests. Now for the campaign itself.

My interests were centered on the Republican campaign because it was evident from the start that the Republicans were destined to win.

The Republican Convention was a very grand affair. arrived in Chicago on the second and stayed until the twelfth of June, and saw the whole operation. I had a friend who has been a member of the Republican National Convention for forty years, and has been one of the leaders in every convention, and he reported each morning — between one and two o'clock — the result of every conference, so that I knew in advance just what the convention was going to do the next day; and it always functioned according to program.

The representatives of the great interests arrived in a body and took charge of the convention from the start. It is the first time they have ever done this. There was Gary, head of the Steel Corporation; Davison and Lamont of Morgan & Co.; F. H. Allen of Lee Higginson & Co.; Atterbury, vice-president of the Pennsylvania Railroad, and Dick Mellon, of Pittsburgh, whose family is, I suppose — next to Rockefeller — the richest in America. Then there were George Baker and Frank Vanderlip and Daniel G. Reid. These men took no chances. They went to Chicago, wrote the platform, and nominated the candidate. They were willing to take Lowden or Wood, but Borah said that he would bolt the convention if they named either one of them. They were holding Knox and Hoover, Harding and Senator Watson of Indiana in reserve, and were willing to take any one of them, but they did not want a bolt in the party.

These financiers are the men who put the United States into the European war. They furnished the money to pay for preparedness parades all over the country; they are out for empire. They wanted to put a plank into the platform providing for a league of nations, or, rather, the Versailles Treaty with mild reservations, and they had prepared such a plank and they would have adopted it, but Borah and Johnson went before the committee and told them they would bolt if they put that plank into the platform. That, of course, destroyed Knox's chances, for he had agreed in advance that he would stand by and carry out such a plank if he were nominated; but without the plank these men would not trust Knox, and that ended his chance for the nomination.

They then canvassed Sproul of Pennsylvania, but Penrose wired that he would not stand for Sproul, who was trying to administer his political estate before he was dead. They finally concluded that Harding was the man least objectionable and most certain to stand right on their plans to exploit the rest of the world. In other words, Harding was from Ohio — which they must carry in order to win — and he was sound on the question of the commercial conquest of the earth by the United States.

The business interests named Harding. They would have preferred a stronger man — Knox of Pennsylvania was the favorite — but Harding was more available, so Harding was chosen.

Just a word as to the record of this latest President of "the greatest community on earth," as published in the "Searchlight," after a careful study of his six years in the Senate:

"Harding probably ranks below every other Senator in initiative, activity and accomplishment,

"Neither his friends nor his enemies can connect his name with a single outstanding issue, good or bad.

"He neither introduced nor championed even one big constructive measure.

"He was absent or dodged 1,170 roll calls and quorum calls.

"All the bills and resolutions he introduced were local or private in character, except eight. None of these eight was of big importance.

"In all matters of politics, economics and spoils he was a follower of the Old Guard bosses — Penrose, Smoot and Lodge.

"On issues at all important he voted with the progressive group only nine times in six years.

"He has voted for the liquor interests thirty times, and against them only twice.

"He favored woman suffrage after much reluctance and indecision.

"He voted for the Cummins Railroad Bill, with its anti-strike provision.

"He stood consistently against conservation, voted for the vicious Shields water power bill several times.

"On every important test between capital and labor, he voted with capital.

"He opposed public ownership in every form.

"On revenue measures, he voted against every amendment to increase the tax upon profiteering and large incomes.

"He voted and spoke for conscription as a permanent policy.

"He opposed disarmament for all nations."

Harding never read the Declaration of Independence and never heard of Thomas Jefferson. Discussing Philippine independence January 28, 1916, Harding said: 'Independence was not the inspiration of the War of the Revolution... The American Republic never gave a thought to the "consent of the governed"; never gave a thought to the violation of "inalienable rights"...I know what is in our hearts...And if we are to go into the Orient for an expansion of commerce and trade, I fancy that the possession of these rich islands will be very much to our advantage.'"

The big bankers, who dominate our foreign, as they dominate our domestic policy, have registered their full determination to take the billions they made out of the war as profiteers and reach out for the oil and iron and coal of the world and, by concessions and the grant of privileges, exploit the great natural resources not only of North and South America, but of Asia and Africa. Vanderlip and Lamont spent all of April and half of May in China and Japan, securing concessions for building railroads and the right to develop the great coal, oil and iron deposits of that country. They had their agents also in Siberia. Their program is to make a contract with Mexico — they are going to call it a treaty — by which they can exploit all the resources of Mexico.' If Mexico will not make the treaty, after Harding is inaugurated, our army will march into that country. They will proceed at once to build a bigger navy than England has, and they are fully determined to use the resources of the navy of the United States to carry out their imperial policy. They proposed to continue to exploit the laborers of this country and force what they plunder from labor on to the other nations of the world by commercial regulations and concessions, which are to be backed up by the full force of the army and the navy of the United States.

We are no longer a republic or democracy or any semblance of either one. The entrance of the United States into the great war extinguished all possibilities in that direction. We are a feudal aristocracy with artificial persons for our feudal lords, the most cruel form of society it is possible to imagine. The old feudal aristocracy was composed of natural persons with some human sympathy; but our feudal lords have none of these attributes.

The situation leads me to repeat what I cannot say too often — that capital is stolen labor and its only function is to steal more labor. This has been true since Lincoln pointed it out more than seventy years ago, and it is equally true today when the power in the hands of the capitalists is greater than it has been at any time in history.

Back of all this program are the voters of the United States. Thrilled by the World War; terrified by the "Bolshevist Menace," as it has been described by the press; lukewarm on the question of mixing up in the chaos of European politics and finance; stimulated and, at the same time, reassured by four years of extraordinary "prosperity," sixteen millions of voters went to the polls on November 2, 1920, and cast their votes for Harding, the nominee of Big Business — the acceptable and accepted representative of the most sinister forces in American public life. Harding's plurality of seven millions — unprecedented in presidential elections, gives the Republican party an assurance of at least eight years of unquestioned power.

The Great War is over. Peace has been restored. Sanity is supposed to have replaced the hysteria of war frenzy. Yet Harding, spokesman of plutocratic imperialism, is in the White House, while Debs, the champion of economic emancipation, is in the Atlanta penitentiary.

32. Capitalism

The people of the United States are playing with fire. They are experimenting with an unworkable system of social organization — a system that has been tried repeatedly during the past three or four thousand years, and that has destroyed civilization as often as it has been tried. The form of the experiments has been different, but their essential features remain the same.

Let me review these features briefly, because they lie at the foundation of our whole public life.

First, there is the concentration of wealth in the hands of a few men — "self-made," "irresponsible" — owing no allegiance to anything save our own destinies and their own ambitions. These wealth-lords, or plutocrats, ruling by virtue of their wealth, have been the bane of every great civilization from Assyria and Egypt to Rome, Spain and Great Britain.

Two per cent of the people of the United States own sixty per cent of the property of the United States. Yet they produced none of it. By legislation, by craft and cunning, by control of Congress and the courts, they took to themselves what others produced. Sixty-six per cent of the people of the United States own five per cent of the property of the United States. Yet they produced all of the wealth and have none of it. Why do not the producers of this wealth have what they produce? Because the making of the laws and the control of the courts is in the hands of those who do not work, and this has been true from the beginning of the Government. The convention which framed the Constitution of the United States was composed of fifty-five members. A majority were lawyers — not one farmer, mechanic or laborer. Forty owned Revolutionary Scrip. Fourteen were land speculators. Twenty-four were money-lenders. Eleven were merchants. Fifteen were slave-holders. They made a Constitution to protect the rights of property and not the rights of man, and, ever since. Congress has been controlled by the property owner, and has framed laws in their interests and their interests only, and always refused to frame any laws in the interest of those who produce all the wealth and have none of it.

In the second place, the wealth-owning class, because of its wealth-power and its hold on the machinery of society, takes a tribute from the mass of the workers. The character of this tribute varies from age to age. At bottom it is the same. The owner of wealth, because he possesses the things without which the masses would starve, compels them to pay him a return for their use. In Egypt and in feudal Europe, the masters owned land and exacted rent. Here, in the United States, the masters own the forests, mines, factories, railroads, banks and insurance companies. These things they own through the instrumentality of corporations and therefore their income takes the form of dividends on stocks and of interest on bonds. The form is immaterial. The fact remains that the few — whether as landlords or capitalists — hold the choice spots of the earth, and the many, for the privilege of enjoying these choice spots, pay tribute to the few who own them.

These masses — the workers — the producers — are rewarded with the least possible amount upon which they are willing to go on working and reproducing their kind. In old times they were chattel slaves; today they are wage slaves. Formerly, their masters took all of their product and guaranteed them a living. Now, a part of the product goes to the workers, but they must keep themselves.

In the past the work done by the slave for his master kept the master in luxury and enabled him to live a life of ease, and, if he desired, of dissipation and waste. Today the rent, interest and dividends paid by the workers to the owners of lands, bonds and stocks enables these owners to live in luxury, in idleness, and, if they desire, in wasteful dissipation. The owners of American wealth, according to the returns published by the Internal Revenue office, state on their income tax blanks that their incomes amount to tens and hundreds of thousands, to millions and tens of millions of dollars each year. The most skilled of the workers seldom make over $100 a week with steady work, and seven-eighths of them make less than $50 a week.

Furthermore, when hard times come, it is the worker who goes on the street and starves. The bondholder continues to draw his interest and the stockholder continues to receive his dividend. The bondholder, under the law, can insist upon his interest. The corporations take care of the stockholder long after the workers have begun to walk the streets looking for a chance to work.

These owners, freed from the necessity for labor, develop rapidly into a leisure class, while the workers, struggling for existence, constitute a labor class. The leisure class controls the surplus wealth of the community. Out of this surplus it feeds, dresses and houses itself; buys privileges, corrupts the machinery of the state; invests in foreign exploiting opportunities; struggles with the leisure classes of other countries for the chance to exploit and rob.

Among the masses, who are laboring and producing without getting the value of their product, there is poverty and want. Diseases waste and ravage; vitality is sapped; energy deteriorates. Perhaps nowhere in the modern world is the picture more clearly presented than among the exploited British factory workers during the forty or fifty years preceding the World War. If the soldiers on the field were common fodder, the men and women of Lancashire and Birmingham were factory fodder. While the leisure class of Britain was shooting grouse and chasing foxes across the ploughed land, the men and women and children belonging to the working masses were huddled in garrets and cellars — the prey of tuberculosis, rickets, anemia and want.

The leisure class, having nothing better to do, plays at ducks and drakes with international affairs, plunges the country into economic and military conflicts, heaps up great debts, and wastes its own and the country's resources, while the workers do the mass-fighting, pay the taxes and suffer from starvation and disease. Between the two classes there springs up hate, class conflict and perpetual dissension. It was not for nothing that Alexander Hamilton wrote, "The various and unequal distribution of wealth."

When I entered the public life of the United States, the economic ruling class was just stepping into power. There was no leisure class to speak of. There was still an abundance of free land for the workers. The America that I knew in my young manhood was still talking, in all sincerity, about "government of, by and for the people." In the brief period of my own public experience we have adopted a species of feudalism more unhuman and more vicious than any of which history bears a record — a feudalism of artificial persons (corporations) using their power to exploit the workers in the interest of the parasites. Within my lifetime we have become a government of corporations whose attorneys are in the House and Senate and throughout the bureaus and departments of the Government, looking out for the interests of those who pay them their retaining fees.

This is capitalism — the control of the machinery of society in the interests of those who own its wealth. This was feudalism in France and slavery in Rome and in Assyria. This is the system of dividing the community into two classes — owners and producers — and of rewarding the owners at the expense of the producers. As I read history, this method of social organization has had and can have only one result. The leisure class rots out and drops to pieces; the workers starve and suffer and die. Sometimes they revolt — particularly in the later years. Generally, they are too weak and too ignorant to do anything more than labor and reproduce.

In the preceding pages I have tried to show how this system was getting its grip on the United States. Out of my own experience in public life I have indicated the activity of the land-grabbers, the bankers, the money-ring, the beneficiaries of the tariff, the trust magnates, the railroad operators and the other masters of the economic world. In Congress and out, year by year, they have taken possession of the country's best resources, robbed the people through monopoly, exploited and plundered the workers by means of low wages and high prices. Then, with their ill-gotten gains, they have invaded other lands — Cuba, Porto Rico, the Philippines, Mexico, Panama, Costa Rica, Nicaragua and Haiti — and there they have repeated the same process, by fair means or foul, gaining possession of the timber, oil, copper and iron, and then forcing the natives to produce these commodities for a pittance wage. Behind them, in these ventures, the plutocrats had the army and navy of the United States to be used when necessary, as they were used against Spain, the Philippines, the Mexicans, the Haitians and the rest. Meanwhile, at home, through the subsidy of political parties — through the passage of legislation — through the courts — through the private control or, where necessary, through the open purchase of coercion of public men, the interests have taken possession of the government of the United States, shaping its institutions, and directing its policies along lines calculated to yield the largest net returns to the plutocracy.

The last move in this direction involved the entrance of the United States into the World War; the conscription of men; the dispatch of an army to the battlefields of Europe; the suppression of free speech and a free press; search, seizure, indictment, trial, imprisonment and the deportation of men and women in open and flagrant violation of constitutional guarantees and long-established precedent.

The Wilson administration and the Supreme Court have demonstrated and established that in time of war the Constitution, with all its amendments, is but a scrap of paper and of no force and effect. Hereafter, all that the people who do the work and produce the wealth have to do it to unite and get control of the Congress and other branches of the government and declare war on some country — any country — and at once proceed to enact laws in total disregard of the Constitution, and all its guarantees, and arrest and imprison all who disagree or protest. It is well for the people who toil to make a note of this fact.

No man who has regard for the welfare of this country, or who is concerned for its future, can fail to be alarmed at the course that it has followed, and is still following, along the road that leads to empire and imperial institutions. There may yet be time, but unless we turn back soon, it will be too late. It behooves the sixty-six per cent of our people to take possession of their Government and enact laws so that every man shall have all he produces. Capital is stolen labor, and its only function is to steal more labor.

33. The Triumph of Christian Civilization

Perhaps I can say more effectively what I tried to write in the last chapter by means of an allegory which tells, in simple form, the story of our blunders.

One hundred years ago a colony of English farm laborers, one hundred in number, composed of men, women and children — old and young — chartered a ship and started for Australia. They were inspired to go by the promise of free land — they and their ancestors having been tenants upon an English estate.

The ship was a sailing ship and the colonists loaded it with their second-hand furniture, second-hand bedding and second-hand farm implements. They also obtained some seeds from a charitable person who was willing to await the success of the colony for the return of his investment; and, with the seeds and agricultural implements, they started from England for Australia by way of Cape Horn. The Voyage across the Atlantic was successfully made; the cape was rounded and the ship stretched her sails as she moved away into the broad Pacific. The colonist, who knew little of sailing routes soon got off from the ordinary track of vessels and, when well out in the Pacific Ocean, ran their ship aground upon a sunken reef which stove a hole in the bottom and placed it beyond repair.

Consternation prevailed among the passengers. Some fainted. Others ran up and down the decks, nearly insane from fear. The cooler heads soon restored order however, and all hands were organized to save what they could out of the wreck. When it became evident that the ship was in no immediate danger of sinking, the faint-hearted regained courage and all went to work with a will.

There were two young men — healthy and strong — who seemed to take no interest in the salvage plans, but busied themselves with trying to release from its lashings the only life-boat upon the ship — a very small boat, which was all that the colonists, out of their meagre funds, could afford.

A study of the situation showed the leaders of the party that their condition was by no means hopeless. The ship did not fill rapidly and about ten miles south of the wreck, land could be made out. There was no wind, the sea was calm. Their one boat was too small to be of any great use, so the voyagers decided to build a raft out of the ship and try to reach the land south of them. So they all started to work — with the exception of the two young men — constructed their raft on the leeward side of the ship and began loading it with their belongings. Before they had gone far with the loading, they found that the raft would not carry over one-half of the colony. So they took the old and the helpless and the children, and half of the most able-bodied, and proceeded to propel the raft to the land, while the others were picking up and putting in shape the remainder of the cargo and the stores.

The occupants of the raft landed upon the island without difficulty. Apparently, so far as they could see, it was a complete and absolute desert. They had noticed, before they left the ship, that the two young men, who had been hanging around the life-boat had disappeared, and that the life-boat, as well as all the arms and munitions on the ship had disappeared with them. These men had rendered no assistance whatever in rescuing their fellow-beings from the wreck, and they had deserted the ship at the critical moment, with the only seaworthy craft that the colonists possessed.

After the first raft cargo had been landed, a few of the men returned with the raft to the ship, loaded their implements and the remainder of the food and taking aboard the rest of the colony, returned to the island.

For the next day or two, the shipwrecked colonists gave their attention to stripping the ship taking such parts as they could detach, to the island, and constructing temporary shelter. After all that could be moved was taken to the camping place they had selected, three of the company were chosen to explore the island, while others were detailed to manufacture a temporary boat in order to see if there were eatable fish in the waters surrounding the island.

Those who had been sent to explore the island soon returned with the report that they had found a body of very fertile land several miles in the interior of the island, that this land was about three thousand acres in extent; that there was a large spring of water in the center of it, and that it appeared to be the only cultivatable land upon the whole island. They reported further that the two young men, who had abandoned their fellows were there in possession of the fertile land, and that when the committee proposed to bring all the other people up to the spring of fresh water and the fertile land, the two young men replied that they, having discovered the oasis, were the lawful owners and they proposed to stand upon their right to retain it. When the committee insisted that the land should not be privately owned but should be the common property of all — as man was a land animal and fertile soil was absolutely essential to his existence — the two young men who had in their possession all of the arms on the ship, first argued that the committee must not undertake to discourage individual initiative — that it would be ruinous to civilization not to encourage individual enterprise and that the land belonged to them by right of discovery. But, when the committee pressed the point and urged the rights of man, the two young men said: "We have all the arms and ammunition that are on this island, and if you undertake to force possession of this land, we shall fire upon you."

After hearing the report of their Committee, the colonists held a meeting and decided that it would be a great mistake to discourage individual enterprise or in any way throttle individual ambition. They and their ancestors had always paid rent to a landlord; they had been taught to believe that it was the rights of property that were sacred and not the rights of man, and so they resolved to move on to the three thousand fertile acres and pay rent for the use of them. So they gathered together the old and the helpless and the little children and moved them first, and then they moved all of their belongings, including their supply of food and seed and implements, without any help whatever from the two young men who were busily guarding the results of their enterprise.

The Colonists set to work at once to cultivate the land and put in a crop. The two young men married the two most likely young women on the island, and the two young women and their relatives esteemed it a great catch.

After the first crop was harvested, the young men, by promising a little reduction in rent, put the whole laboring population at work building them a house that corresponded with the importance of their position. The workers hewed, with their rough tools, the coral rock out of the barren portions of the island and constructed a very splendid residence for the ruling classes. After the house was finished and the workers had manufactured as best they could, out of the wood obtained from the ship, furniture with which to stock it, they began to construct hovels of stone and earth for themselves and their children, and their aged and their sick.

So matters went on for several years, during which about two thousand acres of the fertile land were brought under cultivation. Meanwhile, the population had increased and their labor had made a beautiful park out of the remaining thousand acres which surrounded the residence of their lords. They had also built a heavy wall around the thousand acres so as to protect the park from encroachment.

The leaders of the colony still dreamed of resuming their journey to Australia, and in the little spare time they had between planting, harvesting and building, they explored the island. On the end farthest removed from the oasis, they found a deep and rugged ravine, containing some scrubby vegetation, and coming down from a considerable elevation that suggested volcanic origin. In the ravine they discovered gold in great quantities and immediately began to extract it from the soil. It was placer gold and came out in big and small nuggets.

After gold was discovered, the oldest of the two colonists, who had appropriated all of the fertile land upon the island, took the title of Lord Goldfield, and the whole population turned out for a holiday to celebrate the event.

They attended services in their churches and were told by their spiritual advisers that it was a great providence of God's which had bestowed upon them so kind and beneficent a ruler as the lord of the province; that, in fact, their lord had received his title direct from God; that it was of divine origin and was sent especially to them by the great Ruler of the universe because of his loving care.

In addition to the gold, some of the colonists discovered at the headwaters of the stream upon the banks of which the gold was found, a small band of wild goats. The goats were very thin and their hair was not of the finest quality; but immediately upon the discovery of the goats the lords of the palace had them removed to the one thousand acres which they had walled in as a park around their mansion, and great care was exercised in their breeding so that only the best qualities were reproduced. These efforts met with great success. The inferior goats were sterilized and only those allowed to reproduce who were of the very best quality. The animals became strong and large and covered with a wooly coat, and were thus suitable for beasts of burden, and to furnish wool for cloth, and milk for the children of the rich.

As a result of this achievement, the other young man took a title — the title of Lord Angora, in honor of the discovery of the goats. And again ceremonies were held and a holiday proclaimed and the population instructed in the divine origin of this title.

But while birth control was exercised with regard to the goats, and great care taken to see that they were properly fed, the common people of the colony were taught that it was wicked to interfere with the processes of nature, and as the population had brought with them the usual diseases common to the sexes in Great Britain, there were increasing numbers constantly among the inhabitants of those who were diseased and of those who were mentally defective; in fact, a very large number of dependents had grown up and the slums had appeared, and as they took no care with regard to sanitary affairs, epidemic diseases — the result of the poisoning of the population by their own filth — spread among them and reduced the population from time to time. And the people were taught that this was a visitation by Providence to punish them for their failure to appreciate the glory and goodness of God; that they should read the Bible every day and observe Sunday and attend Church and above all, contribute to the support of the Church and God's representative — the preacher, who had ordered a day of fasting and prayer to appease the anger of the Deity. And the preacher chanted — "God is great and God is good; He provideth our daily food; by His hand we are all fed; give us now our daily bread." And the people cried "Halleluiah, Glory to God." But God's wrath was so great that He would not hear, and the epidemic ran its full course. The preacher then told the people that the only way to prevent future epidemics was to be more devout and that God, above all things, loved a cheerful giver.

The rulers of the island had planned and directed the construction of large warehouses which were used to store the products of the land. Many colonists were improvident. They would sell off what they produced and use up the returns so that they would not have enough to last them until the next crop. As the population grew and life became less bearable the number of the improvident increased. The two thousand acres under cultivation yielded three crops a year; was intensely cultivated and produced an abundance of supplies. The ruling classes, who owned the gold mines as well as the fertile land, knowing that the value of money depended upon its quantity, decided that the nuggets of gold should have a value in proportion to their weight or size, and, of course, they decreed that the unit should be pounds, shillings and pence. They also manipulated the money so that, when the crop was harvested, the money was very scarce and therefore, the prices were very low. They would buy the products of the land and store them in their warehouses and, when the next crop was fairly in the ground and improvident members of the community were entirely out of food, they would make the volume of money exceedingly abundant, prices would rise and they could thus charge several times what they paid for the products of the laborer of the land. They soon found that this was unnecessary for, as they were the only owners of money and had the only warehouses that there were, they could arbitrarily fix the price and thus exploit the population to the full extent of their desire, through their trust control.

But a new problem had arisen. Malthus's theory that population would outrun subsistence had come true. The two thousand acres would no longer produce food enough to supply the population and the serfs began to wonder how they would overcome the difficulty. They never thought of encroaching upon the park because that was private property belonging to God and the descendants of the two young men who had, by their private enterprise, discovered and taken possession of it; and the descendants of these young men never, for a moment, thought of plowing up the park, and they insisted that the miserable population would have enough if they would exercise frugality and industry and would educate themselves; but they were ignorant and many of them were idle and of but little consequence.

So a committee was appointed to explore the neighboring seas with the hope of finding land. The expedition discovered some small islands, almost entirely barren. On one of them, however, they found a human being, clothed in palm leaves, who fled upon their approach; but they called to him and to their astonishment and joy he responded in the English tongue. He had been upon the island for ten years, the only survivor of a shipwreck and had subsisted upon roots, scant vegetation, and the products of the sea, clothing himself with palm leaves.

Of course he went home with the colonists and after ne Had fully recovered, began to preach the doctrine of Socialism. He said the rights of man were sacred and not the rights of property. He said that every man should have all that his labor produces — that man was a land animal and that the land was essential to his very existence, and that no person should own more land than he could use and that, for the idle to demand rent for the use of the land — the common inheritance of all — was immoral and dishonest, and that they should immediately take possession of the thousand acres in the park and put those acres into crops. And many of the people endorsed his views.

But the ruling classes were not idle. They had watched his movements; they sent their paid retainers, their lawyers, among the people and argued that to take the park and not pay for it would be confiscation and robbery; that the present owner had inherited it from ancestors who had acquired it by thrift and industry and enterprise. That if the public appropriated it to the good of all it would destroy all incentive to individual enterprise and stop the wheels of progress and discourage ambition and return the world to barbarism; and they also wanted to know if they proposed to rob widows and orphans.

The ruler had also organized a standing army of trained men under the plea that the colony might be invaded by savages from some unknown island in the sea, and that an army was needed for protection. The army was officered by men who had been brought up from childhood as trained soldiers and taught that they must obey their superior officers even unto shooting their own brothers and sisters, if commanded to do so by the officer over them. And, as the commander-in-chief of their standing army was by law the oldest son of the oldest of the two men who had discovered the fertile land, the army was ordered out, and they captured the socialist in the interest of law and order, and stood him up against the wall which surrounded the one thousand acres, and fired a volley into him and threw his body into the moat.

Civil war at once commenced; the population divided almost equally on the great question of the sacred rights of property, and they began killing each other until half of the people were disposed of. But as the trained men with their guns were on the side of the owner of the property, the people that remained alive stopped the unequal contest, and right and might prevailed; law and order triumphed; the congestion was relieved; the park was saved; the people agreed to continue to pay rent, and Christian civilization pursued its peaceful and solemn course.

34. Looking Ahead

I have had a long experience with the public life of the United States; I have been repeatedly to Europe; I have studied the life of the East at first hand; I have read economics, history, sociology; I have been busily engaged in the life of the world for more than half of a century. If long experience and investigation, coupled with study and discussion, fit a man to understand what is going on about him, then I believe that I have the necessary qualifications for passing on the events that are now transpiring, and for predicting the trend of our economic and political life.

There are certain things that I see very clearly; and certain tendencies that are working toward their logical goals just as inexorably as the sun passes across the heavens. These tendencies in our public life are similar to, though not identical with, similar forces that have operated in other societies during historic times; and they bear a very close resemblance to the forces that are now at work in all of the great capitalist countries of the world.

In the fight over the annexation of Hawaii, I predicted that the road which was then being followed by the United States would lead speedily to empire. Well, the empire is already here — having arrived more speedily than I, in my wildest imaginings, ever dreamed that it would arrive.

At the time of the struggle over the Hawaiian Treaty, few people believed that the United States could ever be an imperial nation. They were skeptical, or else they scoffed openly. Even the representatives of the great interests had little idea of what was happening. They knew that they were serving the men who had retained them, but with the exception of a very few among them they saw no farther than the immediate present. They were lawyers — not statesmen.

As for the masses of the people, they were as ignorant then as they are now. They were swayed by their emotions. "They responded to the "full dinner pail" appeal. They were the victims of an education that taught them to remember — not to think; and they were so busy remembering the glories of seventeenth century Revolutionary America that they had no energy or attention to devote to the problems of nineteenth century plutocratic and imperial America. During the campaign of 1900 I went before the farmers of South Dakota as a man who had served them for a decade in their fight against the exploiters. Mark Hanna, the direct representative of those exploiters, came out to Dakota with half a million dollars, and the half million carried more weight than my eleven years of service in the Senate.

Such experience taught me that, all other things being equal, people will do what their immediate economic advantage prompts them to do. Against the weight of this economic advantage, ideals and abstract ideas will not win with the average man or woman.

Therefore, I reached a conclusion that I have since seen verified again and again — that where the carcass is the vultures will be gathered together. So long as the privileged few hold the reins of economic power, and so long as they are willing to share up with the workers a portion — even a small portion of the plunder — they can hope to maintain their authority.

So I realized that progress was to be made from the tyranny of the masters as well as from the spirit of revolt among the workers, and where the workers had been crushed and exploited for generations, as in England, I realized that it would take a great deal of tyranny before the masses could be expected to revolt.

Thus, the danger of the American farmers and wage earners lay in their very prosperity and in the leniency of their masters. So long as the bread was abundant I did not see how it was possible for forward-looking people to expect any effective progress.

Nevertheless, I expected the present century to yield a crop of revolutions, based on tyranny and starvation, and I predicted such a result in 1900. I made this prediction in reply to a letter from the Red Cross, in which the Director of the 20th Century Department asked me to tell what the world might expect in the new century. The Red Cross request was as follows:

"THE AMERICAN NATIONAL RED CROSS
20th Century Department
Walter L. Phillips
General Secretary, Bridgeport, Conn.
"Miss Clara Barton, President,
Miss Ellen Spencer Mussey, Counsel and 3rd Vice-President,
Washington, D. C.

Frank D. Higbee,
Director 20th Century Dept.,
New York, Nov. 21, 1900.

"Hon. Richard F. Pettigrew,
Sioux Fall, South Dakota.
"Sir:

"The Red Cross regards your position and standing to be such as to make your views on the progress and value of the 19th Century, in comparison with other centuries and your prophecies regarding the 20th Century of great value, and we respectfully request you to forward to us at your earliest convenience from 40 to 70 words in your own handwriting giving your thoughts in that connection. We shall read them at all of our meetings throughout the United States, and afterwards allow the United States Government to take them and forever exhibit and preserve them in the Congressional Library at Washington.

"An engraved invitation is being prepared, one of which will be mailed to you, but the time is short, and we take this method to expedite matters, and hope you will send in your "Greeting" before December 1st, if you can do so.

"We prefer to have the 'Greeting' in your own handwriting rather than type-written because we wish to have each 'Greeting' in autograph form when turned over to the government for preservation for all time.

"Thanking you in advance, I am,

"Very truly yours,
"FRANK D. HIGBEE,
Director 20th Century Watch Meetings.

"Approved:
"CLARA BARTON, President." To this letter I sent the following reply:
"To the American National Red Cross:
"During the century just closed, mankind has made marvelous progress in his control over the forces of Nature, and in the production of things which contribute to his physical comfort.

254

"The early years of the century marked the progress of the race towards individual freedom and permanent victory over the tyranny of hereditary aristocracy, but the closing decades of the century have witnessed the surrender of all that was gained to the more heartless tyranny of accumulated wealth. Man's progress has therefore been material and not spiritual or ideal and the future alone can demonstrate whether any real progress has been made.

"I believe the new century will open with many bloody revolutions as a result of the protest of the masses against the tyranny and oppression of the wealth of the world in the hands of a few, resulting in great progress towards socialism and the more equal distribution of the products of human toil and, as a result, the moral and spiritual uplifting of the race.

"R. F. PETTIGREW.

"Washington, D. C,
Nov. 22, 1900."

It was twenty years ago that I predicted "many bloody revolutions as a result of the protest of the masses against the tyranny and oppression of the world in the hands of the few." These revolutions have occurred — the first in Russia 1905), and subsequently the revolutions in Russia, Hungary, Germany and other portions of Central Europe.

Then, too, there has occurred the "great progress towards socialism and the more equal distribution of the products of human toil" that I predicted at the same time. The progress has been unequal. In the United States and in Japan, it has only just begun. All over Europe it has reached advanced stages, and the same forces of tyrannous capitalism and imperialism that have been at work in Europe, making for these revolutions, and for this revision of the ways of handling economic life are now busy in the United States, where the ruling class is following the old course of empire, and where the workers are beginning to wake up to the fact that they must take charge of their own economic affairs or perish, as have their European comrades, in the inevitable struggle between contending empires.

We have not yet witnessed "the moral and spiritual uplifting of the race," about which I wrote in 1900, but already there are intimations that progress is being made in that direction. A spirit has come out of Russia that has transformed the thinking of the world in three short years, and the end is not yet. This spirit is permeating the masses everywhere, and inspiring the most thoughtful among them with the ideas and ideals of a free economic society.

The closing years of the Nineteenth Century saw the imperialists of the world at the zenith of their power. The World War marked the beginning of their downfall.

Today I see the workers of the world coming into their own. Before this present generation passes, the workers in all of the important industrial countries of Europe will be the masters of the jobs on which they are dependent for a livelihood.

The workers will gain this control only through the course of a struggle during which western civilization will either pass to a new level of industrial

255

and social organization, or else it will destroy itself in the conflict. This is the supreme test of the effectiveness of the present level of working-class intelligence. If the workers have learned enough and can maintain sufficient solidarity to hold the machinery of economic life together, while the transition is being made, the next steps in material and in spiritual progress must come in quick succession. If, on the other hand, the workers fail to make the transition, there must ensue years or perhaps centuries of stagnation, like those which followed the dissolution of the Roman Empire.

Whatever the success of the workers, one thing is certain — if those who do the world's work do not make this fight for the control of their jobs, the madcaps who are now directing the affairs of the great capitalist states will continue with their wars — each more terrible than the last one — until there remain only the fragments of the present civilization, and then the dark ages that will follow, across the war-devastated earth, will be dark indeed.

If through either struggle — that of the workers to get and to hold control of their jobs, or that of the plutocracies for the right to exploit the garden spots of the earth — the present civilization of the West is destroyed, then the ancient civilization of the East, based on the agricultural village, will again dominate the earth.

The beginnings of these changes already are seen in Central Europe, where finances, transportation and manufacturing have been seriously deranged, or where their operation has been completely suspended, and where starvation and disease are consuming a population for which the old order of society can afford no remedy.

The war has been officially over for some time, yet, during the many months since there were open hostilities on the main battle-fronts, the economic life of Central Europe has not recovered its normal tone. There were many who felt that no sooner was the armistice agreed to than there would be a resumption of the ordinary economic activities of the peoples of the warring countries. At least "by the first of the year," insisted the optimists, things would "pick up." The first of the year has come and has gone — for the year of 1919, for 1920 and for 1921, and unless all accounts are at fault the starvation, disease, suffering and misery are more acute now than they were at the end of the war. Certainly the financial reports show that the economic portion of Austria, Poland, Hungary, Esthonia and probably of Germany is growing progressively worse. It is impossible to turn the energies of hundreds of millions from useful labor to destruction for five years without breaking down or wiping out the old impulses and habits that lead to useful labor. War is more than hell. It is chaos, negation and denial of human civilization and progress. The worst that can be said about the present system is that it makes war inevitable.

There is a crisis in the life of nearly four hundred millions who make up Europe. Many of the people are facing a situation that is desperate to a degree that cannot be appreciated by those who have not seen it.

The people of the United States have a unique opportunity in this crisis. I do not speak of their opportunity to give food and clothing. By that means they may push off the anguish of Europe for a few months. I mean an opportunity to show how things should be arranged to guarantee the life, liberty and happiness of a people.

The United States is isolated geographically. Hence it is in a better position to experiment and to work out its new ideas than is any other nation of the world.

Again, nature has supplied the United States with an unexcelled store of all the resources necessary to the building and maintenance of a great civilization. Hence it follows that, unlike the peoples of overcrowded Europe, none of those who live in the United States need lack for food or clothing or shelter. The coal and iron, the cotton and the wheat, the corn and the cattle, the beneficial climate and the generous soil all are present in extraordinary abundance.

Besides that, there are no near neighbors that are in a position to interfere with the internal affairs of the country. Once the American people have decided to reorganize their economic life on a basis of intelligence, there can be no effective check placed upon them from the outside.

Finally, the past few years have given this country an immense surplus in machinery, in liquid capital, in goods of various kinds that represent a great lead over any would-be rival.

Such are the advantages which the people of the United States now enjoy. There is one way and only one way in which they can make good and utilize them to the full. That is for the workers to take possession of their jobs, assume the direction of economic policy, and take the full product that they create.

Under our form of government this can and should be accomplished, not by force but by political action. Those who do the work and produce all the wealth should combine and form a political party with a platform of eight words: "Every man is entitled to all he produces," with a slogan, "All power to the people who do the work and produce the wealth," and take possession of the government in all its branches, drive the lawyers out of office and repeal all laws granting privileges, and enact laws for the public ownership of all utilities of every kind that are now owned by corporations.

By this means, and by this means only, can imperialism be checked, the class struggle eliminated, and the life of the people be placed on a sound and rational basis. In this direction and in this direction only can they hope to attain the life, liberty and happiness of which our forefathers dreamed.

* 9 7 8 1 7 8 9 8 7 3 2 1 4 *